DATE DUE

BLAZERS
Bilingüe/Bilingual

EN CUMPLIMIENTO DEL DEBER / LINE OF DUTY

INVESTIGADORES DE ESCENAS DE CRÍMENES
DESCUBREN LA VERDAD

CRIME SCENE INVESTIGATORS
UNCOVERING THE TRUTH

por/by Connie Colwell Miller

Consultor de contenido/Content Consultant:
David Faran, PhD.
Director, Programa de Ciencia Forense/
Director, Forensic Science Program
Michigan State University

Consultora de lectura/Reading Consultant:
Barbara J. Fox
Especialista en Lectura/Reading Specialist
North Carolina State University

CAPSTONE PRESS
a capstone imprint

Blazers Books are published by Capstone Press,
1710 Roe Crest Drive, North Mankato, Minnesota 56003
www.capstonepub.com

Library of Congress Cataloging-in-Publication Data
Miller, Connie Colwell, 1976–
[Crime scene investigators. Spanish & English]
Investigadores de escenas de crímenes : Descubren la verdad = Crime scene
investigators : uncovering the truth / por Connie Colwell Miller.
p. cm. — (Blazers bilingue. En cumplimiento del deber = Blazers bilingual.
Line of duty)
Includes index.
ISBN 978-1-62065-171-1 (library binding)
ISBN 978-1-4765-1380-5 (ebook PDF)
1. Criminal investigation—Juvenile literature. 2. Crime scene searches—Juvenile
literature. I. Title.
 HV8073.8.M5518 2013
363.25'2—dc23   2012018071

Summary: Describes crime scene investigators, including what they do and
how they help catch criminals—in both English and Spanish

Editorial Credits
Aaron Sautter, editor; Strictly Spanish, translation services; Bobbi J. Wyss,
designer; Eric Manske, bilingual book designer; Wanda Winch, media researcher;
Kathy McColley, production specialist

Photo Credits
911 Pictures/Pete Fisher, 14
AP Images/Isaac Brekken, 6; Joseph Kaczmarek, 10–11; *Philadelphia Evening
    Bulletin*/Mike Mooney, 18; Rich Pedroncelli, 24; Stephan Savoia, 17;
    Toby Talbot, 25
Corbis/Ashley Cooper, cover; Sygma/Stephane Ruet, 4–5
Getty Images Inc./Michael Williams, 20–21
The Image Works/Syracuse Newspapers/David Lassman, 12–13; Frank Ordo, 15;
    John Berry, 8–9
Zuma Press/*Hamilton Spectator*/John Rennison, 22–23; *Palm Beach Post*/Erik
    M. Lunsford, 26–27; Bob Shanley, 28–29; *Toronto Star*/Richard Lautens, 16

Printed in the United States of America in Stevens Point, Wisconsin.
092012   006937WZS13

TABLE OF CONTENTS

TABLA DE CONTENIDOS

ON THE SCENE

A dead body is found on the sidewalk. No one knows what happened. Crime scene **investigators** (CSIs) are called in to look for clues.

[**investigator**—someone who studies crime scenes]

EN LA ESCENA DEL CRIMEN

Se ha encontrado un cadáver en la acera. Nadie sabe qué pasó. Se llama a los **investigadores** de escenas de crímenes (CSI) para que busquen pistas.

[**investigador**—alguien que estudia escenas de crímenes]

5

A CSI unit studies a stolen car. CSIs look for **fingerprints** and other clues. They find a gun hidden in the trunk.

[**fingerprint**—the pattern made by the tip of your finger]

Una unidad de CSI estudia un auto robado. Los CSI buscan **huellas digitales** y otras claves. Encuentran un arma escondida en el maletero del auto.

[**huellas digitales**—el patrón que deja la punta de tu dedo]

A CSI unit is called to a bank. Someone has broken into the bank's safe. A CSI dusts for fingerprints.

Se llama a una unidad de CSI a un banco. Alguien ha forzado entrada a la caja de seguridad del banco. Un CSI espolvorea para buscar huellas digitales.

GATHERING EVIDENCE

CSI units are part of many police forces. CSIs work with detectives and other police officers to collect clues.

REUNIR EVIDENCIA

Las unidades de CSI son parte de muchos cuerpos de policía. Los CSI trabajan con detectives y otros oficiales de la policía para encontrar pistas.

CSI units take lots of pictures. They need to record the scene exactly as it is. Moving anything could ruin an important clue.

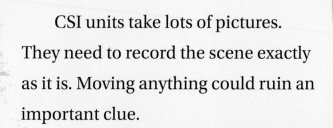

FACT! CSIs sometimes take photos of wounds on injured victims.

Las unidades de CSI toman muchas fotografías. Necesitan registrar la escena exactamente como está. Mover algo podría arruinar una pista importante.

¡DATO! Los CSI a veces toman fotografías de heridas en víctimas lesionadas.

CSIs dust crime scenes for fingerprints. They use tape to lift fingerprints off a surface. Then they put the tape on a fingerprint card.

Los CSI espolvorean las escenas de crímenes para buscar huellas digitales. Usan cinta adhesiva para levantar las huellas digitales de la superficie. Luego colocan la cinta adhesiva en una tarjeta para huellas digitales.

CSIs look for blood at crime scenes. They use bright lights or special chemicals to find bloodstains. They put blood samples in paper bags.

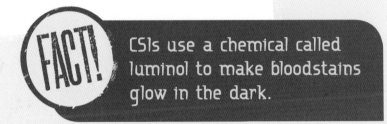

FACT! CSIs use a chemical called luminol to make bloodstains glow in the dark.

Los CSI buscan sangre en las escenas de crímenes. Usan luces brillantes o químicos especiales para encontrar manchas de sangre. Ellos colocan muestras de sangre en bolsas de papel.

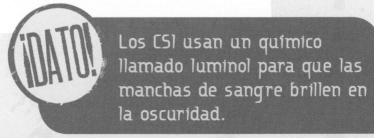

¡DATO!

Los CSI usan un químico llamado luminol para que las manchas de sangre brillen en la oscuridad.

CSI members look for bullets. They look for bullet holes too. The holes can help them learn where the shooter was located.

Los miembros de CSI buscan balas. También buscan agujeros de balas. Los agujeros pueden ayudar a saber dónde estaba ubicada la persona que disparó.

THE CRIME LAB

CSI units take **evidence** to crime labs. Lab workers look for more clues. Markings on a bullet can show which gun was used in a crime.

[**evidence**—information or objects found at a crime scene]

EL LABORATORIO FORENSE

Las unidades de CSI llevan **evidencia** al laboratorio forense. Los trabajadores del laboratorio buscan más pistas. Las marcas en una bala pueden mostrar qué arma fue usada en un crimen.

[**evidencia**—información u objetos encontrados en una escena de crimen]

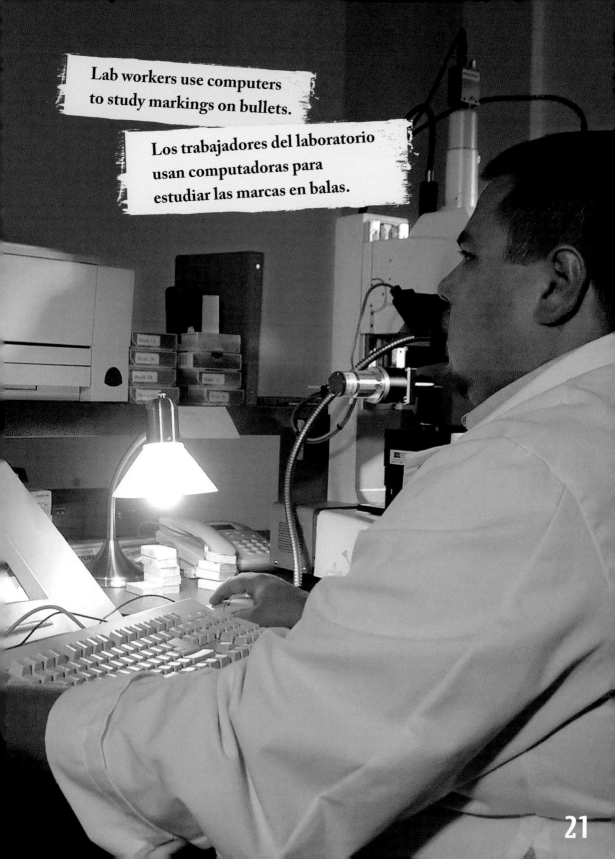

Lab workers use computers to study markings on bullets.

Los trabajadores del laboratorio usan computadoras para estudiar las marcas en balas.

Lab workers use the Automated Fingerprint Identification System (AFIS). This computer system matches fingerprints with known **criminals**.

[**criminal**—someone who commits a crime]

Smeared fingerprints don't have enough detail to make a match with a known criminal.

Los trabajadores del laboratorio usan un Sistema Automatizado de Identificación de Huellas Digitales (AFIS). Este sistema de computación compara huellas digitales con las de **criminales** conocidos.

[**criminal**—alguien que comete un crimen]

Las huellas digitales borrosas no tienen suficientes detalles para igualarlas con las de un criminal conocido.

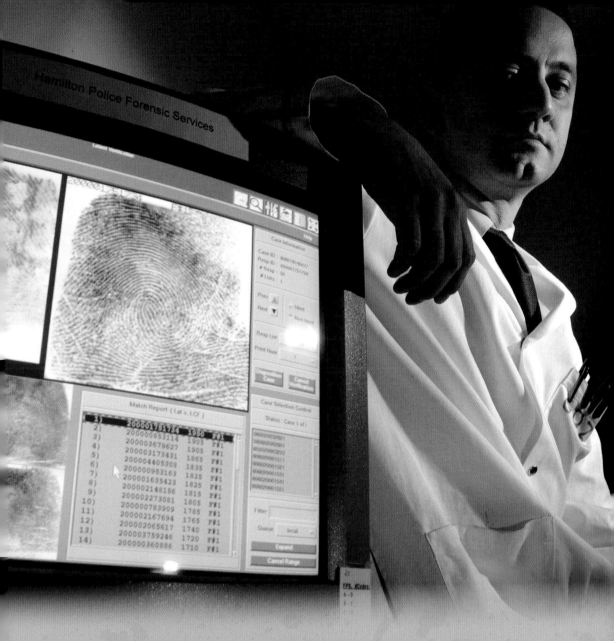

Lab workers test blood samples for **DNA** evidence. DNA is different in every person. It can prove that someone was at a crime scene.

[**DNA**—material in body cells that are unique to each person]

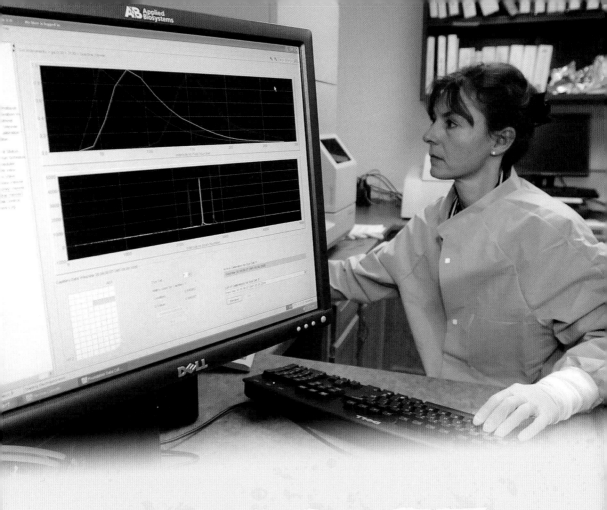

Los trabajadores del laboratorio hacen pruebas con muestras de sangre para evidencia de **ADN**. El ADN es diferente en cada persona. Puede probar que alguien estuvo en la escena del crimen.

[**ADN**—material en las células del cuerpo que es único a cada persona]

SHARING CLUES

CSI units share clues with police detectives and lawyers. Police use the clues to find and catch **suspects**.

[**suspect** — someone thought to be guilty of a crime]

COMPARTIR PISTAS

Las unidades de CSI comparten pistas con los detectives de la policía y los abogados. La policía usa estas pistas para encontrar y atrapar a los **sospechosos**.

[**sospechoso**—alguien que se piensa que es culpable de un crimen]

CSIs share the clues and information they gather at trials.

¡DATO!

Los CSI comparten en juicios las pistas e información que reúnen.

Criminals won't get away when CSIs are on the case. CSI units find the clues that bring criminals to **justice**.

[**justice**—punishment for breaking the law]

FACT! CSIs can study bugs on a body to learn how long the person has been dead.

Los criminales no se escaparán cuando los CSI están en el caso. Las unidades de CSI encuentran pistas que llevan a los criminales ante la justicia.

[justicia—castigo por quebrantar la ley]

¡DATO!

Los CSI pueden estudiar insectos en un cadáver para descubrir por cuánto tiempo esa persona ha estado muerta.

GLOSSARY

criminal (KRIM-uh-nuhl)—someone who commits a crime

DNA (dee-en-AY)—material in body cells that gives people their unique characteristics

evidence (EV-uh-duhnss)—information or objects that provide proof of who committed a crime

fingerprint (FING-gur-print)—the pattern made by the tip of your finger

investigator (in-VESS-tuh-gate-ur)—someone who studies a crime scene to find out how a crime was commited and who did it

justice (JUHSS-tiss)—when punishment is given for breaking the law

lawyer (LAW-yur)—someone who is trained to speak for people in court

suspect (SUHSS-pekt)—a person believed to be responsible for a crime

victim (VIK-tuhm)—a person who is hurt, killed, or suffers because of a crime

INTERNET SITES

FactHound offers a safe, fun way to find Internet sites related to this book. All of the sites on FactHound have been researched by our staff.

Here's all you do:

Visit *www.facthound.com*

Type in this code: 9781620651711

Super-cool stuff!

Check out projects, games and lots more at
www.capstonekids.com

GLOSARIO

el abogado—alguien que es capacitado para hablar por personas en la corte

el ADN—material en las células del cuerpo que da a la gente sus características únicas

el criminal—alguien que comete un crimen

la evidencia—información u objeto que provee prueba de quién cometió el crimen

la huella digital—el patrón que deja la punta de tu dedo

el investigador—alguien que estudia la escena del crimen para descubrir cómo se cometió ese crimen y quién lo hizo

la justicia—cuando se da castigo por quebrantar la ley

el sospechoso—una persona que se cree que cometió un crimen

la víctima—una persona que se lastimó, murió o sufre debido a un crimen

SITIOS DE INTERNET

FactHound brinda una forma segura y divertida de encontrar sitios de Internet relacionados con este libro. Todos los sitios en FactHound han sido investigados por nuestro personal.

Esto es todo lo que tienes que hacer:

Visita *www.facthound.com*

Ingresa este código: 9781620651711

¡Algo súper divertido! Hay proyectos, juegos y mucho más en www.capstonekids.com

31

INDEX

ÍNDICE

ORNAMENTS OF THE METROPOLIS

Ornaments *of the* Metropolis

SIEGFRIED KRACAUER AND MODERN URBAN CULTURE

Henrik Reeh

THE MIT PRESS   CAMBRIDGE, MASSACHUSETTS   LONDON, ENGLAND

MIT Press books may be purchased at special quantity discounts for business or sales promotional use. For information, please email special_sales@mitpress.mit.edu or write to Special Sales Department, The MIT Press, 5 Cambridge Center, Cambridge, MA 02142.

This book was set in Stempel Garamond by Graphic Composition, Inc. and was printed and bound in the United States of America.

Library of Congress Cataloging-in-Publication Data
Reeh, Henrik.
   [Storbyens ornamenter. English]
    Ornaments of the metropolis : Siegfried Kracauer and modern urban culture / Henrik Reeh.
      p. cm.
   Translation of: Storbyens ornamenter.
   Includes bibliographical references and index.
   ISBN 0-262-18237-8 (alk. paper)
    1. Urban beautification. 2. Architecture and society—History—20th century. 3. Kracauer, Siegfried, 1889–1966—Criticism and interpretation. I. Title.
NA9052.R44 2005
720′.1′030904—dc22

2004052418

Contents

Illustrations

All photographs by the author.

Preface

The idea for this book arose during a stay at the J. W. Goethe Universität in Frankfurt am Main in 1986–1987. It was there that I repeatedly came across Siegfried Kracauer's compelling analyses of urban modernity. On every occasion, I was convinced of their vital yet overlooked power—not least because of the dynamic relationship between them and the essays on the urban by his friend Walter Benjamin, also written during the interwar years. Though I had originally envisaged a comparison of Benjamin and Kracauer, in the theoretical light of the former, I realized during my research that there was a distinctive, inner complexity in Kracauer's writings worth the trouble of examining in itself.

Research was made possible thanks to grants from the Deutscher Akademischer Austauschdienst (DAAD) and the Carlsberg Foundation, to which I express my profound thanks. The original publication in Danish was given financial support by the University of Odense, to which I owe a deep debt of gratitude. I would like to express my particular gratitude to the university's publication committee, under the chairmanship of Carsten Nicolaisen, and its consultants, Annelise Ballegaard Petersen, Erik Strange Petersen, and Svend Erik Larsen. I would also like to mention Anne Elisabeth Sejten, whose thoughtful intuition helped me to dot the final *i* before the 1980s were a thing of the past.

This study of Siegfried Kracauer's writings on the modern city now appears in English. I am highly grateful to the Department of Comparative Literature and the Faculty of Humanities at the University of Copenhagen for generously supporting the translation, as well as to the MIT Press for welcoming the book. I also wish to sincerely thank Gwendolyn Wright, Peter Madsen, and Roger Conover for their extraordinary help, as well as John Irons and Alice Falk, Lisa Reeve, Susan Clark, Derek George, and Matthew Abbate, all of whom contributed to the present book in an always professional and cordial manner.

Abbreviations

E = Siegfried Kracauer, *Die Entwicklung der Schmiedekunst in Berlin, Potsdam und einigen Städten der Mark vom 17. Jahrhundert bis zum Beginn des 19. Jahrhunderts.*

FZ = *Frankfurter Zeitung.*

G = Siegfried Kracauer, *Ginster.*

I = Georg Simmel, *Das Individuum und die Freiheit.*

M = Ingrid Belke and Irina Renz, eds., *Siegfried Kracauer 1889–1966*, special issue of *Marbacher Magazin* (no. 47).

O = Siegfried Kracauer, *Das Ornament der Masse.*

P = Siegfried Kracauer, *Jacques Offenbach und das Paris seiner Zeit.*

S = Siegfried Kracauer, *Straßen in Berlin und anderswo.*

U = Ernst Bloch, *Geist der Utopie: Erste Fassung.*

Full publication information is given in the bibliography.

ORNAMENTS OF THE METROPOLIS

Introduction

The Perspective of the Investigation

This investigation of Siegfried Kracauer's urban writings is part of a larger preoccupation with the city and the urban. Taking a critical analysis of discourses on cities and urban culture as its starting point, it aims to gradually define the theoretical principles and the practical conditions for a true humanistic science of the urban.

The adjective "humanistic" has been chosen here to mark the difference between this and what normally falls under the term "urban planning," which strongly dominates the scientific treatment of the city. Urban planning mainly deals with the physical and administrative mastering of the city's complex mechanism. The task of a humanistic investigation of the urban universe, on the other hand, is to contribute to an understanding of the cultural and social contradictions that arise within this particular framework.

One of the main issues facing such humanistic urban research is to determine the importance and place of the city—especially the metropolis—in the development of modernity. The link between city and modernity can hardly be overemphasized. Despite this connection—partly because it exceeds the boundaries of any one discipline—the urban has rarely been the subject of particular attention and analysis on the part of the humanities and the social sciences.

One exception to the relative lack of academic and intellectual interest in the city as a cultural and social space is found in the period between the two world wars. Both modern architecture (the Bauhaus, Le Corbusier) and art and literature (surrealism) defined themselves through their relationship to the city. A number of intellectuals, too, made the metropolis the center of their philosophical considerations and cultural criticism, which, even today, can stand as examples of how the city as a theme can help increase cultural awareness of one's time as well as renew the social sciences and the humanities. Among the intellectuals interested in the urban, Siegfried Kracauer occupies a prominent position.

Siegfried Kracauer (1889–1966)

In 1989, Siegfried Kracauer would have celebrated his centenary. He was born in Frankfurt am Main, but, as a Jewish intellectual critic, he was obliged to flee after the Nazi takeover in 1933—first to Paris and subsequently, in 1941, to New York. Perhaps because he did not return to Europe after the war but remained in the United States for the rest of his life, he is still somewhat overshadowed by the many other famous intellectuals within the humanities and social sciences who belonged to the circle connected with the Institut für Sozialforschung (better known as the Frankfurt School).

Nevertheless, in the 1920s and 1930s Kracauer was one of Germany's most respected cultural editors and essayists. Working for the *Frankfurter Zeitung,* a liberal daily, he was able to explore a number of genres, such as reporting, film and literary criticism, essay writing, and even the serial story. Originally, Kracauer had qualified and, until 1920, also worked as an architect. But prompted by his experiences of the First World War and his increasing interest in philosophy and sociology, Kracauer left what was for him the disappointing profession of a traditional architect and became a co-editor of one of the key trend-setting German newspapers of the Weimar period. After emigrating to the United States, Kracauer mainly made his living as a film researcher at the Museum of Modern Art in New York and at Columbia University, among other institutions. He also occasionally did research for and advised the Rockefeller Foundation. This life in American exile, however, is very different from the intellectual activity investigated in the following chapters. Here, the source material will be limited to a small part of Kracauer's collected writings, that is, to his writings on modern metropolises produced over a period of almost fifteen years—from the mid-1920s to the end of the 1930s—and sooner or later published in books edited by Kracauer himself.

The Subject of the Investigation: Kracauer's Writings on the Urban

Kracauer's writings on modern urban culture remain today some of the most interesting on the subject from the interwar years. With his experience as an architect and his interest in social science, Kracauer possessed a great sensitivity regarding urban phenomena. Since this interest took shape within the broad context of a newspaper, it was not restricted by the internal division of labor of university disciplines. Free of formalized scientific criteria, Kracauer was able to allow his interest in modern urbanity to develop in the comprehensive culture section of the *Frankfurter Zeitung.* Here it was possible for him to publish an extensive series of articles dealing with urban aspects of experience in a way that the present-day reader would hardly expect to find in a daily newspaper—so condensed and philosophically literary do they appear.

To the early part of this journalist/essayist period, with its treatment of the urban, belongs Kracauer's autobiographical novel *Ginster* ("Broom," the pet name of the main character). Initially, this too was printed as a serial in the *Frankfurter Zeitung*, although it subsequently was issued as a book by Fischer Verlag in Berlin in 1928. In this anonymously published novel it is possible, among other things, to find a number of elements that help explain Kracauer's shift from the profession of architect to that of humanistic and even left-wing intellectual cultural critic. In his exile in Paris (beginning in 1933) his interest in urban culture took a new turn, as Kracauer—much like the philosopher and critic Walter Benjamin—concentrated his energies on writing and thinking historically. This impulse found expression in a comprehensive work on the operetta composer Offenbach, who is analyzed in relation to the culture and history of Paris in the nineteenth century.

All these writings have been republished over the past few decades by the German publisher Suhrkamp in Frankfurt am Main. The novel *Ginster: von ihm selbst geschrieben* (*Ginster: Written by Himself*) and the study *Jacques Offenbach und das Paris seiner Zeit* (*Jacques Offenbach and the Paris of His Time*, 1937) have thus shifted in status from books for interwar readers to books for present-day readers. Before his death in 1966, Kracauer also gathered a small selection of his urban essays from the 1925–1933 period. In the volume *Straßen in Berlin und anderswo* (*Streets in Berlin and Elsewhere*, 1964) they have been saved from the usual fate of the newspaper article (oblivion) and instead been handed down to posterity. Also collected as essays in book form are a series of general critical and theoretical studies published under the title *Das Ornament der Masse* (*The Ornament of the Mass*, 1963), after one of Kracauer's seminal programmatic contributions to the discussion of the lot of the intellectual at the beginning of the period of mass culture. These publications constitute the central corpus for the present analysis of Kracauer's writings on the urban culture of modernity.

The Theme for Discussion: Kracauer's Contribution to a Humanistic Science of the Urban

Novel, essay, history—in various ways Kracauer has contributed in all these genres to an understanding of cultural conditions in the specifically modern metropolis. Yet the urban perspective in Kracauer's work has to date been analyzed only sporadically.

There can be a number of reasons for this neglect. First, the cultural sphere of the city is not, as mentioned, a well-established object of study within the different disciplines of the humanities and the social sciences. Second, Kracauer's writings are not organized in the usual theoretical form; resisting an exaggeratedly abstract, theoretical systemization, he has given priority to an essayistic interpretation and presentation that remains close to experience. Third, the city as an overall theme is not surveyed in general; on the contrary, it is analyzed and described from diverse, consciously fragmentary points of view. The city could thus be described as a prominent "locus" in

Kracauer, but it is not a "structure" that can be summed up by some conceptual sleight of hand.

Much analysis and interpretation will have to be undertaken to reveal how Siegfried Kracauer makes the urban sphere of experience a subject of consideration. But as already implied in the overview above, I think that Kracauer's urban writings can be grouped around certain central axes and thus connected to present-day research in social science and history. His writings even seem to clarify certain crucial elements in the particular development of modernity within an urban environment.

Generally speaking, Kracauer's urban analyses involve a critique of the *principle of reality* as applied in traditional urban planning as well as in much social research. City planning operates almost exclusively with a three-dimensional space of a socio-administrative nature. This often means that, for example, the analysis of urban forms of consciousness and cultural phenomena is judged as being uninteresting—unless it has direct relevance for, say, lessening the resistance toward certain forms of urban renewal. This limited interest in the forms of consciousness of the metropolis does not characterize the works written by Kracauer that are now to be analyzed. On the contrary, it is my hypothesis that *Kracauer's writings can be understood precisely as a counterweight to a somewhat restricted understanding of the city* (as is here—in addition—presented in outline form). Briefly (and simplistically) put, the discourse of most urban planners can be said to deal with the city as a *space for construction and administration.* Kracauer, on the other hand, analyzes the metropolis as a fragmentary and contradictory *space for subjectivity.*

How can this urban view be articulated in a way that allows important aspects of a sociological and historical understanding of the city to stand out clearly?

Analyses of the Metropolis and Kracauer's Concept of the Ornament

A unifying theoretical figure recurs constantly in this presentation of Kracauer's many years of work on the forms of modernity in the metropolis—first and foremost in Berlin and Paris. It has been selected by taking into consideration, on the one hand, Kracauer's writings about cities and, on the other hand, his underlying thoughts of an epistemological and historical-philosophical nature. This is the so-called concept of the ornament, which might initially seem to have little to do with reflection on history and sociology. Nevertheless, this concept is the one preferred by Kracauer when, in 1927, he formulates the theoretical basis of his critique of culture in the essay "Das Ornament der Masse."

In systematically analyzing Kracauer's urban texts, I have found a number of variations on the theme of the ornament. These are by no means unambiguous examples of a common thread, and no inflexible theoretical or analytical structure will be postulated to link them. But I will seek to demonstrate how a dynamic connection, a process in Kracauer's interest in the urban, can be understood as variations on the general figure of the concept of the ornament. For Kracauer, the ornament is not merely an essentially two-dimensional decoration of a surface. It also encompasses other meanings and contexts that will be emphasized in the course of this book. To give a taste of the larger argument, let me just mention that the ornament is linked to everything from the scribbles of childhood and youth to a form of writing that, with the aid of almost invisible but radical transitions, links dissimilar levels of analysis. In passing between these two extremes, it unfolds in connection not only with the ornamentation of buildings from the historicist phase in the history of Berlin's architecture but also with other fragments of big cities that, once interpreted, can become the basis for critical awareness. Above all, the ornament is both an intellectual and a real form of abstraction that makes the rationalized everyday life of the metropolis potentially accessible to what Kracauer—in utopian fashion—describes as "Reason"—*Vernunft*.

So it is possible to formulate the hypothesis that Ornament as a concept is the common point by means of which the universe of the metropolis can enter into an active relation with a critically interpreting subjectivity. An attempt will be made to render this hypothesis plausible in the course of this book.

The Dynamics of the Urban Analysis: Architecture, Societal Analysis, History

The presentation follows a tripartite and extremely simple framework—one that I consider capable of establishing a dynamic relationship between the various phases, genres, and issues that have dominated Kracauer's preoccupation with the city.

Part I lays bare a conception of city and architecture that corresponds to that of the young architect Ginster (Kracauer?), until the professional point of view is transgressed thanks to his renunciation of architecture as a profession and—conversely—to the unfolding of a subjective fascination with and interest in the urban universe. This first part of the book is based mainly on the novel *Ginster* and, to a lesser extent, on Kracauer's doctoral thesis on the wrought-iron architecture of Berlin.

Part II analyzes the ways in which contemporary reflection on urban conditions entails a sociologically tinted conception of the city. The city is not only described as a spatial doubling of the human psyche; it is also criticized at points where its space serves to uphold social conditions that are open to criticism. Further, in both spatial forms and social phenomena Kracauer locates tentative utopian characteristics, though these seem to be in danger of being forgotten. With the increasingly worsening conditions for urban (and generally social) memory, the need for historical reflection in an urban context becomes pressing. This second part of the book relies most heavily on Kracauer's essays from the *Frankfurter Zeitung*, collected in *Straßen in Berlin und*

anderswo and—as far as the theoretical essays are concerned—in *Das Ornament der Masse*.

Part III (the final part of the book) presents the particular urban history developed by Kracauer during his exile in Paris. His historical writing must be understood as an attempt—in a situation in which the utility of traditional political practice appeared doubtful—to promote a historical awareness based on cultural relationships. Indeed, one can even speak of him as experimenting with the possibilities of a "collective psychoanalysis" by confronting the depressed political and social culture of the 1930s with one of the early models of urban modernity: Paris in the nineteenth century. The third section thus considers Kracauer's so-called sociobiography (*Gesellschaftsbiographie*), which deals with the relationship between the emigrant composer Offenbach and the Paris of the Second Empire.

To each of these sections correspond differing versions of the concept of the ornament. But the term "ornament" does not constitute the entire subject of the investigation. The issues involved serve primarily to underscore a drive and rhythm in Kracauer's notion of the city, which ranges from a predominantly spatial conception that corresponds to the sociological interpretation by an individual subject to finally dealing with the city as a space of memory for an (imaginary?) collective subject. In this transition, the ornament serves as a point on which both interpretation and presentation hinge. This role must come as a surprise, given the opposition of contemporary modern architecture to every form of ornamentation. But apart from having importance for a critical understanding of the culture of his own time, Kracauer's reply to the repression of ornamentation in modernity is still central past the end of the twentieth century, with the ornament making its comeback in the 1980s in both design and thought (a point that will be returned to in the conclusion of the book).

A comment on the views of modern architecture on the ornament at the beginning of the twentieth century can provide the first indication of the radical nature of Kracauer's writings. As a prelude to the analysis of Siegfried Kracauer's striking position at a time dominated by opposition to the ornament, I therefore intend in the following to examine Adolf Loos's essay "Ornament and Crime" (1908)—one of the most important contributions to modern architecture's self-understanding.

2. THE CONCEPT OF THE ORNAMENT AMONG KRACAUER'S CONTEMPORARIES: ADOLF LOOS'S "ORNAMENT AND CRIME"
Modern Critics of the Ornament

During Kracauer's time as an architect and urban essayist, the ornament was a central theme in the cultural debate. It is not a basic descriptive category of art history but the catchall term for what modern architecture was seeking to distance itself from. "The insidious enemy is the ornament," Richard Schaukel wrote as early as 1908,[1] thereby anticipating modern architecture's attempt to find its bearings by distinguishing itself from the ornamental.

The first cohesive manifesto against what Schaukel refers to as "the ornament disease"[2] was formulated by the Viennese architect Adolf Loos. His essay "Ornament and Crime" (also from 1908) no longer sought a compromise between surface and ornament.[3] After serving as a lecture manuscript in Vienna in 1910 and being translated into French in 1913,[4] it was printed in Le Corbusier's periodical *L'esprit nouveau* (no. 2, 1919). It was thereby confirmed as one of the most important theoretical bases for modern architecture—a status that, to a great extent, Loos's writing has retained.

The Primitive, Uneconomic, Criminal, and Unhealthy Ornament

Adolf Loos's critique of the modern ornament was primarily directed against the refined—but in his opinion suffocating—art craft of the so-called Wiener Werkstätte. He wrote the following about its instigators: "There are certain bigoted spirits; . . . for them humanity ought to continue to suffocate beneath the tyranny of the ornament" (p. 200). But had his criticism been restricted to this local luxury craft and contented itself with recommending Anglo-American aesthetics of items for everyday use,[5] Loos's lecture would never have had such a widespread cultural impact on the public. If he had not included an extensive collection of civilizational and societal fragments in down-to-earth but rhetorically effective argument against modern use of the ornament, his deliberations would have remained confined within a specialized discussion of design of limited general interest.

Instead, the dissemination of the work is prepared for in the simple yet decisive figures of thought that dominate its analysis of the modern ornament. On the one hand, the ornament is given a constitutive role in the early beginnings of the history of art and culture: "The need to decorate one's face and everything around one marks the first beginnings of art. It is the squalling of painting in the cradle," Loos admits (p. 198). On the other hand, historical development has to an increasing extent made the ornament superfluous by promoting clear, uncluttered forms. Loos ends briefly and concisely: "I have come to a conclusion that I have given as a gift to the whole world: *the evolution of culture is moving toward the exclusion of the ornament from articles of everyday use*" (p. 199). The range of the—in itself—radical hypothesis concerning an unambiguous tendency toward the disappearance of the ornament is broadened in the other sections of the article to form a series of morally tinted arguments, including those that disparage and condemn the ornament in a modern cultural context.[6]

The use of ornaments is first conceived as a sign of a backward culture. The ornament may perhaps have had a certain value at an early stage in history, but since, according to Loos, it impedes socioeconomic development in a modern society, it must, in the name of history and economics, be combated. Referring to the fact that present-day use of the ornament in, for example, tattooing is mainly restricted to criminal circles, Loos next subjects it to real moralizing: "A modern person who allows himself to be tattooed is either criminal or degenerate. . . . If a tattooed individual dies in freedom, it is because he dies a few years before committing a murder" (p. 198). From this position, it is not far to a third type of argument that directly pathologizes the modern ornament and its creators: "The artist," full of power and health, has always spearheaded the advance of humanity. The modern creator of ornaments, in contrast, is a laggard or a pathological case, in Loos's opinion (p. 203). This intolerant and totalizing mixing of what taken separately are highly disputable types of argument culminates in the following summary: "The laggards delay the cultural development of peoples and humanity, for the ornament has not only been produced by criminals; it commits a crime, in the sense that it damages the individuals' health and constitutes an attack on the richness of the nations and is thus contrary to their cultural development" (p. 202). Historical assumptions, moral standpoints, and aesthetic precepts combine here to form a rhetorical unity.

The Critique of the Ornament—Against the City and the Profession of Architect

Loos's position acquires further importance for an understanding of how Siegfried Kracauer distanced himself from a prevalent tendency in the cultural debate. In an article titled "Architecture" (1910), Loos widens his rejection of the ornament in a modern cultural context to include a more general criticism of the culture of the metropolis and of the modern architect.

The uneconomic, immoral, and degenerate formal idiom of the ornament is directly linked by Loos to life in the modern metropolis. For him, the metropolis represents the disintegration of all valuable culture. The break made by life in the metropolis with traditional criteria of taste is seen as the cause of the decorative, ornamental style of building in the latter half of the nineteenth century.[7] This tendency, which contradicts Loos's hypothesis concerning a general movement away from the ornament, is allegedly due to a specific urban profession—that of the architect.

Loos goes beyond denying building culture any artistic justification, pointing to its collective, functional, and nonindividualist aesthetic nature. The modern architect, with his lack of taste, is furthermore unfit to produce a good building.[8] The privilege of the architect rests solely on his knowledge of the catalogues of ornaments[9] and on his exact drawings, which the traditional builder is unable to emulate.[10] According to Loos, there is no immediate link but, on the contrary, a contrast between the three-dimensional building and the architect's two-dimensional drawing. It is yet another fundamental argument against the ornament that the ornament, as the basic unit of the architect's drawing, is the source of an impoverished architecture. In a mixture of polemics against and criticism of the division of labor in the building process, Loos makes a frontal attack on the entire architectural profession: "Because of the architect, the art of building has descended to the level of graphic art. Not the person who can build best but the one whose work looks the best on paper gets the most assignments."[11]

Le Corbusier, the Ornamentless Object, and the Antiurban City

Adolf Loos's strongly polemical and multipronged rejection of the two dimensions of the ornament was an excellent point of departure for Le Corbusier's theoretical ideas in the period immediately following the First World War. For that reason, it is relatively unimportant that Le Corbusier disagreed with Loos's belittlement of the artistic dimension in the work of the architect,[12] or that Le Corbusier in both articles and advertisements in the periodical *L'esprit nouveau* preferred industrially produced to handmade products. Loos and Le Corbusier both provide an "apology for that which is banal, indifferent, devoid of artistic intentions"[13]—that is, for *objects without ornaments,* indeed, without a named designer. Like Loos, Le Corbusier bases his deliberations concerning architecture, design, and urban planning on a number of different ideas capable of developing a modern culture, and in his arguments he goes beyond a traditional aesthetic paradigm of design.

The central position of the whole ornament issue in the discussion of aesthetics before and after the First World War has immediate consequences for architecture and urban culture. These effects are foreshadowed by the many arguments of a polemical, moralizing, and theoretical nature concerning civilization that Loos (and subsequently such figures as Le Corbusier) advances in order that he might—with luck—bring about a new architectural idiom. I will provide no detailed proof of the *antiurban consequences* of Le Corbusier's critique of the dense and labyrinthine city. But his battle against what he called the "medieval" city largely involves a negation of every urban culture that is based on a certain density and visible human practice. The widespread public interest in the spatial dimension of modernity, with all its sociohygienic implications, can be linked relatively easily to Loos's arguments against the modern use of the ornament.

Kracauer: The Critical Force of the Ornament in Modern Urban Culture

Given this aversion to the ornament and thus to modern urban culture, subjected to a totalizing criticism, Kracauer's position acquires in advance a special significance. One

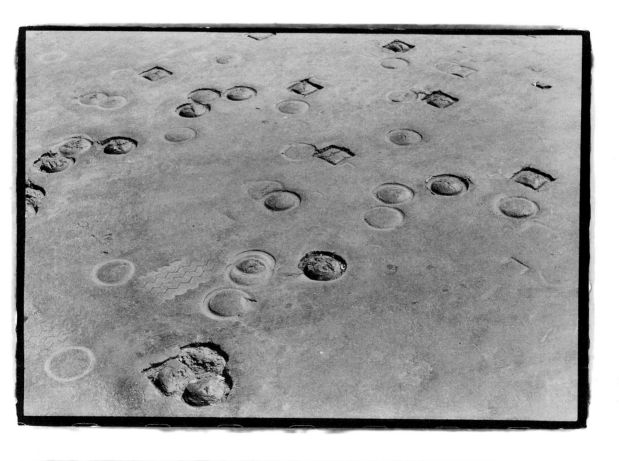
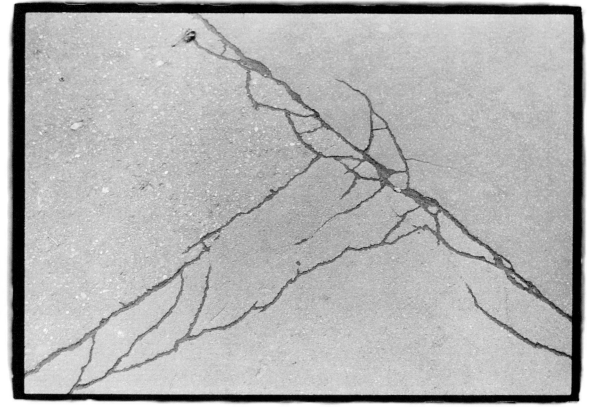

need not make a direct comparison between Loos and Kracauer[14] to clearly see that Kracauer (like Loos and Le Corbusier) goes far beyond the traditional discussion of design and widens the field of the ornament to include modern urban culture as well.

As will be documented in the rest of this work, Kracauer's view of the ornament differs considerably from that of both Loos and Le Corbusier. He is a categorical opponent neither of the ornament nor of the historically developed culture of the European metropolis. Kracauer does not say, as does Loos, "The absence of ornaments is an indication of spiritual force" (p. 207). He neither believes in the possibility nor endorses the desirability of the disappearance of the ornament. At most it can be repressed. Kracauer is convinced that the two-dimensional spatiality of the ornament can be integrated decisively in a specifically urban mode of experience.

So it seems to me that at various discursive and theoretical levels, Kracauer investigates the constantly new ways in which the ornament can support the formation of critical experience and promote *ruptures* in the half-repressed, half-sublimated everyday life of the metropolis. A feature common to many of the in-depth analyses to come will therefore be the tracing of how Kracauer, as he demonstrates the presence of the ornament, suggests fields where civilization's process of repression has met resistance. An overall objective for this book is thus to illustrate how Kracauer's urban writings concretely expose the place of the ornament in modern subjectivity. The presentation of the results of my investigation can now begin in earnest.

PART I

From Everyday Life
as an Architect
to Urban Consciousness

THE FIRST PART OF the book addresses the theoretical and experiential basis for Siegfried Kracauer's analyses of modern urban culture. It takes two different documents as its point of departure—one belonging to social theory, the other being of an autobiographical and literary nature.

In chapter 1, a theoretical link is established between Georg Simmel's classic text "The Metropolis and Mental Life" and Siegfried Kracauer's essays on the urban. The hypothesis is advanced that Kracauer's treatment of the city's sphere of experience is a contribution to the so-called resubjectivization of the objective culture of the metropolis, whose dominance of the subjective spirit is criticized by Simmel.

In chapter 2, an analysis begins of three chapters in Kracauer's novel Ginster. This book is viewed as documenting an attempt at individual resubjectivization with historical perspectives. The relationship of the main character, Ginster, to the urban space of experience is explored via an investigation of his views concerning his employment as an architect and his childhood town "F."

In chapter 3, the complex issue of ornament is introduced directly for the first time, as the status of the ornament in an important urban experience as well as in Ginster's basic aesthetic positions is mapped. Kracauer's doctoral thesis on the premodern wrought-iron art of Berlin is considered as an example of a typological history of art that, in demarcating its subject, reaches beyond tradition. The basic aesthetic concepts foreshadow to a certain extent Kracauer's derived concept of the ornament as organizing experience.

In chapter 4, the themes of the preceding three chapters are gathered in Ginster's discovery of the City as a space for reflection. The textual basis of this analysis is the concluding chapter of the novel, whose action takes place in Marseilles. The mental preparation of a concrete break with dependence on the family and on paid labor as an architect coincides with the visual surface of the Mediterranean city, which appears as mobile ornaments.

To a great extent, the novel Ginster is autobiographical. For this reason, part I, in its reconstruction of Ginster's journey from the occupation of an architect to that of an analyst of the urban, is able to reveal a developmental sequence that has exemplary validity. At the same time, it sheds light on Siegfried Kracauer's views concerning his own decision to abandon the occupation of an architect and, in essay form, to expound a culturally and socially critical view of the modern metropolis.

The Resubjectivization of Modern Urban Culture

I. ANALYSTS OF THE URBAN PRIOR TO KRACAUER
Some Modern Writers on the Urban

Kracauer is not the first person to have thematized the conditions for the subjectivity of the modern metropolis. Both prior to and contemporary with his literary activity, a modern urban awareness was central for a number of writers, literary as well as socio-philosophical. From around 1850—and even before this date—it is possible to discern the self-reflective nature of the modern mentality in such writers as Edgar Allan Poe (*The Man of the Crowd*), Baudelaire (*Spleen parisien*), Flaubert (*L'éducation senti-mentale*), and Rainer Maria Rilke (*Die Aufzeichnungen des Malte Laurids Brigge*). Without mobilizing a sociological framework, each of them articulated in prose the de-personalizing, mobile, and overwhelming culture of the city. No matter whether, like Poe, they referred to London or, as was the case with the other three writers, based their utterances on a Parisian experience, they all supplied a significant part of the foundation for Kracauer and other interwar writers such as Ernst Bloch and Walter Benjamin, both of whom will be regularly referenced in the notes in order to place Kra-cauer's texts in a wider perspective. However, between Poe, Flaubert, and Baudelaire, on the one hand, and Kracauer, Bloch, and Benjamin, on the other, lie the writings of an author whose significance for an understanding of modern urban culture ought not to be overlooked.

The man in question is one of the classic figures of German sociology—Georg Sim-mel (1858–1918), whose lecture "The Metropolis and Mental Life" has, since it was de-livered in 1903, been a seminal text for the broad field of urban analysis.[1] The power of Simmel's work derives in part from its ability to pinpoint empirical characteristics of a city mentality—characteristics whose relevance has remained unchanged. It also provides a theoretical framework for an interpretation of urbanity. Simmel's concep-tual system surpasses both in generality and in its number of academic discourses the one that is made explicit by his successors Kracauer, Bloch, and Benjamin.

It is doubtful whether these three interwar writers were especially familiar with Simmel's urban analysis, which dates from the turn of the century and was then available only in periodical form. But to a certain extent the question of such familiarity matters little, as all three of them, with varying degrees of engagement, found themselves in Simmel's Berlin audience at important points in their intellectual development. From 1908 to 1913, Bloch was a close acquaintance of Simmel and participated in the latter's private seminars.[2] Benjamin mentions that he took part in Simmel's well-attended series of Berlin lectures,[3] whose popularity and magnetic appeal were inversely proportional to their formal academic recognition (Simmel did not gain a professor's salary until 1914—in Strasbourg).

Kracauer's connection to Simmel is more obscure. Everywhere in the secondary literature on Kracauer's work one is struck by the feeling that some sort of close teacher-pupil relationship existed between them. Since the publication of Adorno's essay "Der wunderliche Realist" in 1964, the assertion that Simmel was highly influential in causing Kracauer to give up his profession as an architect and to embark on philosophy and the critique of culture has been widely accepted.[4] This claim is apparently based on a letter, dated February 15, 1962, from Kracauer to a female German student, Erika Lorenz, who, under Adorno's guidance, was writing an unpublished *Diplomarbeit* with the title "Siegfried Kracauer als Soziologe."[5] Despite its importance, this connection and its historical development are very poorly documented.

Not until 1989 did documents emerge that bear witness to the fact that Kracauer was interested in Simmel's conceptual universe at the early age of eighteen.[6] Kracauer was then among the audience at one of Simmel's lectures at the Berlin Art Society. He paid a visit to Simmel the following day, under the pretext of wanting to get some information about his "sociological seminars" (M, pp. 11–12). No real teacher-pupil relationship has ever been documented, however. On the contrary, the name Simmel crops up again only toward the end of the First World War in the chronological table (M, p. 28) found in the first attempt at a Kracauer biography (an exhibition catalogue published in connection with the centenary of his birth in 1889, based on the comprehensive, well-organized Kracauer archive in Marbach am Neckar). In a reply by letter to Kracauer, who at this juncture (November 1917) had been called up for military service, Simmel invites him for coffee during a lecture visit to Frankfurt am Main.

What happened in the intervening decade (1907–1917) is still a matter of conjecture, in part because Kracauer's diaries and notes from the probably crucial years of study in Berlin (1909–1910) are missing.

Kracauer's Intuitive Concept of Ornament—A Differentiation from Simmel

That the meeting with Simmel in 1907 was important for Kracauer is shown not just by a diary criticism of 1912, whose target is the traditional ivory tower and striving academic philosopher—the diametric opposite of Simmel. The inspiration goes much deeper, not least in the field that is the subject of this work: the relationship between the modern experience of the metropolis and Kracauer's use of ornament.

If one reads closely a short extract from Kracauer's diary for 1907, one can confirm that his later concept of ornament is largely anticipated in this attempt to delimit Simmel's view. It is tempting to see in the note from 1907 a first, yet at the same time intuitively precise, formulation of the complex of problems that are going to be examined below in Kracauer's writings on the urban.

Kracauer sets out his position in his diary as he summarizes Simmel's lecture "The Problem of Artistic Style." In line with Adolf Loos (see the introduction) and Le Corbusier, Simmel also makes a general distinction between art craft and the work of art proper. Art craft is linked to the public and thus differs fundamentally from the work of art, which must be thought of as the expression of a personality. From these contrasting affiliations Simmel derives two aesthetic definitions: one is "stylizing" and the other emotionally oriented, corresponding to the article of everyday use and the work of art. As a student of architecture, Kracauer concentrates in his summary on the consequences for articles of everyday use, which, because of their function in ordinary life, "are to spread pleasure and therefore have to be 'stylized'" (M, p. 12).

Although Kracauer is aware that this difference is drawn on a theoretical level, he cannot resist, in a parenthesis, blurring the not very dialectical distinction between design and artistic expression. This does not—as one might perhaps have expected, given Kracauer's participation in ornament-drawing courses as early as his first term as an architect student—take the form of an apology for the decorative element in the designed object. In a foreshadowing of Kracauer's negative and critical concept of ornament, his gaze is turned away from the work of applied art in order to localize, in the very act of artistic creation, elements of the profanely ornamental—or, as he puts it in an extension of Simmel's vocabulary, elements of a stylizing nature. Kracauer's remark concludes the crucial section, the last part of which reads: "He [Simmel] then gave a detailed presentation of the essence behind our articles of everyday use, which are to spread pleasure and which therefore have to be 'stylized,' as opposed to the individual work of art, which causes a commotion in our innermost feelings. (As if Botticelli did not 'stylize' too.)" (M, p. 12).

Kracauer's parenthetical comment does not, perhaps, take Simmel's complex mode of thought into consideration. Simmel would presumably place Botticelli among the geniuses who also "express [their] period" (M, p. 12) in their particular, personal expression and therefore can be assumed, at the formal, visual level as well, to advance toward the general—the "stylized." The crucial difference, however, is that Kracauer, in his resolution of the dichotomy between art and art craft, makes possible the idea of a *personal expression in the formally general.* In the stylized form, which in everyday life

21

works to spread ease, peace, and tranquility, Kracauer indirectly uncovers the possible presence of something personally general—just as the general, thanks to the stylized, was present in Botticelli's paintings. The general forms of art craft are *used* by Botticelli. By means of this figure of thought, everyday articles are indirectly ascribed the privileged role of being able to contain personal expressions of substantial meaning. Art craft, because of its utility function, exceeds the level of the individual subject in favor of a collective, sociocultural subject, a germinal form of Kracauer's later interest in the critique of society and culture.

It can be hard to gain an overview at an exclusively conceptual level of the range of this collective yet still particular expression of something that is apparently unrefined and general. To make such an attempt would also contradict the nature of the expression as a meeting between the particular and the general. For this reason, the remainder of this work will be concerned with the form of expression of individual Kracauer texts, analyzed in order, so that I may give a picture of his concept of ornament that is both general and nuanced.

Kracauer's writings published thus far do not convey in connection with his concept of the metropolis even a very early and lapidary attitude toward Simmel's essay "The Metropolis and Mental Life." In the introductory section to Kracauer's book on Simmel published in 1920 (see below), Simmel's lecture is not mentioned once. Nevertheless, it is one of the basic hypotheses of the present work that *Kracauer's writings on cities must be understood as a historically and socially articulated exploration of the perspectives for a "resubjectivization" of what Simmel calls the city's "objective culture"* (or objective spirit). This hypothesis can be argued with the support of certain elements in Kracauer's essay on Simmel, even though it must first and foremost prove its relevance in the following reconstruction of his many-faceted essay writing on the urban. But to be able to assess the inspiration and the striking shifts from Simmel to Kracauer, we must first subject "The Metropolis and Mental Life" to an analysis.

2. SIMMEL AND THE CULTURE OF THE METROPOLIS
Contexts for a Reading of Simmel's Essay on the Metropolis

Simmel's text "The Metropolis and Mental Life" ("Die Großstädte und das Geistesleben") has in recent times been recognized as one of the decisive, even paradigm-forming treatments of modernity's specifically urban conditions of existence. But even though the text is thus considered a classic of sociology, cultural criticism, and philosophical history, it most often receives a relatively cursory reading. Typically, a couple of Simmel's striking observations are called to attention without these being seen as part of a complex theoretical construction. Even in the essay on Simmel's concept of modernity by the Simmel expert David Frisby,[7] very little effort is devoted to connecting Simmel's experience-organizing (i.e., empirical) hypotheses with the theoretical framework that has enabled Simmel to formulate them. This means that the many theoretical levels in Simmel's text on the metropolis threaten to collapse together.

A reading that fully considers its context in the history of knowledge cannot be undertaken here.[8] The task will instead be limited to presenting the main layers in Simmel's analysis of the metropolis, taking into account the main figures of thought from the individual branches of knowledge. Emphasis will also be placed on the cultural tendencies Simmel uncovered, tendencies that will prove to have a crucial influence on Kracauer's critique of culture.

The Individual and the Culture of the Metropolis

Simmel's analysis—only fifteen pages long, yet for that reason condensed and complex—can seem, for the purpose of theoretical, academic consideration, to break down into a number of strains (sociological, psychological, economic, and historico-philosophical) that may not converge. Yet it should be noted that the title of the essay only indirectly indicates an overall opposition that ensures the presentation's inner cohesion and subtle analysis.

The various levels and the examples contained in them all serve to illustrate the encounter between the individual and the culture of the metropolis. Rather than being a harmonious joining together of individuals in social institutions, this encounter is more of a *confrontation.* In Simmel, the individual is not exposed to a psychoanalytical decentering; he is, on the contrary, kept enclosed within himself so that he thereby may be able to encapsulate a metaphysically irreducible element.[9] But in the everyday life of the metropolis, the individual is subjected to overwhelming pressure. This pressure and its effects are in fact what Simmel is talking about when he refers to "mental life"—"das Geistesleben."

DEVELOPMENTAL SOCIOLOGY

Taking into consideration Simmel's position as one of the founders of German sociology, it might at first glance seem strange that group and developmental sociology (in the strict sense) receive so little attention in his analysis of the metropolis. Nevertheless, halfway into the essay Simmel advances a number of thoughts concerning what the city means in the history of the individual. In spite of the city's many features that break down the individual, which are later emphasized on the psychological and economic levels of analysis, its meaning for the individual is in general *emancipatory.*

The history of the city coincides with the step-by-step emancipation of the individual from social bindings and surveillance structures of smaller groups (see I, pp. 198–200, §§13–18)—including those of the small town (see I, p. 199, §§16–17). The individual's physical and mental bonds are loosened in the city and the metropolis, where *freedom* from an invasive, totalizing social life is at the same time a *loss*. The freedom that can be confirmed at the level of group sociology must in no way be confused with a feeling of emotional well-being. The individual's emancipation from habitual life patterns places even greater demands on him, as that shared life takes place in the technically and socially organized mechanism of the metropolis.

PHYSIOLOGICAL PSYCHOLOGY

When Simmel in the rest of his essay on the metropolis ascribes great importance to a psychological consideration, his reason for doing so is still sociological. For Simmel it is a question of uncovering the conditions of the individual's encounter with social life. The social can be read less from the institutions of society than from the "negative images" that can be observed in connection with individuals.

Simmel's scientific tools in this area are shaped by their origins in a psychology free from contact with Freudian psychoanalysis. The "psychological" (I, p. 192, §2) analysis undertaken by Simmel is characterized as "physiological" (I, p. 196, §9), which clearly reveals that the frame of reference is not a dream analysis based on language and images but rather is biologically inspired. The starting point for Simmel's conclusions is that man is a "creature of difference" (I, p. 192, §2). In his reactions to differences in the world around him, man expends energy to ensure both his awareness and his mastery of situations. In the life space of the metropolis, demands on the individual are aggravated by the general and inevitable "Steigerung des Nervenlebens" (I, p. 192, §2)—that is, an acceleration or intensification of physiological-sensory life. Without the mastery of a comprehensive network of technical and social codes, whose learning calls for a disciplining of man's behavior, survival in the metropolis becomes problematic. A situational awareness that reacts instantly is "the psychological basis on which the type of metropolitan individualities is constructed" (I, p. 192, §2).

In stressing the existence of a "type of metropolitan individualities," Simmel is alluding to a particular individually articulated mentality that carries out the difficult balancing act between, on the one hand, functional reactions (to social and technical events) and, on the other hand, an exaggerated insensitivity to individual differences. Given his postulation of this functional, callous person, it has to be explained how Simmel can describe "the life of the mind" in the metropolis as being of an "intellectual nature" (I, p. 193, §3).

That description does not imply that Simmel credits the metropolitan mentality with a fully developed power of reflection. On the other hand, there is a hint of what was for early sociology (e.g., Tönnies) the central contrast between country and town:

that is, between a traditional form of life that grows naturally within the framework of a *Gemeinschaft* and an "artificial," Babylon-like culture that assumes the form of an anonymous *Gesellschaft*. But Simmel also makes a radical attempt to detach the culture of the metropolis from the condemnation heaped on it in the German political and literary tradition. By accepting the metropolis as a fact of life and thus being able to analyze it as something other and more than a decline in comparison to tradition, Simmel is stepping far beyond most of his contemporaries.

In his positive characterization of the mentality of the metropolis, Simmel is admittedly still dependent on the dichotomy between the metropolis and cultural tradition. The smaller town does not provide norms for him, though it serves as a basis of comparison by representing "temperament and emotional relationships" between people that are part of a development dominated by "the quiet harmony of unbroken habits" (I, p. 193, §3). These qualities of the province are set in opposition to the dominance of reason in the metropolis. Urban reason, despite "the intellectual nature of the life of the mind in the metropolis" (I, p. 193, §3), typically is not open to new people, things, and events. On the contrary, the individual in the metropolis generally regards his surroundings with a blasé and reserved state of mind.

Like Freud after the First World War (in *Beyond the Pleasure Principle*) and Walter Benjamin shortly before the Second World War (in the second version of his essay on Baudelaire and Paris), Simmel distinguishes—within the framework of a physiological system of metaphors—between a surface level and a deeper level of consciousness. The surface level is the seat of reason: "The place of reason is . . . the transparent, conscious, uppermost layer of our minds; it is the most capable of our inner forces at adapting itself" (I, p. 193, §3). Benjamin agrees that the reasonable—"conscious"—layer serves as a *Reizschutz* (protection against stimuli), which in Simmel's physiological psychology becomes a "protective organ" (I, p. 193, §3). But Benjamin, who knew of the psychoanalytical concept of the unconscious (and the repressed), would not share Simmel's confidence that this privileging of reason conversely leads to "the exclusion of irrational, instinctive, sovereign essential characteristics and impulses" (I, p. 195, §7).[10] As early as the 1920s (the time of Kracauer's urban essays), psychoanalysis had become so widespread in the German critique of culture that Simmel's physiologically based hypothesis about "the intensification of nervous life" slid into the background. Instead, writers like Kracauer and Benjamin draw attention to the basically mental structuring of the subject. Benjamin, Freud, and Kracauer as well stress precisely the events that are not picked up by the automatic workings of the "protective organ" but that penetrate into the unconscious. As they break through, the events enable unconscious fragments to return with new force to everyday life. This means that the violence of the metropolis is treated as one of the conditions necessary for both individual and collective memory.

In the absence of an underlying psychoanalytical configuration, Simmel remains focused on the *neutralizing effects* of this apparently transparent, centrally located, but not particularly sensitive reason. His analysis of both the blasé and reserved state of mind implies that the mentality of the metropolis, in its relation to objects and people, excludes essential qualities. A *blasé state of mind* covers over the fact that man as a creature of difference can find himself exposed to so great a number of stimuli that he responds with a "lack of ability to react to the new influences with the . . . appropriate energy" (I, p. 196, §8). The person's psyche becomes *inert*, which, in relation to other people, results in a "negative attitude," a general "*reserved state of mind*" as regards the anonymous individuals of the masses of the metropolis (I, p. 197, §11). The social level is cast into "a quiet aversion, a mutual alienation and repulsion" (I, p. 197, §12).

Simmel's analysis deals with the metropolis at its *level of totality.* He is well aware that there is a finely graded hierarchy of emotions, in which, for example, the street and the department store represent engagement at the lowest and most anonymous level of mental and social contact. But there is no room for the analysis of breaks in the general indifference, whether these take place in the street or in the intimate sphere's inversely proportional worship of consumer goods and human emotions.

Both of these fields—the street and the interior—have high priority in Kracauer, who leaves Simmel's relatively harmonious view of metropolitan culture to examine instead the dysfunctional features of everyday life. The mere possibility of dysfunction (e.g., in the blasé attitude toward technical understanding, resulting in a car accident, or in exaggerated attempts at mastering the cultural sphere) lies undisplayed in Simmel, whose article at this point shows signs of having been written in Berlin at the end of the nineteenth century. Kracauer and Simmel are, however, both critical of urban reason, whose use results in functional mastery rather than in intellectual and social reflection concerning the human conditions in the metropolis.

QUANTITATIVE CONSCIOUSNESS

Simmel anticipates many of the critical theoreticians of civilization (Georg Lukács, Henri Lefebvre, Theodor W. Adorno, Alfred Krovoza, etc.) who, in the course of the twentieth century, concerned themselves with how the capitalist economy makes itself felt in matters of consciousness and thus propagates a culture that focuses on quantity. The exchange value characterizes ever more visibly the aspect of goods that could previously be captured in utilitarian terms. To an increasing extent, this "use value" has to be understood on the basis of a system of needs that is differentiated culturally (i.e., semiotically and socially).

Although Simmel does not use Marx's system of economic concepts in his analysis of the metropolis (or in *The Philosophy of Money,* a work that is much more fully developed theoretically), basing his understanding of economics on the neoclassical idea of marginal value, he has, in a more striking way than the authors mentioned above, concerned himself with the impact of a money-based economy in a specifically *urban* context. The basic theoretical figure for an explanation of the social conditions confronting the individual in the metropolis emerges by means of an analogy between the metropolis, the economy, and the supremacy of reason (I, p. 193, §4). Only when the above-mentioned considerations of sociological evolution and physiopsychology are supplemented by the economic dimension has Simmel's theoretical apparatus been fully set forth.

Simmel does not need to have recourse to a Marxist theory of value in order to demonstrate the impact of the quantitative principle on the life-world of the metropolis. He simply refers to the effects of the production activity being no longer based on commission but destined for an anonymous, comprehensive market (I, p. 193, §5). Consideration of the individual is replaced by this economic context of an objective and formal (though also abstract and potentially inconsiderate) justice. Furthermore, the money economy also assumes importance for the development of particular forms of consciousness in everyday life and knowledge.

"The modern mind has become a schemer," Simmel concludes (I, p. 194, §6), after having proposed that the money economy "reduces all quality to the question of the simple 'how much'" (I, p. 194, §4). Under the gaze of calculating, scheming reason, the quality of things recedes into the background.

The city of the money economy is also of importance for the development of intersubjective relations. The urge of the individual to reproduce himself by means of income establishes a general climate of competition that does not stop at a discreet aversion to collectivity but is heightened in the attempt to escape the mass culture and mass economy that envelop everybody. Both the advanced division of labor and a widespread tendency to extravagant conduct are explained as part of the individual's efforts to attract the attention of an anonymous public.

The blasé individual who rules via reflexive actions proves to embody a number of colorful characteristics that express individualism more than they do individuality. The extravagance is not linked conceptually with psychoanalysis's (later) theory about narcissism. But Simmel implies the social basis of narcissism in his explanation of extravagance, which is characterized as "the only means, via a detour through the consciousness of others, to salvage some sort of a feeling of self-worth and . . . the awareness of filling a particular space" (I, p. 202, §25).

This last quotation indicates the extent to which Simmel's use of radically different levels of scientific analysis is fluid and permeated by transitions. At no point is it denied that interaction between various separate levels is necessary to understanding the relationship between a culture of reason and a money economy. The psychological and the economic levels of analysis are kept relatively independent of each other, without dominance being attributed to either. In Simmel, economic determinism's "in the last instance" is omitted, whereas it would become central in, for example, the Althusser-inspired, so-called structuralist Marxism of the late 1960s.

Although Kracauer concerns himself in depth, from the mid-1920s onward, with Marx, especially the early writings, he never adopts a mechanically materialistic mode of thought. Doing so would have distanced him so much from Simmel's methodological relativism that a theoretical relation between the two would be harder to demonstrate. Kracauer's basic aversion to ambitious constructions of theories makes him rather less explicit, more object-bound in his considerations than Simmel, whose work related to concrete themes did not exactly shun a conceptually creative perspective. Even after publishing the seminal programmatic essay "Das Ornament der Masse" (1927), which will be dealt with in chapter 5, Kracauer was inspired by Marxism primarily when establishing a framework for the concrete investigation of cultural phenomena. He chose for his point of departure the organization of production, whereas Simmel, as mentioned, concentrates on the medium of the circulation process: money. In both instances, the critique of culture builds on an analogical construction with several levels on an equal footing. This common feature is important and overshadows the difference in the natures of their critiques of the urban. Simmel could otherwise have found a basis for a critical involvement in his well-developed perception of the place of the metropolis in the development of history. Instead, it is Kracauer who shoulders this task.

The Metropolis: The Role of a Sociomental Place in History

The enumeration of the theoretical levels and the concrete observations that belong to them focuses the question on the unifying point: the metropolis. Only the metropolis remains an anchor: "The only thing that is certain is that the form of the metropolis is the most fertile soil for this interaction" (I, p. 194, §5) is how Simmel concludes his thoughts about the relationship between psychology and economics. Shortly afterward, he defines the city's status as the social arena where methodical relativism finds a model in reality: "It is the conditions of the metropolis that are both the cause and the effect of this essential characteristic [i.e., the calculating mind]" p. 195, §6).

The metropolis occupies a special position in modernity by being at one and the same time the point of departure for epoch-making experiences and the model for an epistemological position. Kracauer later stresses the radical difference between the pursuit of culture in a small provincial town and in the metropolis, where all classes and strata are part of a relatively uniform mass public (O, p. 313). Similarly, the term *Groß-stadt,* "metropolis," also means for Simmel an essential change in relation to the tradi-tion-bound town.

Simmel does not primarily treat the metropolis as a *morphological* feature—that is, as a city that can find an adequate cartographic representation and be defined by its size and by its specific administrative, political, and ownership structure.[11] The metropolis for Simmel builds on real relations, but has a quality added to it as a *cultural place* (in the philosophical sense),[12] functioning as the setting for cultural relations that—like the theoretical levels in Simmel's article on the metropolis—have a tendency to become detached from each other.

Because of its totalizing nature, the metropolis avoids the daily reminder of its dif-ference from the country, appearing instead as an independent, fragmented, but inte-gral form of culture. It assumes such dimensions that its contrast with the rural is resolved into a new quality. The metropolis serves as a place for social and cultural practice. It becomes a supposed intersection between—and thus an ideal reference point for—a number of different points of view regarding urban reality. That these perspectives are only rarely collected in a common vanishing point is precisely one of the metropolitan culture's challenges to the social analyst.

Simmel advances a common denominator for the many discourses analyzing the urban in his essay by letting the metropolis assume a privileged place in a reflection on the philosophy of history. In light of the individual's history of development, which becomes the focus of Simmel's diverse thematic interests, the metropolis is no longer one single place among many. It becomes *the place* (the definitive place)—the place where the polarities of modern life unfold. From being, in the first sections of the es-say, a potential meeting place for examples, tendencies, and discourses, the metropolis, toward the end of the presentation, is ascribed "a completely new value in the univer-sal history of the mind" (I, p. 204, §28). The metropolis becomes the essential cultural sphere for subordination to what Simmel calls the "objective mind" (technology, insti-tutions, culture):

> The deepest reason for its being precisely the metropolis—no matter whether it is always justified or fortunate—that directs one's attention to the most indi-vidual personal existence would seem to me to be this: The development of modern culture is characterized by a predominance of what one could call the objective mind over the subjective, that is: within both language and law, pro-duction technology and art, knowledge and the objects of domestic surround-ings, a certain amount of mind is embodied, whose daily growth is followed

only very incompletely and at an increasing distance by the mental development of the subjects. (I, pp. 202–203, §26)

For Simmel's metaphysical concept of the individual, the metropolis is the greatest challenge to date. The relation between the subjective and objective mind shifts there in favor of the heavy and hard-to-master expressions of civilization: knowledge, technology, buildings, media, and institutions. The dominance of objective culture is the real and generally formulated basis for the blasé and quantifying mentality. So the question is what *potential for development* Simmel's conceptual apparatus can outline regarding the individual's (but also, more generally, subjectivity's) signs of increasing powerlessness.

Simmel's essay "The Concept and Tragedy of Culture" ("Der Begriff und die Tragödie der Kultur"), published for the first time in 1911, provides tools for a different strategy than the text on the metropolis, which—with a concept of history polarized between a subjective and an objective mind as its point of departure—limits itself to concluding that "our task is not to accuse or forgive, simply to understand" (I, p. 204, §29). The somewhat later text presents a more fully developed conception of history, and thereby also implies the possibility of combining the hermeneutical strategy for an understanding of urban culture with the perspective of cultural criticism.

The article on the tragedy of culture operates with a historical process of the mind that is divided into three, allowing the concept of culture itself to depend on this process taking place. Culture is defined in its pure form as the movement of the mind "from enclosed unity via unfolded diversity to unfolded unity."[13] For life in the metropolis to be converted into culture Simmel requires, in other words, that the subjective mind, in an initial movement, be exteriorized into an objective (projected) form. But the crucial, almost Hegelian condition for the happy outcome of the total process is that a subsequent movement resolve the objective mind in a third form. The objective mind, which dominates the individual under modernity, must in principle be *reappropriated* by the subjective instance before the concept of culture finds fulfillment in history.

Although the conditions for the reappropriation are not particularly promising, the abstract possibility of completing the movement still exists. A general explanation of the tragic—in a classical sense—derailing of the development is also provided. Simmel thematizes "the tragedy of culture" as a structure of destiny (*Schicksal*), which, in a fateful way, makes it possible for unsuccessful development always to be present in the very concept of culture. Before the three-part process is completed there is an important and real risk that the objective mind will make itself independent of the control of the subjective instance:

It is the concept of all culture that the mind creates something independently objective, through which the development of the subject passes from itself to itself; but by that very fact, the integrating, culture-determined elements involved must necessarily undergo a self-development that either uses up the forces of the subjects or always pulls the subjects into their orbit, thereby bringing them up to their own level: the development of the subjects can now no longer take the same path as the objects; if they nevertheless follow the latter, they lose themselves in a cul-de-sac or in a state of emptiness as regards their inner and own life.[14]

The subjects neither can nor ought to follow the objective mind further, but must insist on a perspective different from the development of this objective culture that has made itself independent. That remains "the great project of the mind: to overcome the object as such by creating itself as an object and, thereby enriched, to return to itself." In modernity, generally speaking, this project is infrequently fulfilled, although Simmel insists that over the whole history of the mind, it "succeeds on innumerable occasions."[15]

Even in the culture of the metropolis, objective culture has a "chance of resubjectivization" (I, p. 140, §34). The only difficulty is that the general problem—which consists of indicating concrete paths to the subjective mind's reappropriation of that which it (according to Simmel's speculative concept of history) itself has exteriorized—is even more acute in the metropolis. The individual's confrontation with objective culture is inevitable, taking the form of polarizations of individual and mass, of body and space, of the labor force's necessary reproduction and the prevailing conditions of production, and so on. The discrepancy between the individual's qualifications and the total social and technical division of labor is not easy to overcome, either conceptually or in an actual life.

To a great extent, Simmel defends a strategy of individual self-development (*Bildung*) as the only realistic answer to a situation that affects all individuals. But this strategy, whose justification in the long term is Simmel's concept of the metaphysical individual, is surpassed by Kracauer, whose conception of the individual and subjectivity is marked by his experiences in the First World War. As a result, Kracauer sees the problem mainly from a social perspective.

3. THE RESUBJECTIVIZATION OF OBJECTIVE CULTURE — KRACAUER'S AND SIMMEL'S STUDY OF THE METROPOLIS
Kracauer's Emphasis on "The Philosophy of Money"

Kracauer's published writings present no real stance toward Simmel's article on the metropolis and the strategy of cultural criticism whose possibility is implied in "The Concept and Tragedy of Culture." The two articles are not directly mentioned. It is also possible that Kracauer was not familiar with "The Metropolis and Mental Life," published in the 1903 yearbook of the Gehe Foundation. Given this background, it may seem surprising that in what follows, Kracauer's urban essays will be read against Simmel.

Yet the hypothesis concerning Kracauer's attempt to contribute in a social and historical perspective to the resubjectivization of the objective culture of the metropolis is far from baseless. First, Kracauer's urban writings, whose inner cohesion is reconstructed in the present book, show that he actually followed such a strategy during the interwar years. Second, the published introductory section of his much more comprehensive book on Simmel[16] contains certain indications that support the idea that his subsequent writing about the city is inspired by Simmel on precisely those points Kracauer criticizes in Simmel's work. These points will now be dealt with briefly, after which a number of analyses of Kracauer's writings will attempt to uncover how the programmatic ideas were fulfilled.

The metropolis is mentioned only once in the introductory section of Kracauer's 148-page-long manuscript "Georg Simmel: Ein Beitrag zur Deutung des geistigen Lebens unserer Zeit"[17] ("Georg Simmel: A Contribution to the Interpretation of the Mental Life of Our Time"). This is in connection with fashion—a metropolitan phenomenon ("eine großstädtische Erscheinung"; O, p. 236)—and not in a comment on Simmel's essay on the metropolis. Even if he was unfamiliar with "The Metropolis and Mental Life," Kracauer is nevertheless in contact with its conceptual world, since he draws attention to Simmel's 1900 book *The Philosophy of Money* as being the "finest example" (O, p. 238) of that fundamental idea in Simmel that there is a mutual link and interdependence between the most diverse points in the totality. The metropolis is probably included in the "core principle of Simmel's thought" (O, p. 217)—revealed precisely in connection with *The Philosophy of Money*—that "All the utterances of mental life . . . are connected to each other in innumerable ways; none [of them] can be detached from the contexts in which they find themselves with others" (O, p. 218).

The Philosophy of Money is at the center of Kracauer's interpretation of Simmel. Since this title is also listed in footnotes in Simmel's essays on the metropolis and on the concept of culture (considered in the secondary literature to be Simmel's works of cultural criticism) as the work that motivated the essays' briefly expressed thoughts, the link between Kracauer and the texts that convey Simmel's thoughts about the metropolis is established as certain.

The Defense of Things, History, and the Link between Individual and Society

At his modest distance from *The Philosophy of Money*, Kracauer notes three points where he feels he can identify weakness in Simmel's work: first, the threat against the individual object; second, the absence of historical awareness; and third, Simmel's conception of the individual. All three points are later important in Kracauer's own urban writings.

First, Kracauer's insistence on a delimited ornament as both the starting and finishing point of the written interpretation underlies the critical observation that Simmel, in his attempts to establish mediation between the individual object and the totality, tendentiously dissolves the object and "loses himself in the infinite" (O, p. 241). This problem, which is of immediate importance to any interpretive practice applied to fragments, is articulated by Kracauer in practical experiments within the problematics of the ornament.

Second, Kracauer is apparently trying to overcome the relativistic tendencies in Simmel's thought by appealing to history. At any rate, in his introductory delineation of Simmel's work he draws attention to history's unobtrusive position: "Likewise he [Simmel] lacks a conception of history in the grand style; interpreting the course of history is alien to him; the historical situation in which people find themselves at a given time is something he does not consider to be important" (O, p. 209). The criticism is concealed in remarks about Simmel, but can nevertheless be read as a hint of Kracauer's own intentions regarding historical consciousness.

Third, in the presentation of Simmel's view of the individual one can see an early sketch of Kracauer's later attempts to mediate between history and the single individual. Kracauer seems—judging by the following quotation—not to approve of Simmel's generally metaphysical view of the individual: "The unity of meaning and purpose [double meaning of *Sinneinheit*] that Simmel denies the world he assigns to individuals.... Only Simmel detaches human individuality completely from the world totality, while nevertheless considering all other complexes on the basis of their interwovenness in the whole" (O, p. 243). As can be seen from his book on Jacques Offenbach, Kracauer does not turn against the individual as such, but feels it is necessary to illuminate the individual in terms of the surrounding society. Kracauer finds such a method of analysis represented in Simmel's work on Goethe. Here, an intense, integral relationship is developed between the *individual* and *history:*

> On one single occasion, in his book on *Goethe,* Simmel has attempted to grasp *the individuality of a life* at the root. According to him, the secret behind the figure of Goethe is, among other things, concealed in the fact that the writer himself "knows perfectly well that obeying his own law corresponds to the law of things," in that each of his experiences, as well as everything that comes to him from the outside, fits in a wonderfully fateful way into the stream of his total personality, and, having melted into it, finds creative expression. (O, p. 247)

It is precisely this analogy between the individual and society that Kracauer attempts to develop in his book on Offenbach and Paris, which will be dealt with in the third part of the present volume.

It should by now have been shown that Kracauer is a discreet spokesman for the particularity of the single thing, the central position of history, and mediation between the individual and society. But it has not been proven, in a stricter sense, that Kracauer consciously distances himself from Simmel in his analytics of urban culture in order to promote the resubjectivization of the city's "objective culture." Against this background, the seemingly paradoxical hypothesis nevertheless has to be advanced that Kracauer is intuitively so close to Simmel regarding the question of the threatened position of subjectivity in the metropolis that he—consciously or unconsciously—can have omitted any direct comment on Simmel's position. This unvoiced but critical continuity may have protected a joint urban inspiration that would lose its effect if openly and bluntly proclaimed. But given the writings of Kracauer now available, any explanation of the fact that he deals only indirectly with Simmel's attitude to modern urbanity in the introductory chapter to his book on Simmel must remain conjectural.

This first chapter has attempted to reconstruct the relationship between Simmel and Kracauer concerning the points that are central for the investigation of the ornaments of the metropolis. At a number of different levels, the close link between Simmel and Kracauer has been demonstrated. Adorno may possibly be right in claiming that "Simmel's influence on him [Kracauer] was really more at the level of a turn of thought than of an elective affinity with an irrationalist philosophy of life."[18] Only Adorno tendentiously reduces Simmel to his final vitalistic period, thereby avoiding any detailed consideration of the question of Simmel's substantial inspiration of Kracauer. In connection with the issue of the metropolis, this influence seems to be decisive.

An overall methodological problem arises because Kracauer's published writings do not directly express an attitude toward Simmel's analysis of the metropolis. So it must remain a *hypothesis* that Kracauer's own essays on the metropolis can fruitfully be seen as a socially and historically oriented attempt to promote the resubjectivization of alienated, objective urban culture. The plausibility of this hypothesis will be demonstrated in the following pages.

The first section, which has already been introduced, will concentrate on Kracauer's anonymous fictive autobiography, *Ginster.* The progression of the main character of the novel from experiencing a boring, everyday life as an architect to identifying hope in the city space will be established in detail. This in itself will provide an opportunity to see how Kracauer constructs the link between the individual and urban society. To a certain extent, the novel is a reply to Simmel's biographies of, for example, Rembrandt and Goethe. However, the main character has less in common with these geniuses than with the "type of metropolitan individualities" outlined by Simmel in his essay on the mental life of the metropolis.

A concluding quotation from Simmel's essay on the concept and tragedy of culture must stand as a symbol of Kracauer's fictional doppelgänger, Ginster. Anticipating later remarks, the observation can be made here that *Ginster* is a historically concrete display of the type of personality that lives under the increasing dominance of objective culture. In describing the situation of the individual, Simmel states that

> at several points there [is] more of a decline in the culture of the individuals concerning spirituality, sensitiveness, individualism. This discrepancy is basically a consequence of the growing division of labor—for that requires of the individual efforts that become more and more one-sided and, if pushed to the extreme, often allows his personality as a whole to waste away. At any rate, the individual becomes less and less equal to coping with the spread of objective culture. (I, p. 203, §27)

The next three chapters will illustrate this situation, using material from Kracauer's novel *Ginster.*

The Everyday Life and Urban Perception
of the Architect

I. THE INDIVIDUAL IN CRISIS
AND THE ANONYMOUS AUTOBIOGRAPHY

Siegfried Kracauer's book *Ginster: Von ihm selbst geschrieben* forms the literary point of departure for the rest of part I, whose task is to reveal the forms of the individual re-subjectivization of the city. This autobiographical though anonymously published novel, which appeared first as a serial in the *Frankfurter Zeitung* in April 1928 and later that year in book form (Fischer Verlag, Berlin),[1] is a peculiar document that can be taken at many levels: as a portrait of the age, as literature, as a philosophical essay.

The book, despite being spoken highly of by such writers as Thomas Mann and Joseph Roth, has subsequently not really drawn any particular attention in studies of comparative literature.[2] And yet it is neither dusty nor irrelevant, being of interest as an aid to understanding Kracauer's authorship, including his attitude toward the city as a field of experience, and—more broadly—as a source document for how the cultural traumas left by the First World War were treated between the wars.

In terms of genre there can be no doubt: it is a novel, told in the third-person singular. Yet it has no "high" literary form in the traditional sense. Kracauer has transferred his language of the philosophical essay ("in which only the never-ending struggle against this world's normal laws and organizations are outlined," Joseph Roth writes in his review)[3] from the cultural pages and the periodicals to the domain of the novel.

The novel can be read as a biographically and historically precise analysis of the opposition between the individual and totality, in which category Simmel placed his essay on the metropolis. But the individual is not any traditional, "autonomous," bourgeois subject. On the contrary, he finds himself in a precarious situation, as seen by the fact that the book was published anonymously under a title that was not even accompanied by a nom de plume. The complete title was *Ginster: Von ihm selbst geschrieben* (*Ginster: Written by Himself*).

This anonymity, not revoked until the book's reissue in the early 1960s, was not due only to a wish on the author's part to avoid recognition. In the circles in which his "confessions" could be the starting point for gossip, people knew that they were looking at the work of S. Kracauer, editor of the *Frankfurter Zeitung*. It is rather Kracauer's view of the postwar individual (and thus of himself) that led him to omit the traditional mention of the author. Kracauer has elsewhere stressed the importance of the war for literary thinking and writing, when referring to Kafka's "The Great Wall of China": "They [the fragments of the story and aphorisms] were written down in the years of the war, revolution, and inflation.... It was perhaps not until these intrusions that Kafka was capable of assessing and constructing the confusion in the world" (O, p. 256). The author's choice of anonymity leads on the one hand to his identity being concealed, or suppressed, and on the other hand to the identity slipping into the title itself under the nickname, pet name, and cover name Ginster (which means "broom"), not so much to place the individual at center stage as to mark what is perhaps the only—albeit nominal—fixed point in an individual's life. Here it becomes the fixed point for a novel.

The life of the main character is communicated via writing to other "broom" people. For Ginster has admittedly written the work himself, even the title, but he has not found any reason—or the strength—to sign the work "Ginster" (let alone S. Kracauer).[4] He retreats unnoticed to the position of an unknown person, which he shares with his readers. *Ginster: Von ihm selbst geschrieben* can thus be ascribed to the wish to take part in a general process of experience. For though the individual is weak in the culture of the metropolis, he can still write, write (about) himself.

The anonymity of the individual recurs in many of the incidents to which the novel gives cohesive form. Ginster is drawn into a succession of events in which his opinion is not asked for. He apparently conforms to an alien principle of reality (that of history, the family, or the division of labor). But as an individual he is not completely dissolved or neutralized. Precisely because his behavior is naive and docile, this individual sometimes gains strengths that recall Simmel's observations about the so-called objective culture's ability to break free of—and turn against—the subjective instance. Here, though, the opposite occurs: the individual's endless series of "understatements" enables him at certain points to avoid the dominance of objective culture.[5]

This subtle form of criticism (which makes use of an almost unconscious and highly indirect form of cunning [Hegel]) also allows a relationship to the *city* to shine through. It is all the more central, as Kracauer is building on his own experiences as an employed architect in his treatment of Ginster's professional life. All things considered, *Ginster* is valuable as the autobiographical, sociophilosophical novel of an individual who is being threatened. On the one hand, the book is based on the particular, which Kracauer seeks to translate into the language of the novel; on the other hand, he is determined to let the story have general historical perspectives. Kracauer speaks of his intentions in a letter to Ernst Bloch: "You will realize—I am quite sure of this— that throughout the work I have done nothing except depict myself with great accuracy. Every fact is correct. (Though naturally much else has been changed or invented.)"[6] In the following, *Ginster* will, for practical reasons of analysis, be considered as Kracauer's individual self-reflection, unless sources currently available suggest that something else is possible. The aim is not so much to discover the whole truth about Kracauer as a private person (this is not possible, nor would it be satisfying) as to reconstruct his later views concerning formative characteristics in the relationship between individual and city.

In the next section (2) of the chapter I therefore intend to reconstruct Kracauer's analysis, through Ginster, concerning the *profession of architect* in the—perhaps not exclusively—specific context represented by the First World War. In the final section (3), the investigation into the nature of the architect's job is dropped in favor of an analysis of architect Ginster's *relationship to the city*. The city belongs to the architect's leisure time, in which it is possible to get away from family and work. But as a residual category, the experience of the city remains limited; it is seen in the light of job and family. Beyond this polarization into work and leisure, where leisure is subordinate to work, a third, undeveloped force can be discerned: that of the ornament. With its nature of surface and formal abstraction, distraction, and will to art (*Kunstwollen*), the ornament implies the possibility of new relationships to space and city. More of this in chapter 3.

2. THE EVERYDAY LIFE OF THE ARCHITECT

In an isolated moment of agitation and intoxication, Ginster goes so far as to exclaim: "I am twenty-eight years old and hate architecture, my profession" (G, p. 124). The somewhat pathetic and declamatory tone must be seen as a consequence of his long-standing acceptance of an "architecture" that, according to Ginster, has served the purpose of supporting his mother and himself as well as, in connection with the outbreak of the First World War, delaying his call-up to the army. At the time of this quotation, that call-up has just taken place.

The Dreaming Space of the Architectural Project

The war marks the beginning of the story—both Kracauer's novel and Ginster's relationship to architecture via wage labor. Formerly, he has studied and, among other things, gained his doctorate, less in order to guarantee himself socially than as "incognito" (G, p. 9) to have a certain inner guarantee of academic worth. The day war is declared and everyone is mobilized for the sake of the nation, the possibility is also extinguished of realizing the novel's only architectural project that is able to produce in Ginster a spontaneous joy of designing.

At that time, Ginster is the collaborator of an artist-craftsman, in the vicinity of M. (Kracauer had studied, among other places, in Munich), who has been assigned by a ceramics firm to make a preliminary design for a swimming pool. Since the purpose of this project is apparently to create an architectural symbol, Ginster and the aging artist-craftsman, whose work has a touch of kitsch about it, can indulge in considerations of the basic principles for this architectural dream assignment.

Two different artistic temperaments meet in an architecture that is already, when the discussion begins, diametrically opposed to the national mobilization, by virtue of not being monumental in its exterior. Ginster and the artist-craftsman are more interested in making the swimming pool an interior, a space for the self-expression of the subject, temporarily screened off from history. Ginster formulates a spatial principle of a certain architectural radicalism. He proposes a neutralization of the monumental that allows the comprehensive building project to appear without a facade:

> "I have thought about it," Ginster remarked, "entrances and the front hall ought to be kept invisible. At present, people are building monumental portals everywhere, behind which there is nothing. Modern railway stations are suitable places for funeral ceremonies on a large scale. How anyone can buy a fourth-class ticket in them is quite beyond me. The swimming pool ought only to have side entrances. Most of the people who use it normally only come up to the floors via the backstairs." (G, p. 14)

In Ginster's imagination the monumental aspect can be resolved in civil society in a different way than in Kafka's novel *The Trial*, where public surveillance is extended in the form of anonymous court actions in attics intended for laundry drying and so on.[7] The idea is precisely to promote public spaces in the city interior that also protect individuals against the widespread desubjectivization caused by society. The swimming pool is meant to support unconscious, individual reflection, which ought to be able to flourish during the relaxing, exhausting, and self-forgetting sessions of swimming.

Ginster's employer does not comment on this spontaneous political reflection whose analogy between architectural form and social patterns could have wide-ranging consequences for design. Instead, he allows his own variety of a Jugendstil inspiration—Ginster does not avoid describing pictures of sunsets, bulging coffee jugs, and hand-beaten metalwork—to find expression in the idea of an oval swimming pool ("I don't like corners . . ." G, p. 14). There are to be wavelike patterns on the walls and a general exploitation of reflected light. The pool has the appearance of an almost live, organic—though potentially bombastic—imitation of nature.

Still with the intention of enhancing the influence of the swimming pool on subjective life, Ginster adds—uncontested—a more modernist equivalent. Remembering his childhood, he recalls the double feeling swimming gave him of freedom and returning to a maternal universe. His eyes used to wander upward in a dreamlike movement, as they ought to do in a future swimming pool: "I used to like to swim on my back and look up into the lit-up glass above me. In the roof above the pool we must insert a large kaleidoscope that is set in motion by machinery and that gleams in constantly changing brilliant patterns" (G, p. 15). But his architectural dreams are not in any way anchored in reality. The circumstances of war prevent this vision in praise of the subjective mind from being realized. The Jugendstil idea of a harmony between form, technology, and nature proves to be as far removed from the actual situation as Ginster's attempts to detach individual reflection from society as totality. The nation is put on a war footing; the time for dream projects is past.

Through this meeting of two generations, Kracauer presents, almost as in a parable, the break in architecture around the First World War. The representative of the older generation has "dull eyes" (G, p. 14), and the young architect soon learns that he has to obey a different code of architectural ethics if he is to get a job as an architect. A new ideological alliance between technology and architecture is in the offing. This means the end of a couple of decades of art nouveau in European countries.[8]

Furthermore, it represents a radical forgetting—even repression—of the subjectively reflexive dimension in architecture that Ginster defends in the situation referred to.

Architecture as Wage Labor—Ginster's Incomplete Identification with the Creative Process

Ginster spends the first two years of the war employed as an architect at the drawing office of Mr. Valentin in his home region of F. (Kracauer came from Frankfurt am Main). The firm is bourgeois in mentality, very much a family business in the sense that the office adjoins Mr. and Mrs. Valentin's apartment. It is more like an empty bedroom or a living room.

Mr. Valentin shows no signs of having any thoughts of an independent, design-oriented, or even functional nature. Whether the job concerns a staircase with an adjoining gallery in a shop or a comprehensive competition project for a cemetery in honor of fallen soldiers, his only remarks have to do with the number of steps and the widths of the graves. A partition on the landing presumably interests him more than the gallery that the staircase leads up to. The projected elements are not seen by Mr.

Valentin as form or space, let alone as visual experience. This annoys Ginster, who is also capable of appreciating partitions and closures if they add a moment of surprise to the planned surfaces (G, p. 59).

What is important for Ginster in an architecture carried out professionally is tied to the nature of the work as a *transitory process*. His interest in architectural form and functions is linked to their being part of a creative movement or a receptive moment of observation. The exclusively visual comes into its own only when it is part of a technically, visually, or intellectually enriching experience. For example, the shop staircase mentioned—which Ginster projects with far too exact drawings (G, p. 71)—loses its importance once it is realized and then taken over by its users. At this later stage, Ginster the architect does not identify himself in any way with the object that he has designed: "The shop looked like any other shop: over the gallery banister textiles hung, and the display tables, on which spools rolled, covered the calculated staircase. Ginster completely renounced any feeling of affinity when his path took him past the shop" (G, p. 85).

The completed work process and the everyday use of the finished article do away with whatever imaginary relation may have existed between the architect and the project at the drawing stage. The truly exciting aspect of Ginster's work as an architect lies, in other words, in its nature as ornamental "exteriorization" (Simmel). The actual building, although ordered by a client, is part of an individual's mental process of objectivization. In order to maintain even a limited aesthetic relation to his job as an architect, Ginster has to learn to ignore not only the owner's relationship to the buildings but also their future use, their *finality*.

The use of the planned work becomes a problem in connection with some factory building projects, which owe their existence to the increasing demand for soldiers' boots and grenades. Under these circumstances, an identification with the *form* is absolutely necessary to make it possible to implement the work assigned. Ginster is brought into a situation in which he has to defend the outlined design of the building against its finality—represented by the engineer who demands to have the requirements of the machinery expressed and impressed on the facade. Most important, however, is the almost metaphysical fascination he feels in connection with the building's relation to nature. On each visit to the building site in the city woods outside F., Ginster observes with excitement the changing interaction of the factory halls with the tops of the trees. The aesthetic experience is devoid of any nostalgia about nature:

> With a host of workers around them, the red brick walls broke through the greenness. Higher up everything was still open—a void—with only the poles of the scaffolding pushing up into the sky, each pole separately. The way in which

they rose out of the brick, free and without foliage, made them seem to Ginster closer than the tops of the trees next to them, which constantly sighed in the wind. Nor did he like woodland cabins that tried to give the impression that they had not been built but had simply grown out of the soil. (G, p. 98)

The man-made vertical feat of strength exerts a certain fascination. The feeling of beauty is not, at its essence, produced by the actual building he himself has designed. The relationship between the building (the end) and the implements used to erect it (the means) undergoes a radical volte-face. The projected work has value only as the occasion of an unintentional beauty (the scaffolding):

> In his eyes the red walls were only being built in order to make the scaffolding possible. The walls shot up all too fast; each time he came, they had risen even further. Each time he was amazed to find that the joining together of individual bricks could result in such an amplitude. . . . All by itself. Soon the scaffolding would have served its purpose. Then there would be no more maze—nothing but smoothed surfaces. (G, p. 99)

Ginster's interest is centered on the dynamic and the transient. He thereby rejects architecture's official cultivation of the finished, naked building in favor of the changing interaction between building and environment. Ginster's personal thoughts and comments are on the boundary of—and to a certain extent outside—what is thought of in modernity as being the architect's sphere of activity: physical form and its function.[9]

The Anti-monumental Monument—A Dystopian War Cemetery

The tension between Ginster's basic unease with his everyday life of architecture and his occasional identification with his work becomes more pronounced in connection with a competition to design a war cemetery for fallen soldiers from his hometown, F. (Frankfurt am Main).

To begin with, Ginster declines out of pure professionalism to work on a project whose realization could come to house the earthly remains of his fallen friend (G, p. 106). In continuation of his personal grief at the death of this friend, Ginster begins by sketching a cemetery whose aim is to form a framework for the individual task of mourning:

> Cemeteries ought not to be as easy to grasp as a timetable; they should rather be a maze, like the stony confusion under the pines [at the cemetery in Genoa]. If things had gone in accordance with Ginster's conviction, the graves would have been organized so secretly [*heimlich*] that each of them showed itself only to

those who wished to mourn at them. And yet he normally attached no feelings to [such] venues. (G, p. 106)

In a mixture of aversion and nostalgia, the wish to create a critical work and an identi-fication—never openly formulated—with the competition entry, Ginster ends by giv-ing up the maze and the individual task of mourning. His description of the intentions behind the project are so unambiguously political that the inserted symbol loses its subtle force and becomes openly displayed. Instead of sketching the possibility of a posthumous reconciliation with the war, Ginster pursues a monumental and totalizing strategy. This second project rather pursues an *inhuman* perspective by letting the ap-pearance of the cemetery be in accordance with the actual principles of the war and of army organization:

They [periods of war] called for a complex in which their horrors were repeated. Instead of using the existing sketches to date, Ginster now designed with his ruler and set square a cemetery system that looked like a military organizational diagram. "Victory is a question of organization," Hay had so often ex-plained. . . . His cemetery fulfilled Hay's requirements, insofar as it denied every feeling of secrecy [*Heimlichkeit*]. (G, p. 106)

The analogy between military organization and the war cemetery, coupled with Ginster's distancing himself from military discipline and war in general, must result in a *symbolic architecture.* At the center, on an elevation, a cube is placed that is without decoration except for the names of the fallen soldiers and some edifying inscription or other on its front, facing the main entrance. With the sides of this cube as the starting point, four avenues spread out—three smaller, one larger, but all aligned with identical burial plots "in serried ranks" (G, p. 107), likewise without any ornamental additions. Ginster does everything to underline the "violence" (*Gewalt*) of the avenues' "per-spectivizing effect." He adds sentry-box-like columns at the entrance to stress the image of identical, imprisoned corpses. The symbolism is heavy and apparently im-possible to misunderstand: "The monument looked down on the troops as if it was tak-ing a muster; there was, however, not the slightest irregularity to be discovered. . . . Any attempt at escape would have been doomed to failure" (G, p. 107).

This architectural sketch follows a completely different strategy from that of the swimming pool project mentioned earlier. The main aim is no longer to promote the conditions for a predominantly individual mental reflection; it is rather to instill a feel-ing of horror at a collective and political level. In terms of design, the result, according to the description, is a monument that underlines its own monumentality to such an extent that it loses its legitimacy as a symbol and, instead, spreads doubt about and disgust at the war. Thus, the *intention* of the monumentality is anti-monumentalist. The assumption that barbarity is certain to exercise its own critique is the basic strategic thought underlying Ginster's project.

Ginster has faith in the strength of human reason that transcends his otherwise widespread lack of faith in the world. It does not occur to him for a moment that an extremely centralized complex is precisely what can evoke a fascination with war as a heroic action in defense of the fatherland and as a necessity. Through his necessary gestures toward his employer at legitimization, Ginster himself makes the first contribution to adapting the project's intention to the ideological universe of wartime—and thereby to transforming it into its own opposite. In his two-syllable communication with the owner of the drawing office, Valentin—who later takes all the credit for the competition project—Ginster makes repeated use of references to prevailing tendencies in architecture and in the construction of complexes. He argues, for example, that a highly placed monument "would be more modern" (G, p. 103) than one that discreetly fits into the overall design, and also that "war monuments must have unprotected edges" (G, p. 108), thus avoiding ornamentation of the central cube. With a retrospective irony that shows the project's potential for different interpretations, Ginster summarizes his own project: "During the war years, simplicity was the solution in leading circles" (G, p. 107). The project ends up winning first prize at the competition. Although Ginster claims that he can "scarcely remember the project" a couple of weeks later (G, p. 108), the entire relevant chapter in *Ginster* is suffused with anger toward Valentin, who has neither shown any real interest in nor participated in the work, but who finally misrepresents it.

Valentin's public presentation of the project, where he makes no mention at all of Ginster's efforts, displays how easily the intended anti-monumental hypermonument can lend itself to other interpretations. In his speech Valentin makes use, for example, of individual fragments of Ginster's deliberations:

> In my plan I have been sustained by the firm conviction that the mentioned similarity, which must be seen as typical of the spirit of the fatherland [*vaterländisch*] in the finest meaning of the word, demands that every addition of ornamentation be renounced—therefore, instead of curved lines, I have drawn some that are just as unshakable as the ranks of our soldiers, a host of parallel ranks, next to which there are lines of square tomb plates. (G, p. 111).

Ginster's attempt at using architecture to express a humane message, to create a critical monument, has failed—as far as his employer is concerned, at any rate. Ginster is left without any illusions concerning architecture as a field of activity of ethical and aesthetic worth. In a later effort in Q. (by which Kracauer means Osnabrück), as he works under the title *Hochbauingeniör* (G, pp. 84, 188)—a title that helps secure Ginster exemption from the army after a couple of months' military service—all critical intention has been toned down. An idea of putting up tombstones in the gardens of the workers' houses, whose design was his original assignment, is more an expression of impotent sarcasm than a serious attempt to practice social criticism by means of architectural design.

Discursive Architecture—Intentions and Projects

Ginster's—and Kracauer's—basis for "hating" architecture is limited and, by itself, can scarcely articulate a more general criticism of this form of expression. And Ginster already restricts the valid scope of his animosity toward architecture by adding that it is his "occupation" that is being condemned. The value of his simple but exemplary deliberations should not be dismissed, however.

Ginster's criticism operates at levels of variable generality. With the example of the swimming pool, he shows how the limitation on experimenting restricts the possibilities for individual reflection. A collective social criticism, as outlined in his intentions behind the war cemetery project, is indeed averted by the dominant institutions of architects, here exemplified by the architect Valentin's presentation of the project.

Broadly speaking, constructive reason is directed at profane objectives, such as finding expression in connection with the conversion of a shop and the erection of new production facilities for the war industry. For the employed architect who does not completely allow himself to be reduced to salaried work and its realistic projects, as in Ginster's case, the only possibility that remains is to isolate individual aspects of architectural space in their progressive context. Ginster limits his identification to, for example, the activity of drawing and the observation of the building's development in relation to its surroundings. He is without any great expectations. Even the attempt to use broad—ornamental, in Kracauer's sense of the term—charcoal sketches (G, p. 104) in the cemetery project is subjected at the presentation of the winning project at F.'s architectural society to Valentin's purely technical verdict: "unfortunately, the copies are somewhat indistinct. We were too lavish, ladies and gentlemen" (G, p. 111).

Ginster's situation is a special one, but his exemplary, concrete experience with and criticism of architecture as a profession carries general weight. The novel *Ginster,* through its literary and retrospective nature, gives a certain type of insight into Siegfried Kracauer's otherwise almost obscure life as an architect. It would be wrong on the basis of *Ginster*—as often happens in the secondary literature—to reduce Kracauer's critical reflections to the idea that from the beginning architecture was simply a case of a *Broterwerb* forced on him by his home (G, p. 22). A development takes place that moves through disappointments and adaptation to the possible—in parallel with the increasing ethical and political demands being made on architecture as a profession.

But fulfilling the demand that *Ginster* should be read with greater subtlety does not resolve some important methodological problems. These arise from the use of a text of fiction (the novel) as a source to shed light in part on the author's biography and in part on his theoretical standpoint. In Kracauer's case, a number of things in the interplay of biography and novel weaken the justification for the secondary literature's quite uncritical use of *Ginster* as a reliable source shedding light on his own life. *Ginster* was written almost a decade after the end of the First World War and is therefore a historical reconstruction of a sequence of events. In this book Kracauer suppresses, for example, the fact that he, under the influence of the general enthusiasm for the sudden spirit of national solidarity at the war's outbreak, both composed a military song, "Auf der großen Fahrt" ("On the Long Journey"), and wrote an article on how the war served to release the individual from loneliness and to organize freedom.[10]

In a similar way, the possibility exists that his portrayal of his life as an architect seeks more to *legitimize* than to explain or motivate his actual change of profession. Until recently, the lack of accessible documents has posed a practical obstacle to distinguishing between Ginster and Kracauer. This lack has been partially remedied, since some documents relating to his family and to architecture have been published in connection with the centenary of Kracauer's birth.[11] A sketch of the war cemetery for fallen soldiers discussed above shows that the bombastically alienating architecture described in *Ginster* is hardly as devoid of ornamentation as the novel might suggest.

The discursive presentation of an architecture completely devoid of decoration and particulars proves—when compared with one of Kracauer's sketches—to refer to a design that is more neoclassicist than premodern. The small dimensions of the cemetery—there are only four tombstones in each row—makes one immediately think not of the major provincial city F. (Frankfurt) but rather of a village with 2,000 to 3,000 inhabitants. The central monument is not a pure cube—it has a superstructure, divided into four layers, which it supports. A band of niches, alternately projecting and recessed, is repeated in the stones of the soldiers' graves.

The intention to arouse horror presented in *Ginster* has—if one is to judge on the basis of this one drawing—been only roughly translated into an architectural idiom. The complex spreads a feeling more of desolation and emptiness than of horror. This emotion, seen with present-day eyes, is far less than the grim atmosphere involuntarily evoked by Verdun or by the American cemeteries, so radically devoid of ornament (but thereby so much the more monumental), for soldiers who fell in the Korean and Vietnam wars. The possibilities and needs of the autobiography to reconstruct and rationalize an individual life-story and a visual architectural dimension of reality must be just as little underestimated as the link between collective historiography and topical social relevance. As a fictional processing of experience, *Ginster* appears in certain respects to be less a portrait than a touched-up interpretation of Kracauer's life.

3. THE *LEBENSRAUM* OF THE CITY: GINSTER IN HIS CHILDHOOD CITY F.

From Constructing Buildings to Reflecting on the City

From a biographical point of view, there can be no doubt that Siegfried Kracauer leaves, at the beginning of the 1920s, his profession as an employed architect to earn a living as a writer. This shift is more than just one of profession—and, at this distance in time, it is possible to show a certain dialectic in his development. First, Kracauer moves from an essentially constructive to a predominantly reflective mode of existence. Second, this change means he has a different object. The limited building project is replaced by the city's themes, which are admittedly fragmentary and ornamental but which include more dimensions than the three-dimensional space of architecture. Constructive, limited design is replaced by its opposite: mental and writing activity that is endless when it comes to reflection.

The retrospectively constructed dialectic between two stages of life's path does not of itself guarantee that there is a particular dynamic relationship between these two opposites. Ginster's muted frustration at his work as an architect is not compensated for by a counterreaction in city life that could explain why one day he—under the name of Siegfried Kracauer—makes the general and mobile forms of the city the object of his professional activity.

The Burden of Intimate Knowledge of One's Home Region

Even if *Ginster* was written after a change of profession, Kracauer has included little about his path to writing essays on the city in the novel's course of events. The retro-projection of the finishing point is moreover extremely limited in the quantitatively important sections on life as an architect in F. in the first years of the war. Only in the very brief mention of the Berlin of his time as a student is strolling through the city featured as an important activity. Ginster's lack of any social anchor is sublimated in extensive *flânerie* (G, pp. 23–25), which refines and displays solitude in public spaces. On one single page Kracauer offers a wonderful, condensed depiction of the point of view of the city researched by Walter Benjamin under the unifying figure of the *flâneur*. Kracauer presents in a literary form the paradigm of this figure—the wanderer who is at the same time disinterested, pensive, and alienated. Later, in M. [Munich], Ginster prefers to go to a dancing school, by means of which the city is reduced to "a sort of habit" (G, p. 9). Ginster's period as a practicing architect is linked to his native city, F. This link is crucial, since F. is perceived as the epitome of a basic unfreedom.

That the city (represented by F.) does not seem to be an enticing alternative point of view to spatial contexts, frozen by the architect's profession, has to do with the fact that the architect Ginster's relationship to the metropolis greatly resembles that of the son Ginster to his mother. The binding roles in wage labor and in family are linked to the city F., which, with biting irony, is characterized as an ambitious provincial city in the following portrait, based on historical facts:

> Ginster came from F., a metropolis that had grown throughout history, situated by a river, among middle-sized mountains. Like other cities, it exploits its past to increase tourism. Coronations, international conventions, and an association's shooting contest took place within its walls, which had long since become public parks. A monument has been erected to the gardener. Certain Christian and Jewish families trace their origins to [distant] ancestors. Even families without ancestors have succeeded in becoming banking families that have links with Paris, London, and New York. High places and the stock exchange are separate only in terms of space. The climate is warm; the population not living in Westend, the area to which Ginster belonged, is hardly taken into account. *Since he actually grew up in F., he knew less about the city than other cities with which he was unfamiliar.* (G, p. 20; my italics)

This acerbic characterization of F. (Frankfurt am Main, the city in which Kracauer was born and grew up) was written at a juncture when Kracauer had realized Frankfurt's relative mediocrity ("among middle-sized mountains," etc.). Yet the final sentence avoids the cheap scoring of a point by, en passant, making an observation that is banal in terms of urban sociology and urban philosophy, but basic nevertheless: familiarity with a city is not the same as a knowledge of it. While familiarity often remains silent and implicit, knowledge tends toward becoming externalized. These two registers of experience have to be brought into an active relationship to each other in order to substantially contribute to urban self-reflection.

At the outbreak of the First World War, Ginster already knows his home city, F., all too well. So well that he does not even try to convert his familiarity into either objective facts (as in the characterization just quoted) or into knowledge, knowledge of life. For Ginster, F. is *the restrictive city*. It appears in a childhood memory, when Ginster is whistling on the back platform of the tram (a motif that returns in the very last pages of the book) and is interrupted by the conductor, who impresses on him that "whistling's something he could do at home," not in a public space (G, p. 20). Right from his childhood, the public spaces of the city have been associated with suppressed expressions of joy and a corresponding disciplining of the self.

Street Form and Street Life—From Suburban Noncontemporaneity to the Labyrinthine Immobility of the Inner City

Against this background, it is less surprising that the interpretation of F. is so limited. It consists essentially of a sociomorphological typology that polarizes the city into suburbia and city nucleus. The broad suburban street with its culture-creating elements of popular life contrasts with the medieval city center, whose spatial maze corresponds to a feeling of mental and social closeness.

Ostend, which lies just outside the former ramparts and the present park, represents what is typical of suburbia, or rather the outer precincts. Its description has its starting point in Ginster's drawing office, but it could just as easily have been based on Kracauer's home until 1930, which was also situated in Ostend. (No information is provided about Ginster's family home.) The description focuses on the meeting between space and social life. The smooth facades of the broad, straight streets find their counterpart and transformation in a traditional Jewish courtyard and street life. The lack of contemporaneity between the space of the street and its life adds an exotic touch to F., which is otherwise presented as a quite colorless city.

> Smooth facades to the houses, backyards behind them, out of which Jews poured forth. They wore caftans and had flowing beards; two men conversed as if there were four of them—Jews that seemed like imitations—they looked that genuine. The broadly laid-out streets, through which there even drove trams, were artificially hemmed in by the caftans. (G, p. 58)

Ginster seems to be fascinated by the striking and unexpected contrast between modern form and traditional culture.

Such a compensatory feature is not to be found in the inner city, inside the ramparts. The historical city is identified so greatly with the unaesthetic lifestyle of Valentin that, dank and unchanging, it becomes an image of Ginster's futile, tangled life. The labyrinthine basic pattern that could have interested (and in other contexts—e.g., Marseilles—does interest) Ginster as a space for discovery is one-sidedly interpreted as analogous to the moody enclosed personality of the architect:

> "I'm just off for a little walk," said Mr. Valentin. It turned out that it was impossible to get him outside the old city, in whose neighborhood he had settled down. It had narrow lanes [really secret passages] that fortunately were always partially in shadow. If they had been covered like a junk stall, Mr. Valentin

would have felt even more at home in them. For him the war was too spacious, a palace with huge entrance halls, where one could be seized with agoraphobia. (G, p. 59)

The maze of the old city, which in the case of Frankfurt disappeared forever during the bombing raids at the end of the Second World War, returns repeatedly in comparisons and metaphors connected with Valentin. Valentin's arguments are "full of corners like the streets of the old city" (G, p. 60). His private flat, which, as mentioned, adjoins the drawing office, was "difficult to get an overview of—a maze like the old city" (G, p. 61). And when he attempts to write an application to get Ginster exempted from military service, his formulations are "a self-created old city maze" (*Altstadtlabyrint;* G, p. 88).

The old part of F. and the city F. in general cannot serve as a sphere that offers Ginster a chance of changing his life. F. is linked to the depressing occupation of an architect, not to its opposite. The city lies—quite literally—in the shadow of salaried work. Ginster's relation to the city remains subject to the restricting principle of reality that is prevalent in general forms in practical architecture and that, in extremely petit bourgeois forms, organizes his daily life in the drawing office. Ginster has an unconscious, purely functional relationship to F. during the time he is an architect there. A single exception to the rule leads to a confirmation of the limiting nature of urban life: "Apart from that, Ginster . . . moved around the city in a system of lines. . . . Various systems do not even intersect each other" (G, p. 122). Ginster uses the streets he has to use only for practical reasons—to get to the drawing office or, once a week, to meet with a couple of not particularly valued, let alone friendly, acquaintances for simulated men's talk in a music café with "a skylight; three musicians unfit for war" (G, p. 92). If one ignores a single (unpleasant) meeting (G, p. 94), Ginster glides unnoticed through F., as if Frankfurt with its half a million inhabitants was a real "metropolis," as is claimed in Ginster's introductory description of his hometown (G, p. 20).

Ginster's general passivity toward his hometown as a city portrayed in gloomy terms does not result only from its labyrinthine *form*. To a far greater extent, the explanation has to be sought in the fact that the *life* that unfolds in the city is perceived by Ginster to be oppressive. Instead of enticing Ginster with a worldly alternative, the labyrinthine aspect of his childhood city becomes in Ginster's memory the sign of an existential situation that does not allow the individual's creative development, let alone any hope of possible change. As an analogy of the futile and erring life situation, the medieval maze of the city becomes a confirmation of the immobile everyday life of the individual.

The limited job of architect does not select the city as its utopian opposite. On the contrary, the perception of the city, in the case of F., is dominated by the unacceptable life-horizon. In F.'s tradition-dominated and immobile city there is no dynamic tension between the life of the individual and its spatial surroundings. Not until the reality principle of the frozen life-form is exceeded can even F., on occasions, acquire an innovative function in Ginster's consciousness.

In its capacity as an anonymous novel of recollection that seeks to establish a link between the individual and the collective during the First World War, *Ginster* sheds light on the relationship between the everyday life of an architect and his leisure experience of his childhood city, F. It must not be forgotten that Kracauer has written his memoirs *after* having switched from being an *architect* to being a *writer.* In the novel's reconstruction of history, certain events and architectural projects are interpreted in ways favoring intentions that were not always evident at the original moment or successfully translated into reality.

With this proviso, the novel *Ginster* can be said to offer important insights into the relationship between Ginster's limited view (caused by the division of labor) of the city's spatial constructions (the object of architecture) and his leisure experience of the city's civil, cultural, and spatial aspects. His frustration at his limited job as an architect, which he makes at best only subjectively acceptable by concentrating on marginal aspects of the actual process of drawing and building, provides no basis for hope in the urban sphere of experience. His experience of the City, which is moreover Ginster's native city, is weighed down by his apparently unalterable life situation. Only in exceptional and utopian moments does awareness stir in him of the city as a possible reservoir of change and hope.

Beyond Functional Space: The Ornament

In the universe of the ornament, the novel *Ginster* reveals another, more original basis for Kracauer's later urban analyses than is supplied by his life as an architect in F. That life, on the contrary, closed off the city—his native city at least—as a field of reflection.

Just as in Kracauer it is never a question of a general *theory* concerning the relationship between ornament and city, it would be a mistake to see in *Ginster,* which remains literary in its form, a *concept* of the ornament. Nevertheless, the ornament—that usually two-dimensional abstraction of perspective's three dimensions—features in crucial passages as a central theme that enables one to undertake an analysis of its significance at the level of an individual life-story.

Kracauer's *ornament-figure*—let me, by way of introduction, use this vague expression so as not to claim that a positively formulated concept of ornament exists—is extremely comprehensive, exceeding the word's traditional meaning, "decoration." The semantic breadth of the term "ornament" is, for example, expressed in a passage set at the time when Ginster accepts his call-up to the army. With a host of other soldiers he is waiting on the platform of F.'s main station, when a memory from his childhood surfaces. This image, without Kracauer's ever making use of the term ornament, comprises various different dimensions of the complex of problems that are to hold center stage in the final chapters of part I of the present work, as well as—at a level of social analysis and of reflection on his own time—in part II.

I. THE ORNAMENT AND EVERYDAY LIFE

The Ornament—Between Image, Memory, and Narrative

With its blend of time past recalled and time present, this crucial scene from *Ginster* shows that the ornament basically has the nature of something exceptional and negative. The event consists quite simply of a meeting between past and present. As a child, Ginster, after setting out from home on a Sunday afternoon, spent time on his own in the huge station hall. He had fled from a family life he found oppressive because of the complete lack of tolerance shown toward his particular method of producing an ornament, though one unsuitable for his sex and age: knitting. Even during the mobilization, in his adult life—Ginster has been called up and has declined an offer of exemption—knitting has a magical touch. Out of a single row, structures of net can be produced that, while joining together to form a surface, are at the same time almost transparent. And they are also constantly being threatened with annihilation, with becoming unwound. Ginster the soldier is slightly surprised when confirming and commenting on his childhood fascination with knitting: "Obviously, it had amused him to create with the long, gleaming needles a regular web, one that could be run through with the selfsame needles and immediately become loose threads, had they not been secured" (G, p. 142).

Ginster sees himself as a child, sitting on a bench in the station hall, busy producing small knitted nets. In recalling this incident, which takes place when he is once more breaking with the home—and in the same interior space as the first time—knitting becomes the compressed expression of the station hall's comprehensive scene. As a dramatic visual substitute for the family, the human crowd, train technology, and the station building combine as coordinated factors in the child's eyes to form a *mass.* This mass also appears, in the interior space of memory, as if it were in a process of constant change:

> Again and again . . . sorrow and defiance had given way and, in the feeling of bliss at being so lost in a milling crowd that incessantly renewed itself and reengaged itself, he had strewn magnificent gleaming nets over the vaulted glass roof, nets that mixed with the smoke from the locomotives disappearing into the dark. (G, p. 142)

The material forms of knitting and the life of the station are experienced in the child's eyes in figures that remind one of art—for example, Monet's paintings from London, Rouen, and the garden in Giverny. In the eyes of the artist, light converts matter (water lilies, weeping willows, and water) into color fragments, which—translated into oil painting—can be (one hopes) fixed on canvas by a Monet. In F.'s station hall the same light brings about a sparkle that lights up humans and objects, giving them unfamiliar shapes. As if they had a new inner life, phenomena actually dissolve into light structures that can only just be held together in cohesive images of sight and recall: "Finally, the entire glass hall had become a huge sparkling, and from the people light penetrated outward as from colored paper wrappings beneath which candles are burning. Intoxicated by the light, he had gleamed the most himself, with a small patch of wool in his hands hanging forgotten between the needles" (G, p. 142).

The shift from ornamental expression (through knitting) to experience and intoxication in ornaments (through the gaze) is, of course, recorded as an adult's recollection, processed through language that is far removed from the world of a child. But a link to the original experience is established via Kracauer's underlining of the visual ornamental structures. These manifest themselves in the knitting, the milling crowd of people, the imaginary radiant net, the glass roof, the train, and the smoke, finding their climax in a specifically urban sunset. This gives the ornament the status of a *figural principle* vital for both the psyche and the world of images, a principle that is certainly visual but that cannot be depicted in defined images.[1]

The Ornament and the Everyday Will to Art

In the recalling, narrative medium of language, the ornament establishes a series of transitions—broken, concentrated in fragments—between gaze and psyche, between sight and mind. The perceptive richness of the analyzed passage reflects Kracauer's attempt to widen the field of aesthetics to also include everyday life. In such situations he seems to confirm reminiscences of a *Kunstwollen*, a will to artistic expression that in aesthetic theory has traditionally been confined to the sphere of the highbrow—the work of art rather than art craft. The expressively shaping force of the "true artist" is modified and restricted in the artistic expression of the everyday by a number of social factors, a modification that seems only to increase Kracauer's interest in the hitherto unnoticed ornamental expressions.

A striking example of the close relationship between the everyday and art that finds expression in ornaments can be observed in an episode from Ginster's time in the army. He has been given the task of polishing windows with a piece of rag that is full of holes—something that makes carrying out the practical task a hopeless affair before he even starts. Ginster's interest is drawn to the possibility of letting this rag produce ornaments:

> To his horror, an impenetrable smeary mess gradually emerged, which admittedly filled him with a certain triumph, since it corresponded to the rag [which Ginster had] immediately seen through. Just as Ginster was about to stop work, he noticed that it was possible to cause certain patterns to appear, depending on the polishing technique used. If he stirred the smear in circles, it formed scrolls. Perhaps it was possible to produce artificial frost-flowers with the aid of the folds in the rag. "Come down!" someone shouted up at him. In confusion, he descended the ladder one rung at a time; the entire squad had gathered at the foot of the ladder and was laughing at him. "You're completely useless." (G, p. 160)

Through the intervention of a special form of willfulness, the impossible task is transformed into a possibility for absentminded aesthetic expression. Since Ginster's activity is on the borderline between introverted and external expression, it may seem pretentious to view this mixture of distraction and stubbornness as an everyday version of the will to artistic expression. But such passages cover Kracauer's interpretation of the relationship between the *psyche, everyday life,* and *art* during the modernity that is accentuated by the First World War. By this means he also lays the foundation for an account of his own connection to architecture. The discovery of an ornamental will to artistic expression in the everyday makes possible a critique of the limited potential for personal development in the profession of architecture.

2. GINSTER'S THEORETICAL PROGRAM OF ARCHITECTURE
The Ironically Reconstructed Choice of Profession

The hypothesis concerning a generally present, average will to artistic expression in modern subjectivity can—still using material from the novel—be supported by an analysis of Ginster's theoretical "manifesto" of architecture and art. This takes the form of a lengthy synthetic passage of recollection,[2] whose discursive levels must be analyzed separately.

The main hypothesis stresses precisely the fact that the will to artistic expression is not restricted to the sphere of the highbrow but can, in the form of the ornament, be found in modernity's metropolitan individuals. The outlining of this position begins with the following passage, where Ginster, with a certain degree of self-distance, presents the underlying reason why he was advised to attend the school of architecture: "From an early age, Ginster was fond of drawing ornaments. In the blank margins of his school notebooks systems of spirals shot upward, tapering as they rose. They radiated outward to right and left from a vertical line: leaves that had become fine lines and that joined up with themselves" (G, pp. 21–22).

Everyone can give a little nod of recognition at this and think back to an inattentive, absentminded nervousness that was converted into semiautomatic, unpremeditated decorations on notepaper. But the claim that there lies a form of artistic expression in this activity that can even be ascribed a norm-giving function vis-à-vis the space-forming practice of architecture needs further justification. The passage quoted, which serves to introduce the novel's programmatic section, places the widely assumed correlation between a child's apparent "abilities" and his choice of education and profession in an ironic light.

He [Ginster] would most have liked not to become anything at all, but his parents wanted him to be able to earn a living. Everyone should have an occupation, and the first wages one had earned oneself were a source of happiness. He would have felt happier if he had been given the money—but the family had only a poor relation in America. On the basis of his spirals, he was advised to choose architecture. Just how this plan emerged it was impossible later to discover. (G, p. 22)

The juxtaposition of doodles and the commonsense decision to choose to study architecture appears in *Ginster* to be somewhat grotesque and accidental.[3] The irony is complete insofar as his reasons for choosing architecture indirectly make Ginster himself focus on these half-unconsciously drawn ornaments.

With a peculiar stubbornness and a wonder that corresponds to a mentally central (but unconscious) force, the production of ornament survives as the technique of observation and interpretation for the entire history of art and architecture.[4] Ginster notices how "the outlines of the art history books formed ornamental figures" (G, p. 22). He does not try to decode them in order to arrive at a constructive, functional, or symbolic perspective. On the contrary, these illustrations are subjected to a process of abstraction that allows them to appear two-dimensionally. Kracauer expresses Ginster's gaze as follows: "If he looked at them [the outlines] independently of the significance they acquired in connection with the elevations, they appeared to be black-and-white compositions of strokes, letters, or empty surfaces, whose beauty corresponded to their purposeless existence" (G, p. 22). In line with the pictorial art trends of the period, whose sources of inspiration include African art and expressions by mental patients alongside the development toward abstract art, Kracauer does not consider the naive—in both senses of the word, the simple and the original—to be inferior, even when it applies to "inartistic" childhood activities. In Ginster's relationship to architecture, analyzed earlier, his love of the ornament is found at a number of levels. At the receptive level of observation, for example, one might mention his relationship to the scaffolding and building in the woods; so, too, the spatial form of the ornament finds constructive expression in, for example, his exaggeratedly exact staircase drawings and his soft charcoal sketches for the military cemetery.

It is perhaps surprising that Ginster never considers translating his fondness for the "purposeless existence" of the ornament into a commitment to pictorial art proper. One reason is that the basis of legitimating his work, that of being a "breadwinner," would be lost. A second is that Ginster would scarcely credit himself with having a talent for a mode of expression that is purely visual. Behind these reservations is also the fact that Ginster does not think of artistic activity as something outside his everyday life, that is, exclusively in professional isolation. On the contrary, the interest in the ornament is constantly placed in a state of tension with more "immediate" reality, leaving it few possibilities within traditional modern public art (if one excludes, for example, surrealism and certain tendencies emerging in the 1960s). The critical function of the ornament in relation to its mental, social, and spatial surroundings is crucial for Ginster—and for Kracauer.

This critical dimension (which also includes the ornament's resistance, persistence, and nonidentity) is reduced in the architect's work process to an extremely limited field that includes neither the finished work of art nor its societal functions. As shown in chapter 2, Ginster is disappointed in his encounter with salaried work and the conditions for architectural construction.[5] As an employed architect he cannot control his own "ornament production," but has to make do with unexpected ornamental additions in projects and construction work. Only in architecture as a process can ornaments come into being.

From Construction to Reception

Architecture as a process has low priority in the professional contexts that Ginster faces. On the other hand, the building possesses the ability to appear as an ornament in a phase *after* it has assumed material existence. Ginster tries to define his real aesthetic intentions as a shift in emphasis from architectural construction to the reception of what has been built: "Instead of letting strangely interwoven figures result in buildings, he would have preferred to dismantle all useful objects into figures" (G, pp. 22–23). The splitting up of the "useful objects" into "figures" is an act less material than visual and analytical. The spatial elements are detached from the total mechanism in order to enter into a new process as fragments, according to criteria other than mere technical functionality (which is not excluded, however).

Referring to Simmel's definition of the tripartite process of culture, one could say that Ginster wishes by this formulation to *displace* himself from the first position of the subjective spirit, where it (in this case, the architect) exteriorizes himself in the objective spirit (project, building), to reach the third and final—though not always achieved—stage where the objectivized spirit (the material structure) is reappropriated by the subjective factor (through analysis and reflection). (But, on account of conditions of ownership and the dimension of time, the empirical subject is seldom the same . . .)

This deconstruction is not subject in advance to a new unifying purposefulness. In his examples of Ginster's reflection, Kracauer outlines the characteristics of an *aesthetic* form of interpretation that naturally gives high priority to the visual aspect, with its potential for letting the subject become self-reflective.

Ginster exercises a figural contemplation that, in various ways, fulfills the demand that the appropriation of space be dynamic. This aspect is ensured by means of shifts of scale. Sections of the material are subjected to shifting degrees of magnification

FRISEE AUX LARDONS ŒUF MOLLET 25
ENDIVES AU BLEU. ET NOIX 22
FILETS DE HARENG..... 18
QUICHE LORAINE 18
ONGLET BEARNAISE 42F
BAVETTE .ECHALOTES 40
PAVÉ AU ROQUEFORT 45
ENTRECÔTE AUX HERBES 44
PLAT DU JOUR
AILERON DE RA
SAUCE AIGRELETTE 43F
DESSERTS-MAISON
TARTES: TATIN, POMMES, FRAMBOISES
CITRON, CHOCOLAT, C. CARAMEL

under the microscope. Slowly moving objects (plants in an aquarium), which are observed over time, are also advanced as a methodological example. Changes of substances such as a drop of ink dissolving in water develop further the idea of visual diversity contained in the individual substance. At any rate, the stable totality is pushed aside in favor of its elements' fragmentary metamorphosis.

That metamorphosis is the point of departure for a comprehensive visual abstraction. "The figures came toward him from all directions" (G, p. 23) is how Ginster's situation is summarized. This interpretation can, in principle, just as easily involve drops of blood, ink, plants, rain puddles between tramway lines, railway lines, and light in the windows of city apartments. Everything is contained within the common denominator of the ornament. "The lights burning in the apartment complexes in the evening not only illuminated the family tables but were fragments of a gleaming mosaic" (G, p. 23), Kracauer concludes the series of examples, as if he wished to stress that the aestheticizing (i.e., disinterested) look could be included as the final stage of a social analysis.

The ornament is used for an untraditional processing of the everyday and a polysemic reality. One can talk of the eye's sociopsychic reflection undertaking a description, an interpretation, and finally a critique of socially determined space. For example, Ginster, when he visits a clinic to get a doctor's certificate for a (simulated) heart condition, experiences the consultation rooms under the sign of ornamental abstraction. The clinical space dissolves into pure whiteness, from which the nurses can be distinguished only because they are in motion. The only anchor is of an ornamental nature— a network of strokes on the white walls: "Like threads they seemed to measure the whole building," a building that, in strong sunshine, "would dissolve completely; only the network of strokes would continue to exist" (G, pp. 82, 83). The ornaments survive the visual abstraction, remaining as traces of a comprehensive material reality. In a condensed form, this can be made the object of a denaturalizing interpretation.

At no point does Ginster reject the diverting patterns of childhood. When his project for the military cemetery has been chosen for the first prize he is celebrated by the family as an architect, a role with which he is unable to identify himself. A little later, he goes into the city—that is, "to the arcade café and drew lines unconnected to a point in the middle of the marble table" (G, p. 109). He does not detach the ornaments from "reality," as might result from, for example, raising them to the level of pictorial art. As the above quotation makes clear, instead of forcing enlarged and stiffened "ornaments" onto reality in the form of architecture, he retains the visual ornaments as the point of departure for a critical analysis. This takes place in a way no longer practical and expressive but analytical and contemplative. Material reality for Ginster tends to become a gleaming mosaic.

The question is, what status of reality can be ascribed on the basis of these investigations to the ornament in its numerous variations. First, the ornament is a conceptual designation for a *figural abstraction* that refers to innumerable formal idioms, ranging from the organic through the inorganic to the point and its disappearance. These visual abstractions can, second, become part of *expressive processes,* even though Kracauer normally has recourse to ornamental abstractions in descriptive (i.e., receptive) moments. In this form the ornament can, third, become a bearer of *experiential processes.* Initially, the experiential form of the ornament is silent, forming the basis for a system of visual metaphors only in its conversion into autobiography.[6]

Siegfried Kracauer's perception of everyday ornaments, as seen in *Ginster: Von ihm selbst geschrieben,* ranges between, on the one hand, the visual abstraction of reality into ornaments and, on the other hand, the subject's connection with and reflection on "reality" precisely by means of these abstract, ornamental forms. The ornament is both an encroachment on reality and reality's adequate but selectively abstracting form of articulation.

Kracauer thereby distances himself from the concept of the ornament in the history of art. He can do so with a good conscience, since in his doctoral thesis (1914) on the ornamental art of forging in Berlin and Potsdam from the seventeenth to the beginning of the nineteenth century he used an art-historical point of view. Since this piece of work bears particular witness to Kracauer's fascination with the ornamental—and is thus immediately connected to the theme of the present discussion (the ornaments of the metropolis)—its methodological characteristics will be investigated in the following section.

3. THE TYPOLOGY OF THE ORNAMENT — WROUGHT-IRON ARCHITECTURE IN PREMODERN BERLIN
An Object on the Periphery of Architecture

Kracauer's interest in the ornament is not restricted to his childhood drawing and to his metaphor-laden rewriting of everyday experiences. In his doctoral thesis on ornamental wrought-iron work in premodern Berlin (from the seventeenth to the beginning of the nineteenth century), the theme is a particular ornamental architecture.

The subject is a logical extension of a line whose beginning can be traced back to Kracauer's first term as a student of architecture—or perhaps even back to his diaries from 1903, which also include small drawings and ornaments (M, pp. 2–3). In the summer term of 1907, Kracauer followed a course at the Technical University in Darmstadt given by Professor Varnesi in "ornamental drawing." At the same time, he studied "the history and theory of ornamentation" under *Privatdozent* Dr. Hülsen (M, p. 7). Kracauer's interest in the ornament continued during his next two terms of study in

Berlin, where, once more at the Technical University, he studied "the architecture of antiquity" and "ornamental drawing" under Professor Strack, alongside such technical disciplines as "high-rise construction and statics" and "the science of building construction" (M, p. 16). The ornamental drawing course continued during the 1908–1909 winter term. After this, Kracauer moved to Munich, but there are no examination records from the ensuing period.

In 1915, Kracauer's thesis on Berlin ornamental wrought-iron art was published as a book under the precisely focused title *Die Entwicklung der Schmiedekunst in Berlin, Potsdam und einigen Städten der Mark vom 17. Jahrhundert bis zum Beginn des 19. Jahrhunderts* (*The Development of the Art of Forging in Berlin, Potsdam, and Some Towns of the Mark from the 17th until the Beginning of the 19th Century*).[7] Since Kracauer no longer undertakes this kind of typological and art-historical treatment of the subject in his later work, many of its analyses reveal the basis for his love of the world of ornament.

Kracauer's first book can be seen as an architectural and art-historical demonstration at a point in time when Adolf Loos's "Ornament und Verbrechen" (mentioned in the introduction to the present book) was becoming a paradigm for a new phase in modern architecture. By emphasizing the relevance of the premodern ornament, Kracauer adopts a position that deserves more than the silent thumbs-down that has been reserved for his book in the secondary literature.

This is the first book publication listed in Kracauer's bibliography (O, p. 352). Even Inka Mülder, whose thesis *Siegfried Kracauer—Grenzgänger zwischen Theorie und Literatur* has the subtitle *Seine frühen Schriften 1913–1933*, which implies that it ought to include a treatment of this book (published in 1915), seems to reduce it to an academic labor of necessity to join the profession of architecture, which she gives the blanket term *Brotberuf*.[8] She does not even comment on the book.

Though Mülder's reference to Kracauer's "first publications of articles and numerous unpublished theses" may justify her claim "that his true interest lay in philosophy and sociology,"[9] that is no real argument for dismissing the doctoral thesis on wrought iron. This thesis is perhaps not explicitly sociophilosophical or revolutionary in its methodological deliberations. But both the subject matter of the book and its handling contain original facets that, under any circumstances, have to be included in a treatment of Kracauer's attitude toward the ornament of the metropolis.

By limiting the subject matter of the thesis to "such works of the art of forging which are closely related to architecture" (E, p. vii), Kracauer has already adopted a slightly distanced attitude toward architecture's traditional sphere. His analysis deals with an area that is peripheral to architectural design, being located half inside and half outside what is traditionally architecture's field of interest. By means of a systematic analysis, Kracauer focuses the reader's attention on the small elements of a building

that are often overlooked, ranging from grave railings and skylight and window latticework to banisters and balcony railings. Yet these ornamental details help shape the
distinctive character both of the individual buildings and of a city or region.

Kracauer's analysis is certainly meant as a practical intervention in city architecture
around 1910. For example, he recommends in the final chapter of his thesis a return to
the forms of a number of hitherto unnoticed grave crosses from the 1650–1700 period,
which he prefers to open iron Bibles with sayings and the name of the dead person: "It
is to be deplored that these simple crosses are no longer to be found in present-day
cemeteries. . . . It would be a welcome development if these old unassuming pieces of
work came into use once more" (E, p. 107). In the organization of his entire work Kracauer generally paid attention to the idea that it should be able to be used to revive the
anonymous, marginal forms of architecture: "So that the [reproductions] could also be
of practical use to architects and craft workers, the main iron thicknesses were also frequently listed, a number of details added, and sometimes photographs used to help
clarify the effort of that which was depicted" (E, p. vii), he writes, to remove any possible doubt about his intention.

Time-consuming efforts in connection with this book were presumably also involved in Kracauer's painstaking measurements and reproduction of the described
works in order to increase the possibility of these forms being realized in, for example,
Berlin. The book contains 140 illustrations on 120 pages, which were set using a modern font, unlike the gothic script normally used in German books at the time. By means
of the finest of line drawings—at least sixty of the book's richly detailed illustrations
are his own—he provides ample evidence that his acts of drawing have long since exceeded the nervous scribbles in the margins of his school notebooks. Precisely in connection with these wrought-iron railings in innumerable versions, Kracauer's drawing
gives him the opportunity of attaining a visually mimetic (imitative) relationship to the
flickering objects that few people would otherwise be able to distinguish from each
other. Only then can they be dealt with discursively and sorted typologically in art-
historical description and commentary.

*Anonymous, Complex Craftsmanship—Art-Historical Commentary
with Perspectives on Cultural History*

The paradigm for Kracauer's work is art-historical. As his title indicates, his work
builds on a corpus that is delimited in its geography, time, and subject. His fixed assignment consists in giving a reasoned presentation of the material in relation to a
temporal axis. This is achieved by his giving the objects depicted in drawings and
photographs what could be called *a doubling effect* via a description of their history
in terms of style. Since Kracauer does not restrict himself to what the French

archaeologist and epistemologist Jean-Claude Gardin defines as a compilation but also ventures into the area of explication,[10] his description in part depends on the assumption that particular stylistic periods may differ in their artistic value. This means that aesthetic judgments are occasionally passed during the presentation.

Kracauer probably satisfies the conventions of the history of art and architecture.[11] His analysis of the ornamental art of forging, especially various forms of latticework, lives up to Quatremère de Quincy's generalizing concept of type as regards form (as presented in his *Dictionnaire d'architecture,* 1796). But through its interest in the anonymous group of wrought-iron craftsmen, Kracauer's work also connects with another definition of type—one that is characterized by its taking into account the sociological forces that are involved in connection with presenting and acquiring a given object.[12]

A broader sociohistorical framework of presentation has thus contributed to making the typological study of the ornaments in the various types of latticework relevant for Kracauer. This cultural history perspective can be summarized in three points.

First, the art of forging (*Schmiedekunst*—the overarching concept used by Kracauer to sum up his subject) is not primarily a highbrow phenomenon. Despite the ongoing comparison of the developments in architecture at the French and German courts, the main creators of this form of culture remain less architects and kings than the German craftsmen, who, during all periods of history, have forced inspiration coming from outside to undergo their personal interpretation.

These smiths also constitute history's blank spot. They vitalize research and indicate its boundaries. Even the Berlin smiths have in the vast majority of cases remained anonymous: "Practically no names have been handed down. Most of the art metalwork that comes under consideration has been carried out by the guild of locksmiths" (E, p. 7), Kracauer notes. The executive body that ensures the distinctive character of the objects is not made up of identifiable individuals. Posterity views them merely as members of the guild that is collectively responsible, and whose inner conditions are unknown. Thus the basis is formed for considerations of *art craft.*

Second, it is worth emphasizing that art craft is based not on the individual genius but on an almost historyless tradition that, through its techniques, stretches back to the Middle Ages.[13] Those engaged in the ornamental art of forging combine everyday work with the nonprogrammatic creation of art. Kracauer does not fail to call attention to a particularly successful unity of past and present, of craft and art in certain sections of "the development of ornamental wrought-iron work." In connection with a number of banisters from quite a short period (probably 1760 to 1770), he advances his hypothesis of a special Berlin rococo. The works mentioned "all bear witness to so unified a spirit, [and] are—without the chance taking over of foreign motifs—so created out of the conditions of the craft, that it is possible within wrought-iron work to speak of a Berlin school of the rococo" (E, p. 53). To explain why this particular balance and cohesive spirit are not more widespread, Kracauer advances the hypothesis that the style contains so many natural, unformalizable characteristics in its individual expression that its further dissemination was impossible for technical reasons alone: "That such an art that has sworn by its lack of rules was unable to form any school is understandable, since it was too difficult to imitate and practice" (E, p. 67).

This hypothesis concerning the particularity of ornamental wrought-iron art in Berlin is based on a romantic conception of the Middle Ages. In one of his numerous parallels between the art of forging and the medieval period, Kracauer observes that the smith's work process had a decisive influence on the design of the end product: "One could surmise that only a rough plan existed for the making of these banisters; during the actual work something new was constantly being hit upon, and much has been left to the discretion of the smith himself—just as in the richly decorated portals of many medieval churches" (E, p. 77). The concrete work process dissolves what is codified, but at the same time—via independent variation on traditional forms and techniques—it produces that which is truly original.

The individual piece of wrought-iron work builds on an endless and noncommunicable tradition, but it is, third, something close to the opposite of a *simple*—that is, simplistic—architecture. A premium is placed on the *complex* in the aesthetic judgments passed in the course of the thesis. The constantly recurring adjective used to characterize a particularly successful example of the art of forging is "rich" (*reich*), which underlines the distance between such work and the simple, formal, and substantial. The epithet "rich" refers not to precious materials (bronze or gilt), only to a differentiated and complex formal idiom. Kracauer appreciates the simultaneous presence of many motifs that intercommunicate and that together form a whole characterized by balance and visual harmony. The artistic imagination of the craftsman ought to engage in a composite, natural mode of expression. This forces one in the position of observing art into a demanding process of reception:

> In constant alternation, the shell work is interwoven with leaved branches from which clusters of grapes hang. From time to time, quite slender palm leaves appear in the midst of everything; and there is furthermore no shortage of rosettes strewn here and there. Only gradually does the eye extract the details out of the richness of motifs. (E, pp. 64–65)

Resubjectivization is already here hinted at as a problem even for the individual who is working scientifically.

"Ornamental Amorphism"

The romantic accent in Kracauer's text on the art of forging goes so far in praising the naturally complex—as opposed to the formally abstract—as to furnish these main tendencies within the architectural idiom with national signatures. France, which is the point of departure for much inspiration within Berlin's art of forging, clearly represents either parallel or centered lines. On the other hand, the Berlin craftsman tradition in all its "conservatism" (E, p. 86) uses iron for more distinctive figures. Unlike French smiths, who let the wrought iron reproduce earlier forms in stone and give the iron a smooth surface, their German counterparts try to respect the iron as a material that is suited to its own independent forms of architectural expression (E, p. 31). This exploration of the detail produces, at best, an "ornamental amorphism." This early text, which is characterized by a romantic aesthetic view, thus nevertheless contains a central element of Kracauer's later—more derivative—concept of the ornament. The expression is used in emphasizing two favorable examples of German bourgeois wrought-iron work that display a distinctive, almost natural, and extremely organic form of abstraction:

> In French wrought-iron work this ornamental amorphism is rare; there one finds a far greater number of parallel sequences among the scrolls and the connections between them. The difference between the French and the German way of decorating things would thus seem to be radical—at least as far as the art of forging is concerned. (E, p. 74)

And in connection with an "exuberant, almost overloaded" banister Kracauer exclaims ecstatically: "How freshly and naturally the branches and leaves have been treated! With such a love of detail!" (E, p. 75). These exclamations have been taken out of context, but they nonetheless express in an extreme form Kracauer's basic aesthetic position at this juncture before the First World War. That position can be even more concisely illuminated by his emphasis on three elements in wrought-iron architecture. These three factors—whose existence, in the history of secular buildings, is most frequently treated separately, or even suppressed—are all mentioned in the final sentence of the introduction: "Even those items of wrought-iron work that exist today still have enough of the Beautiful and Individual that one can become absorbed in contemplating them with Joy" (E, p. viii). The three elements—beauty, individuality, and joy—sum up Kracauer's early aesthetic position: the anonymous yet masterly art of wrought-iron work, whose amorphous yet intellectually cohesive and detailed yet harmonious latticework constitutes a neglected yet decisive element in premodern Berlin.

It is not possible, given the existing source material, to assess precisely whether ideological or institutional considerations may have caused Kracauer to adopt arguments in his thesis that differed radically from his own convictions. For example, the idea cannot be ruled out that the period immediately prior to the First World War lent a certain national-romantic tinge to passages in this piece of examination work. And yet the thesis shows so many characteristics bearing structural analogies to how he developed the issue of ornament in his later work that Kracauer's first book may be described as a premodern, Jugendstil-inspired attempt, by means of an art-historical analysis of an object on the periphery of architecture, to find a basis for an architecture that had room for the beautiful and for the individual—as well as for joy.

These three general categories are not repressed in Kracauer's later sociohistorical and more modernist work on the issue of ornamentation. But they take on a sublimated nature by virtue of no longer being conceived of as positive and immediately accessible fixed points. In the course of his writing, Kracauer cuts himself off from the idea of a direct, though quite fragile, transfer of premodern ornaments to the urban modernity of Berlin, or of some other place. Accordingly, the localization of beauty, individuality, and joy assumes forms other than mere categorization and commentary.

To the extent that these three fields are not indirectly treated (e.g., by an investigation of their opposites: the ugly, the general, and grief), beautiful, individual, and joyful ornaments are articulated as integral parts of the metropolitan present. They cannot be detached from it just like that. Because of their presence in a complex and polysemic age, ornaments assume a potential place in the reflections of individuals and of the whole culture of the metropolis. They are part of a comprehensive context that, according to Kracauer, is in need of change. The ornaments even occasionally give premonitions of this change. A first outline of such foreshadowing is given in the final chapter of *Ginster,* which is the theme of the conclusion of the first part of this work.

Both Kracauer's doctoral thesis on Berlin's wrought-iron ornaments (published in 1915) and his autobiographical novel *Ginster*—though the latter was written a decade later—constitute sources of his thoughts about ornamentation up until the end of the First World War.

Already in his art-historical thesis, the ornament finds itself on the periphery between the three-dimensional spatiality of architecture and the truly beautiful (and disinterested) arts. This in-between position implicitly links the wrought-iron ornament to everyday life in the metropolis. Despite its links with tradition, the ornament is part of Kracauer's own age, distinguishing itself by covering a complex formal idiom that is

the result of craftsmanship. Kracauer tries to promote these ornaments by including in his thesis meticulous measurements of them for the use of architects and others.

The novel *Ginster* shows how the concept of the ornament also played a decisive role in Kracauer's sociologically and historically reflective period. There it is both more derivative and internally more differentiated in its meanings than in the study of the art of forging. Ornamental drawings from his childhood—as they lead to a choice of profession that is presented as something between an arbitrary decision and a misunderstanding—form the basis for Ginster's architectural studies. Symmetrically around this event, the ornament plays a main role in Ginster's perception of the history of both art and architecture as well as the metropolis (exemplified in the railway station). The outlines of a reflective, spatially borne form of experience can be made out, without its privileged location yet being made precise. The sphere of experience offered by the metropolis will be introduced into this empty space in the next chapter, which will be the fourth and final one of part I.

Discovering the City as a Reflective Space

I. THE CITY AND THE INDIVIDUAL'S MENTAL PREPARATION FOR DISRUPTION
Developing Urban Consciousness

From the moment Ginster is called up for military service and is thus taken from his salaried work as an architect and from his life with his mother, aunt, and uncle, it is possible to trace a development in his relation to both F. and the general experiential universe of the City. The signs are sporadic, but are found at crucial points in the narrative.

As he is on his way to the railway station with the other conscripts, the facades of his childhood city already seem "strange" to him, even though he can recognize the locations without any difficulty.[1] A couple of months later in K., the images of F. in his memory form the prelude to a nightmarish dream that—also with an urban backdrop—announces Ginster's successful attempt to be exempted from military service.[2] Although his native area assumes a menacing nature in these images from his memory, it serves as the sign of a well-timed evasive action. Ginster's time as a soldier is framed by urban experiences.

His stay as an engineer-architect in Q. (Osnabrück) immediately afterward also promotes Ginster's urban sensitivity, via his initial doubts as to whether he has come to a city at all (G, p. 195). His discomfort at the omnipresent false coziness of the half-timbered houses causes him, in an imaginary countermeasure, to prefer a solution with "smooth concrete walls" (G, p. 218). In this overornamented urbanity Ginster does not recommend—as does Kracauer in modernity's Berlin—a return to, for example, wrought-iron ornaments, stressing instead the necessity of a contrasting element: the raw concrete.

Ginster remarks sarcastically: "a little more war would not have harmed the city" (G, p. 203). The sought-for cultural opposites, when they finally occur, take the form of a provincial echo of the workers' uprising in Hamburg in 1918. All at once, Q.'s citizens are transformed into brothers and sisters who are described by Ginster as a "public at a market festival" (G, p. 223). His doubt of the authenticity of their sudden radicalism gives him yet another reason to resign his post and take the train to F. The conclusion is a minimal but demanding personal revolutionary program: "just don't live in one place and have a two-room occupation" (G, p. 226). In a moment of overweening confidence Ginster decides to go all the way along the path of which the war, by forcing him to leave his family and restrictive salaried work, had shown the contours. This means in concrete terms that on his arrival in F., he spends the first night at a hotel, so as to sense if but for a moment the possibilities of not holding a fixed position (G, p. 230).

The liberation of the individual in an anonymous public space is the theme of the last chapter in the novel. The action takes place in Marseilles five to six years after the war. In light, above all, of Adorno's criticism one can think whatever one likes about the chapter's literary and philosophical qualities,[3] but there can be no doubt that it has been "precisely thought out."[4] It can thus be seen as a novelistic version of a political and epistemological urban manifesto. Ginster's development differs somewhat from the contemporary political radicalization of the German intelligentsia (like that of Ernst Bloch and Walter Benjamin, mentioned earlier). He may indeed represent an intuition of cultural revolution (G, p. 239), although he does not imagine it will be carried through by militant political practice (G, p. 240). Apparently apolitical, but individually more authentic, Ginster pins his hopes on the discovery of a socioaesthetic field with nihilistic overtones. In the course of the period after the end of the war he has been initiated into this "Nothing" (G, p. 241). His revolutionary wish to shun the family-bound dwelling and his job as an architect is still unfulfilled (G, pp. 239–240). But meanwhile it has been strengthened by a mental and existential rupture that Ginster, with dramatic conviction (as if he were in a theater), announces to the woman accompanying him on a walk through Marseilles's exotic urbanity. The concrete experience behind the ambitious formulations will be dealt with below.

The Urban Analogy of Emancipation from the Mother: Marseilles

In the intervening period, Ginster has neither moved away from home nor escaped his monotonous everyday job as an architect. At a symbolic level, however, he has partially escaped from his angst-filled relationship with his mother. This is the effect of an act of initiation that probably begins in an urban space but that, in its concrete form, is sexual. During a visit to D., Ginster has decided to go to "a certain notorious district" (G, p. 236) in order to buy himself a form of unashamed sexuality that he has experienced only in relations involving money. The amoral (not immoral) situation is confirmed by the fact that the prostitute refuses to indulge in any emotional intimacy along with the physical act for which money changes hands. The alienation between Ginster (who, to begin with, attempts to adopt a personalizing style) and Emmi, the prostitute, thus improves the chances for Ginster's rebellion against his own moralistic and stifling superego.[5]

Even so, the shift in Ginster's consciousness is not completed in reality until he meets the city that corresponds to this unashamed sexuality. While his experience with the prostitute frees Ginster from a timeless unity with his mother, the later walks through Marseilles create a surprising mental distance from the social and spatial environment that until now have supported dependence on his mother. The problematic identification with the hometown of F. and the family home situated in it suddenly seems to have lost its legitimacy. Ginster's pathetic mention of having "gotten to know death" (G, p. 237) thus refers to a feeling that reality has developed through history and is therefore capable of change over time. Life suddenly stands like a colored image against a dark background; eternal life is not guaranteed by a religious belief or a psychic fixation on the mother figure. Unashamed sexuality and anonymous urbanity are like markers that frame Ginster's hope of one day being able to lead a different sort of life.

It may seem surprising that sexual initiation has its social counterpart in the anonymous sphere of the City rather than in an immediate, personal context. Relationships between individuals are once more abandoned in favor of a dynamic and reflection-fostering urban universe. This aspect is underlined by the fact that the city in the final chapter of *Ginster* is Marseilles. In the novel's dedication "To L., in memory of Marseilles 1926 and 1927" one can sense the importance of this culturally mixed Mediterranean city in Kracauer's life: "L." is without doubt Lili, then Kracauer's lover and later his wife. Furthermore, Marseilles—because of its cosmopolitan strangeness—has a special status among the cities of Europe. It becomes the opposite of the cities of northern Europe (including Germany), whose special historical features Marseilles nevertheless casts in a new light.

Kracauer lets Ginster select Marseilles—and the city's poor harbor area in particular—as the urban analogy of the state of symbolic initiation: "Why am I telling you this right now—because in this miserable harbor area I at last come across a world that corresponds to the state in which I find myself after [having been with] that girl.[6] Here I almost feel at home" (G, pp. 237–238). He is "almost at home" in that which is geographically and culturally very foreign, says Ginster.[7] This is probably the most positive remark one finds in the novel. Considered matter-of-factly, Ginster's approach to this area is limited to a visual register. Despite his momentary physical presence, there is never any question of his one day actually wanting to live there. The feeling covers an existential utopia. The feeling of home defies the geographically real location F., as it is linked to the foreign city. But there is not necessarily an insuperable opposition between the feeling of home and the actual strangeness. In connection with what Simmel described as the subjective spirit's exteriorization of itself in an objective culture, radical alienation was a compulsory stage in the history of culture. Ginster's choice of

Marseilles as the most "homelike" place can be interpreted as supporting the necessity of the same movement from the strange back to what is familiar but as yet not understood.

Strangeness—A Condition for Urban Reflection

Kracauer's deliberations concerning Marseilles cannot be rejected as an invalid recognition of the urban simply because a foreign city is involved. Simmel, in his analysis of "the Stranger," had already shown how this sociologically basic figure is not restricted to its primitive form, the commercial traveler. Considered more closely, strangeness and manifestations of the Stranger turn out to be present in the most banal, intimate everyday situations—in the form of a blend of distance and proximity, as when a feeling of difference from other people accompanies actual coexistence with them.[8] Strangeness cannot be avoided but has, instead, to be explored as an opportunity for gaining a historicizing view of the city. By means of his reflection as a stranger in Marseilles, Ginster also undergoes a change—at least personally—in his view of the metropolis of modernity. But the themes thrown up by the metropolis need to be elaborated.

The decisive perspective at the end of *Ginster* is the selection of urban space as a sphere of experience that is superior both personally and socially. Ginster's interest in the city has previously been made impossible—or at best highly sporadic—because personal reflection was contingent on his work and family situation. Not until Marseilles, far away from M., F., K., Q., and Berlin, are his reflective energies released in an ecstatic form.[9] They correspond to a time of vacation, but they also usher in a new period for Ginster (and Kracauer, who did not, however, wait until he had experienced Marseilles . . .).[10]

2. THE ORNAMENT — THE MATERIAL OF URBAN REFLECTION

The Ornament—From Acanthus Leaf to Sign of Historicity

Decay in the visual surface of the city is something that, at a general level, is reminiscent of death as a borderline experience. At the same time—and at a more concrete level—it involves conditions favorable for the ornament. When the surface of the city dissolves into ornaments, it is a sign that cultural forms are brought about historically and are subject to change.

As a quite open reply to Kracauer's analysis of wrought-iron ornaments in Berlin, *Ginster* notes the presence of the acanthus leaf in Marseilles. It is one of the city's few intentional ornaments; as if in a second phase, after having been subjected to the ravages of time (decay) it is transformed into a flowering though unintentionally ornamental profusion:

Soft yellow sunlight from time to time embraced faces and objects, carefully painted spots on a waiter's dinner jacket. Behind the waiter, who was sitting at the bottom of a staircase, acanthus leaves spread out indistinctly—the house was an old patrician building. Its streaked latticework no longer hid any riches, and the once so imposing facade became one with the walls of the neighboring jumble of houses to form one vast mishmash. Hole upon hole—window panes were often missing, too. The postman must have had a hard time of it, Ginster rejoiced inwardly. At one point a huge crack had opened up that laid bare the skeleton of the houses. In its darkness lay a heap of beams, sections of roofs, rubble, and railings. Perhaps the incomprehensible ball of wool could be straightened out at one tug and then could have gleamed beautifully. (G, p. 235)

In the composite urban culture of Marseilles the sphere of the ornament becomes broader. Starting from marked-off points in an immobile architecture, the spatial form of the ornaments really spreads out, beyond the three dimensions of abstract perspective, as they tend to encompass the entire urban surface in their net.

The ornaments of the metropolis coincide with a completely different version of the figure of the maze than the one that Ginster linked in F. with his childhood city's sealing in of itself and what already existed. The maze of Marseilles exceeds in complexity the unfathomable network of streets in F. The boundary between outer and inner space dissolves in favor of a maze of innumerable aspects—as many as the gaze can cope with. The radical confusion and advanced process of decay mean for Ginster that the maze, which was the framework of a quasi-natural immutability in F., now symbolizes the very possibility of change. The maze invites one, at any rate, to explore the culture of the city further and thereby becomes a potentially liberating place. The maze of Marseilles points to the possibility of happiness and beauty being able to derive from their apparent opposites:[11] "yes indeed, if happiness were to rise out of these alleyways, if beauty were to look them in the face and yet be beautiful" (G, p. 238), Ginster hypothetically concludes his praise of the ornaments of decay. The ornaments are dismissed by the revolutionary woman accompanying him with the exclamation "Let's get out of here" (G, p. 236). The difference between the resubjectivization of the metropolis and the militant political mode of thought cannot be emphasized more clearly.

The question of the extent to which Ginster's attitude toward the poor district of Marseilles is romantic is open to discussion. If the term is taken to mean that Ginster's stroll through the maze of the city has idealizing characteristics and overlooks the actual everyday life of those living there, then it is to a certain degree apposite. But on the other hand, Ginster's view of the city is influenced less by unchangeability than

by historicity. The traditional Mediterranean city adds in a surprising way a feeling of disruption to the image of the modern metropolis. His position is by no means unambiguous.

So calling Ginster's view of Marseilles romantic is truly well justified only if one is referring to the philosophical superstructure of German romanticism. It is correct that Kracauer—in line with the Schlegel brothers (from the last decade of the eighteenth century), as Walter Benjamin demonstrates in his dissertation on German romanticism's conception of art criticism[12]—outlines a disintegration of the clearly defined subject, which is replaced by active contact with agencies hitherto normally confined to the role of passive objects of the eye, of thought, and of subjective control. The individual thus enters into a relationship that is diametrically opposed to the suppression and limitation of the subjective forces of which the army and division of labor earlier in *Ginster* are excellent examples.

The Diffusion of the Individual and of Meaning in the Reflective Medium of the City

Within the framework of the city, which (with a certain degree of caution) can be considered as a secular and sociohistorical analogy to German romanticism's conception of the "reflective medium" of art criticism,[13] the *individual* also undergoes a certain type of disruption. But this is more an extension, an expansion, a diffusion that involves greater sensitivity to the components of the urban scenario.

Ginster contains a passage where the motifs of this complex of problems are brought together. The main character, Ginster, finds himself at the moment in question in a café located in the immediate vicinity of Marseilles's answer to the boulevards of Paris, la Canebière. In the text, Kracauer presents step-by-step Ginster's reflections on the complex world of appearances of the southern metropolis.

The process contains both "active" (projective) and "passive" (receptive) aspects. All of them are concentrated in a small toy bird. It is perched on its whirring tin ring on the table in front of Ginster, constituting a type of ornament that opens up a passage for the senses to life in the city. This spinning fixed point, which even eludes the eye's control,[14] grants access to a basically disrupted image of reality. Synthesizing subjectivity meets its boundaries, which at the same time indicate the conditions for experience in the metropolis. For this reason, the text can be considered to be *Ginster*'s most comprehensive outline of Kracauer's principles of urban analysis. They are introduced one by one in the ensuing passage.

The first part of the passage presents a replete, hot Ginster who, via the toy bird, is sucked out—or actively projects himself—into the metropolis behind him. The reflection has, at any rate, the nature of an *identification:*

He [Ginster] had just eaten dinner and, from the chair at Café Riche where he was seated, he gazed at la Canebière behind the walls of air balls and a haze of voices. From time to time, he spun the ring; the heat dissolved him. Certainly he was still sitting there, yet at the same time he was a donkey cart containing ice puddings, the red-brown surface of an awning, a smiling Indian, the small lady who gleamed like a firecracker among the taxis. In actual fact, the women here were rather full-bodied. (G, p. 231)

This identification also means an *unceasing fragmentation* of the image of reality—as is clear from the following passage:

The arms of a mulatto flapped as if they did not belong to his body; it seemed, in fact, that nothing but separate parts were wandering about. A straw hat, teeth, and the corner of a handkerchief formed a complete Negro; the Mohammedan over there consisted of a full beard and mackintosh. Part of a breast, the red fez of a colonial soldier, headlines, coats, a turban, a steering wheel, flowers—Ginster had the impression that the separate parts were constantly being shaken into new constellations that once more fell apart. (G, p. 231)

Ginster regards the life of the café and the street as the expression of a tower of Babel. The crisis of semantic systems really puts observing, describing, and interpreting subjectivity to the test:

Like individual words in a school grammar, he had the feeling that they [the parts] could combine to form instructive sentences. The general's daughter chats with a venerable elderly man; this Greek woman is wearing a white dress with light bright-green ribbons, her cousin is a beautiful, melancholy woman; these gentlemen are leaving the president's garden: at random he spelled his way through several sentences that had taken form at that instant. When the contours shimmered too much, the fragments dissolved into an irregular language of light that he was unable to decode; or the noise level increased, its thunder sweeping across the entire grammar like a cloud. (G, pp. 231–232)

The situation is full of contradictions. On the one hand, Ginster bears witness to and participates in visual contact between separate cultures. On the other hand, these cultural phenomena, their distinct shapes and linguistic expressions, are hard to perceive and to describe.

This crucial passage illustrates three ways that boundaries are transcended. To begin with, the subjectively registered distance between the individual and the collective is overcome. Next, Ginster feels that the division between distinct material objects dissolves. As mentioned, Ginster adopts a visually limited point of view, focused and made possible by a metal ring that spins around a toy bird. This is the immediate form of more basic conditions of awareness and interpretation that are at stake in an intense urban culture such as here in Marseilles. A totalizing view of the object at a comfortable distance is impossible, simply because the gaze is established from within the object. Despite his feeling of alienation, the analyzing subject is an element in the scene.

The intensity and constant change of life in the metropolis neutralizes further the internal semantic and sociological systems. Language becomes light, sound becomes spatial volume. As in Charles Baudelaire's poems in *Les fleurs du mal*—which, according to Walter Benjamin, cannot be conceived without Paris as a sociohistorical background—the boundaries of the individual registers of perception are exceeded. The interactions and endless dynamism of the register of the senses were turned by Baudelaire (in the program poem "Correspondances," among other works) into an important basis for poetry.

In his point of departure for the analysis of the reality of the metropolis, Kracauer is confronted with the same problem. In something between lyrical text and intoxicated experience, Ginster exposes the interplay of the human senses. Only the focus of attention here is not poetry or literature in the narrow sense of the term but a sociohistorical reflection on the experiential universe of the metropolis's culture. The listing of the states of tension between apparently opposed forms of the senses seeks to strengthen the description of the subject's urban reflection.

The basic position grounding this deliberation can be summarized as follows: supported by "ornamental" forms of a fragmentary kind, the subject, immersed in the nature of the metropolis, allows his senses to move in all directions. The establishment of a new experiential universe between subjective and objective ornaments constitutes a possible result of this process. Every situation has the nature of an experiment, and Kracauer's writings can be considered to be reports that can be generalized only with difficulty. The movement beyond three-dimensional constructional space that dominates modern architecture and urban planning results in Kracauer in a strengthening of space to reflect on urban culture. A precise analysis of the written "traces" (as if they were reports of dreams) becomes imperative. This will be attempted in part II of the present work.

From the instant Ginster is called up for military service, his urban experiences are, at crucial moments, part of a slow release from the symbiotic relationship to his mother and the intellectually restrictive life of an architect. But his desire to break free of these bonds builds only gradually. Two meetings, at different levels, are of importance. The visit to a prostitute gives him access to an anonymous sexuality without feelings of guilt. The walks through Marseilles's urban maze open Ginster's eyes to the active, historicizing reflection of urbanity. In this way, Kracauer links sexual initiation to urban space, thereby anticipating an important motif in Walter Benjamin's book of reminiscences *Berliner Kindheit um neunzehnhundert* (written in 1932–1933).[15]

In this connection it is of less importance that the city's answer to breaking through sexual boundaries is linked to the foreign city of Marseilles. The feeling of almost being "at home" here becomes natural, without the logical consequence of taking up residence. The consequences at an intellectual level, however, should not be underestimated. No mention is made of whether Ginster, building on sexuality procured by money and on his reflections on the metropolis of Marseilles, is able to fulfill his reiterated wish (G, p. 239) of escaping the profession of architect.

Kracauer, in contrast, develops a rich body of urban analysis during the eight-year period from 1925 to 1933. This can be seen as setting Ginster's aesthetic reflection on the ornament against the sociocultural and historical situation of interwar Germany. From the café of la Canebière in Marseilles, Ginster observes how boundaries are broken down—first, between individual and collective; second, between the separate elements of social reality; and third, between human language and semantic systems in connection with various human senses. The city's surface dissolves into ornaments that can participate in many different contexts. The link with both individual and collective everyday life is central to an urban analysis dealing with culture and society. Kracauer's distinction between ratio and Reason in the programmatic essay "Das Ornament der Masse" seeks to provide a societal and historico-philosophical perspective for the resubjectivization that is to be investigated in part II at a social and contemporary level.

Conclusion to Part I

It has been possible to reconstruct important fixed points in Siegfried Kracauer's interest in the city thanks to his autobiographical novel *Ginster* and his early dissertation on wrought-iron work in premodern Berlin. If one is to believe the novel *Ginster*, which provides the most important material for analysis in part I, that interest is not the positive outcome of his profession as a practicing architect. On the contrary, it is the result of dissatisfaction with the limitations of the everyday life of an architect. For this reason, the first part of this book has shifted from Ginster's exemplary criticism of the pragmatic architect's three-dimensional conception of space to his attempt to transcend the division of labor and adopt the modern metropolis as a *space for subjective reflection.*

In chapter 1, the sociological and historico-philosophical basis for Kracauer's essays on the city is outlined, using Georg Simmel's classic text "The Metropolis and Mental Life" as the point of departure. Certain theoretical differences between the two thinkers—for example, Simmel's physiological psychology versus Kracauer's psycho-analytically inspired analyses—are less important than their shared perception that the culture of the metropolis is crucial for the development of modernity. Simmel has pointed out objective culture's dominance of the subjective mind, and Kracauer's urban essays ought to be read as an attempt to correct this disparity.

Chapter 2 begins the analysis of Kracauer's anonymous autobiographical novel *Ginster*. This analysis is further developed in chapters 3 and 4. Chapter 2 concentrates on mapping Ginster's relationship to his job as a salaried architect in his hometown of F. We discover, first, that Ginster finds personal satisfaction only in marginal areas of the profession of architect. Second, his experience of the city of his childhood—as a result of his bonds to his family and his profession—concentrates on the quasi-natural and stuffy or claustrophobic characteristics of the mazelike city.

Chapter 3 lays bare the ornament's avoidance of architecture's three-dimensionally governed space. The two-dimensional spatial form plays a central role in both Ginster's memories of childhood and his perception of the unconscious characteristics of the history of art and architecture. This form is part of the basis for Kracauer's doctoral

dissertation on premodern wrought-iron ornamentation, which he seeks to revive in modern Berlin.

Chapter 4 deals with the city's assumption of a privileged position in Kracauer's analytics of culture. In the fragmented and decayed surface of Marseilles Ginster finally discovers a reflective space that recalls his feeling of unashamed sexuality experienced in connection with a visit to a prostitute. The strange, almost anonymous prostitute and his anonymous walks as a stranger through Marseilles pave the way for the fulfillment of Ginster's revolutionary resolve from the last days of the First World War, when he decided to rid himself of the habitually familiar and the daily drudgery of work. Whether Ginster leaves home and gives up his job as an architect is not stated in the novel, which concludes in Marseilles. But Kracauer—the author whose experience provides the basis for *Ginster*—begins to write a wide range of urban essays beginning in the mid-1920s, the results of which are the source material for part II of this book.

In the course of the first four chapters, the figure of the ornament has had a central, recurrent meaning. At the end of this first stage it is possible to speak of *four different types of ornament*. They diverge increasingly from the immediate meaning of the word to concentrate on the ornament as an experience-organizing agent.

The first type of ornament coincides with the traditional, art-historical meaning of the word. In both the study of wrought-iron work in Berlin (Kracauer's first book) and various drafts of architectural projects (in *Ginster*), the ornament corresponds to a visually decorative element in a larger spatial context.

Already the concept's second level assigns a superior meaning to the subjective factor, since Ginster, in answer to the narrow reality principle found in the job of architect, links an individual aesthetic enjoyment to certain tensions between the planned architecture and its context.

At the third level of the issue of ornamentation the link is broken to the traditional artistic-constructive concept. Nevertheless, the ornament remains visually fixed, since it constitutes the compulsory mediation between reality and subjectivity. As both observation and interpretation of the life space develop, two different registers of subjectivity are mobilized: those of vision and writing.

At the fourth—and provisionally last—level the ornaments of subjectivity are placed in a historico-philosophical perspective in nihilistic tones. This forms the experiential basis for part II, which, however, tones down the nihilistic characteristics in favor of a more contemporary and socioanalytic treatment of the city and its cultural universe. The ornament's link to societal conditions already means in *Ginster* that both subjectivity and urbanity are marked by the concept of transience. By underlining the intensity of life in the awareness of death as its boundary and—analogously—by linking the beauty of the city with crumbling decay, Kracauer places the issue of ornamentation in a specifically modern context.

The ornament of modernity that is foreshadowed in the otherwise tradition-bound metropolis of Marseilles contains the possibility of a coincidence of the *beautiful,* the *particular,* and the *joyful,* which was also Kracauer's justification for the analysis of wrought-iron work. But it becomes increasingly apparent that these qualities occur in connection with the ornament's negativity. The ornament that Kracauer investigates at levels of sociohistorical reflection have a decorative effect on the surface of reality, but they also have the critical function of facilitating experience.

The meeting in the ornament between a critical and an uncritical dimension becomes a more pressing theoretical problem the moment that Kracauer decides to devote himself to an analysis of the city and its sociality. Part II, which deals with Kracauer's essays on the contemporaneity of the metropolis, will therefore begin with an analysis of his perhaps best-known essay of cultural criticism and philosophical history, "Das Ornament der Masse": in English, "The Mass Ornament" or, probably better, "The Ornament of the Mass."

From Individual City Cognition
to the Encounter with the
Metropolitan Crisis of Memory

THIS SECOND PART OF the book deals with Kracauer's socially oriented treatment of the city and its culture. The section is relatively comprehensive since the texts analyzed are heterogeneous and therefore only with caution can be integrated into a common framework. But the textual material, consisting of Kracauer's urban essays from the Frankfurter Zeitung (1925–1933) along with several important critical essays on culture from the same newspaper, is so rich and versatile that it is well worth closer scrutiny and a thematic interpretation.

This analysis of Kracauer's urban essays in journalistic form will take up four chapters.

In chapter 5, the cultural criticism frame of reference for Kracauer's journalistic activity with the Frankfurter Zeitung will be presented and discussed. It will become clear that the 1927 essay "Das Ornament der Masse," without being directly concerned with urban ornaments, ascribes to them a central function in the strategy of cultural analysis. That Kracauer carries out this program will be demonstrated in the three subsequent chapters.

Chapter 6 deals with the mediation between individual and city effected by urban ornaments. In his interpretation of the city's visual and morphological reality, the individual (represented by Kracauer) meets certain destabilizing structures in his own psyche. This discovery turns out retroactively to affect the conception of urban sociality.

Chapter 7 concentrates on the city's role in societal reproduction. A critique is carried out, above all, of the space in which the unemployed are held in isolation from public life. This uncovers a passive waiting consciousness, whose active version is central to Kracauer's conception of the urban intellectual critic.

Chapter 8 maps out the attempts made by the intellectual to develop—in an almost photographic sense—utopian characteristics in the metropolis. The confrontation between the aesthetic form of criticism and the social reality of the metropolis encourages a more thorough elaboration of the disturbing, dystopian characteristics of the city. This shift serves to underscore the importance of the urban work of remembrance which undergoes radical changes in the modernity of the interwar years. The consequences of this for Kracauer's intellectual work will be dealt with in the third and final part of this book.

Ornament, Ratio, and Reason

Siegfried Kracauer's essay "Das Ornament der Masse" bears witness to the development that—in a programmatic, proclamatory form—was outlined in the last chapter of *Ginster.* It became clear to Ginster in Marseilles that he, as an individual, had to go beyond the boundaries of oppressive intimacy and seek in the city's collective medium of reflection a social mediation of his personal problems. So it is from a social point of view that Kracauer, no longer an architect but now a writer on culture for the renowned *Frankfurter Zeitung,* publishes the essay "Das Ornament der Masse." This essay, from June 9 and 10, 1927, is anything but a light piece of newspaper journalism. It adds a perspective critical of society and culture to the host of empirical variations on the issue of ornament dealt with in part I, thereby forming the framework for the part of Kracauer's work that addresses social history and essay writing and is analyzed in this second part of the book.

I. THE CONCEPT OF MASS ORNAMENT
The Consciously Created Mass Ornament

Kracauer's essay represents a challenge to the hypothesis that ornamentation is connected to the city. Whereas the term "ornament" is featured prominently in the essay's title,[1] neither the article's empirical material nor its theoretical considerations immediately suggest concentrating one's critical cultural interest on the city (or the metropolis). Even though one should not forget that Kracauer also dealt with other cultural spheres of modernity during this period—mainly contemporary film—it is nevertheless my hypothesis that "Das Ornament der Masse" not only supplements the treatment of ornament in *Ginster* in its analysis of society and culture;[2] it can also offer guidelines for interpreting Kracauer's urban essays from the *Frankfurter Zeitung* during the 1924–1933 period.[3] I hope to demonstrate that the cultural, social, and historical conclusions from "Das Ornament der Masse" can, with due caution, be extended to encompass a close connection between *ornament, critique,* and *urbanity.*

The first hurdle to be overcome in seeking to demonstrate a link between "Das Ornament der Masse" and Kracauer's urban essays is that mass ornament is far removed from the irreducible and experientially organizing ornaments featured in *Ginster*. The mass ornament does not possess any humane qualities; on the contrary, it represents a desolate, rigid, and formalized structure. Rather than serving the critical intuitive awareness of the single individual, as in *Ginster*, the category of the ornament is primarily linked in "Das Ornament der Masse" to the conformity of the mass.

This is especially obvious in the specific material for analysis, which mainly consists of the so-called Tiller Girls[4]—gigantic Anglo-American (or Anglo-American-inspired) dance troupes from the period just after the First World War. With their almost military discipline they enthralled the mass audiences who thronged their performances in sports stadiums, in huge theaters, and in front of the screen at the weekly film revues shown all over Germany. Kracauer analyzes the elements of this cultural product. He shows how this "dance" culture involves the training of each individual girl, who is drilled into executing precisely codified movements. This turns her into a neutral element in a serial body-machine. The individual becomes an unconscious part of a whole of which she is unable to gain an overview. The whole can be seen only, if at all, from the point of view of the spectators. It takes the form of geometrical shapes whose constant changes take place within the register of two-dimensional figures that appear to be inhuman. The mass ornament, formed by the dance girls, appears to the numerous mass (of spectators) as an ornamented physical mass.[5] This is what prompts Kracauer to write: "Ornaments of thousands of bodies . . . bodies in bathing suits devoid of gender" (O, p. 51). The stadium becomes the stage for the self-objectivization of the mass, thereby producing a special kind of ornament.

The Tiller Girls share a common feature with Ginster's military cemetery: in their fetishized mass appearance they suppress all organic life. But whereas the military cemetery for the fallen soldiers presupposes a form of moral fellowship and a politico-aesthetic intention, the mass ornament of the dance girls is, in Kracauer's eyes, without any substantial cohesive force. Briefly, his analysis is as follows:

> The ornament is an end in itself [*Selbstzweck*]. . . . The girl units train . . . in order to produce innumerable parallel lines; and the training [*Ertüchtigung*] of considerable human masses would be desirable in order to generate a pattern of undreamed-of dimensions. The final result is the ornament, for whose closed uniformity [*Geschlossenheit*] the substance-containing structures are emptied [of their content]. (O, p. 52)

Precisely here, Kracauer, with an unmistakable historical intuition of the political developments of the 1930s, senses the danger that the ornament—now made independent and devoid of content—would become an end in itself and thereby allow itself to become involved in mythic (i.e., not linked to reason) historical projects. For Kracauer the mass ornament becomes a dystopia, a terrifying opposite to the critical and utopian ornament found in *Ginster.*

The Taylorization of the Production of Culture

To Kracauer's way of thinking, the interest in an ornament—whose formal abstraction of the organic material of the human body is interpreted as an impoverishment—runs parallel with the introduction of a new theoretical level.[6] This approach implies putting the ornament into a socioanalytical perspective.

As he develops elements from the Marxist critique of capitalism, Kracauer notes that the mass ornament is produced using techniques that are reminiscent of the Taylorized organization of production: "The hands in the factory correspond to the legs of the Tiller Girls. There is an effort to measure not only manual but also mental dispositions using psychotechnical tests of suitability. The mass ornament is the aesthetic reflection of the rationality that is striven for in the ruling economic system" (O, p. 54). Furthermore, he stresses a structural similarity between the ornament and capitalistic profit, since both cherish an unlimited ambition to grow that lacks any external substantial definition of purpose. The ornament, devoid of content, thus has its point of departure in the principle of "capitalist production" (O, p. 53), which likewise makes no specific demands regarding content as long as the abstract aim (the realization of profit) is met.[7]

The accuracy of this comparison—at that time, quite original—between mass entertainment and the rationalist organizational forms of the production process can of course be discussed, and obviously one would have certain theoretical and empirical reservations about a simple analogy between the production of goods and the production of entertainment. These reservations would prove even more urgent if Kracauer, in his analytical work, let the city be a pure reflection of the capitalistic organization of production.[8] But Kracauer does not do so. The link with the urban-reflexive ornament (see part I) is indirectly reestablished via Kracauer's conception of the possibilities for a critique of the mass ornament.

The Critique of the Ornament: The Distinction between Ratio and Reason

In his argument for adopting a critical point of view concerning a culture that to an increasing extent is assuming the form of "mass ornaments," Kracauer repeatedly dismisses any kind of highbrow nostalgia. He advances the idea that traditional cultural norms and values are not, from a sociohistorical point of view, relevant for modern interwar capitalism.[9] On the other hand, the impoverishment of human culture by the mass ornament is assumed to involve certain critical possibilities. Because of the extreme lack of organic elements in its organization, it gives such a distorted image of society's basic mechanisms that the critical sense of the mass public can be mobilized and protest against this reality itself.[10]

In terms of method, however, it is far more crucial that the mass ornament's reduction of the human being to a mere functional element of a mechanism alien to life is precisely part of a comprehensive historico-philosophical construction that leads Kracauer to make a distinction between two different types of ornament.

His considerations are based on a historical conception of the concept of reason. Basically, reason is a demythologizing force that slowly, indirectly, but irresistibly makes its influence felt at nature's expense. Thus the "historical process" unfolds as the fight of "weak and distant reason" against the "natural powers" (O, p. 55). But this process becomes distorted under the conditions of a capitalist society, which makes it necessary to distinguish between two basic forms of reason.

Ratio and *Reason,* the names given to the two forms of reason, are both linked to the historical process. Ratio, however, is something specifically capitalistic, whereas Reason adopts the position of negativity in this historical phase.

This means that Ratio, via its societal function, is the expression of a limited, distorted form of reason. At first sight, it does involve a break with the power of external nature. It is, however, so closely linked to a capitalist form of mastery that it assumes the nature of "darkened reason" (O, p. 57). Ratio is characterized precisely by its not being able to take "the ground of Man" (*Grund des Menschen*) into consideration (O, p. 57). Here Kracauer is referring especially to the conditions that cannot be reduced to—or even be made to harmonize with—a capitalist finality. For this reason, Ratio results in practical cynicism and in formalism of thought. Moreover, its sidelining of the human principle creates fertile conditions for new mythological forces.[11]

Unlike Ratio, Reason is not characterized by the blinkered view of rationalism. On the other hand it is—especially under capitalist conditions—utopian. Reason is linked to the superior "process of demythologization" (O, p. 58); and since this process is not yet complete but only temporarily distorted, Reason has to be outlined mainly via exemplary and—in a capitalist context—negative definitions. For example, in the period of the Enlightenment it has shown itself in the world of fairy tales (*Märchen*) in the form of values such as truth and justice (O, p. 55). Furthermore, bourgeois revolutions have benefited greatly from the "fortune of reason" (*Glück der Vernunft;* O, p. 56) in their fight against the church and the monarchy.

As something utopian, Reason has to be defined by distinguishing it from the forms of practice and thought found in abstract rationality. This is achieved by insisting that it has to take into account the particular. By this term Kracauer understands something that he (just as negatively) describes as "man" (as shaped by history). It is of vital importance that this sensitivity to and respect for the particular is not achieved by reverting to mythic concretism. On the contrary, it is fundamental to Reason to be able to understand and act in relation to the nonidentical without relinquishing the ability to use the power of abstraction (O, p. 58). All in all, Reason is a term for a negative, demythologizing force that does not become addicted to the abstract subordination of complex experiences.[12]

Ratio and Reason—Historically Exemplified

Given these general characteristics of Ratio and Reason, we can now examine an example of the analytical development of these two theoretical registers.

A decade later, in December 1936, Kracauer himself indicated how a politico-sociological analysis could be inspired by both the concept of mass and that of reason in "Das Ornament der Masse." This occurred in the research program "Masse und Propaganda (Eine Untersuchung über die fascistische Propaganda)" ("Mass and Propaganda [An Inquiry into Fascist Propaganda]"), which was prepared for the exiled Institut für Sozialforschung (which had moved to New York). In it, Kracauer, using the concept of the mass, outlines the opposition between Ratio and Reason, between the lifting of an enchantment and the resuscitation of mythic forces.

The decisive political task in the actual historical situation is determined as being "to cause the masses [by which Kracauer means the proletariat, middle classes, and unemployed] to disappear . . . as a mass" (M, p. 87). He is in no way advocating the physical removal of the population or the like—rather, he is urging the necessity of a "communist" development of society that can abolish social need and the capitalistically motivated class divisions. But this development is prevented by the overall political situation in Germany, characterized above all by resistance from "the dispossessed middle class" (M, p. 87).

This means that the only practical possibility is a reintegration of the masses into capitalist society—which does not solve the problem, but only fixes the situation in an intolerable form. Fascism is the main agent of this process, but "fascism is a mock solution," as it cultivates the masses' "mass nature" to excess and, in its systematic political staging, "seeks to give rise to the impression that the mass is in fact integrated" (M, p. 87). That development is underpinned by the use of terror and propaganda. Fascism exploits politically the aesthetic forces that Kracauer a decade previously had analyzed in connection with the mass entertainment provided by the Tiller Girls. This time, though, it is a question of the tautological self-reflection of the masses. The final separation of stage and spectators is done away with in the mass processions of fascism, replaced by one part of the masses' observation of another part. "Everywhere the mass is

forced to observe itself (mass meetings, mass processions, etc.). The mass is therefore always present to itself—often in the aesthetically seductive form of an ornament or a striking image" (M, p. 88). Via their totalizing abolition in the form of the masses, basic social problems are given a mythic treatment. "With the aim of underlining the importance of the masses, all the mythic forces that can be developed in them are emphasized," Kracauer notes immediately afterward. Despite signs of a crisis in the fascist organization of society, mythic Ratio temporarily dominates.

Doing away with the mass as a mass, to be replaced by a real social existence, remains a utopian aim. The factors of *Entzauberung* (disenchantment) and Reason are hard to locate positively in the historical development of Germany in the 1930s. This is one of the reasons why examples of a fully developed utopian form of reason are so few and far between. In the series of texts illustrating utopia that will be systematically dealt with in chapter 8, only one can be considered a valid illustration of the utopian concept of reason. Concrete utopian reason is located neither in the production process nor in the urban sphere in the immediate sense, but rather in the condensed version of public space found in the theater (or the circus).

The essay in question is "Akrobat—schöön" ("Acrobat—Wooonderful"; FZ, October 25, 1932). Here the three Andreu-Rivel clowns are considered to be a cultural phenomenon of such great inner generic cohesion that they can serve as a point of departure for an analysis outlining principles for a different historical and mental form of logic. Their act has ceased to have a subordinate role in the circus performance—with its blend of sudden ideas and coherence it appears as an independent (but self-dissolving) work. This makes the clowns a practical example of the "fairy-tale reason" previously mentioned in the analysis of "Das Ornament der Masse" (see especially O, pp. 55, 63).

In the clowns' performance Kracauer does not see a drama that aims at simple distraction. On the contrary, he hypothesizes that a particular kind of logic unfolds beyond the many individual ideas that provoke such mirth. The "hierarchy of values" is exposed to a refined critique, since the clowns place "apparent bagatelles . . . center stage" at the expense of the "important" sides of reality (S, p. 139). By doing so, they act against the unambiguous subordination of means to an end that they have jointly set themselves. The clowns find themselves in an inverse relationship to the end, which is forgotten in favor of beautiful deviations. Yet these, in one way or other, nonetheless serve a purpose, since the realization of the imaginative end (here, the acrobatic creation of a bridge) "is achieved entirely by detours that are of greater importance than the end itself" (S, p. 138).

This "stubborn policy of nonfulfillment" (S, p. 140) reminds one in its negativity of Kracauer's love of Marseilles and the popular nature of Paris. But the purpose of his analysis here is first and foremost to investigate the hypothesis concerning the performance by the clowns as a potential source of insight into a particular childlike or fairy-tale-like logic on which a utopia is founded. The existence of an independent "imagined sequence in the child" appears "completely categorized" in the clowns' performance (S, p. 140). The logic of the child is not affected by the accusations of adult reason of being "absent-minded and distracted" (S, p. 141). On the contrary, the logic of the child (and of the clown) includes a large inner coherence that makes plain the connection with the issue of ornament, referred to in the following quotation by the word "arabesques": "Stated briefly, the childlike excesses are not isolated chance acts but are closely interconnected; the sudden ideas are under strict control and the stream of arabesques follow an organized sequence" (S, p. 141).

Kracauer thus locates a subtle critique of a rational relationship between the end and the means in the clowns' performance. All in all, there is a "meaning in the meaninglessness" (S, p. 142). It is just that its logic is that of the "fairy tale" (S, p. 141)—which is different from that of the rational. Its development of all the specific sudden ideas into a child's logic presents the outlines of a utopian force. In this way, the acting of the clowns "intimates a *reality . . .* that is not identical with our own, that is just as oblique to our everyday [concept of reality] as is that of fairy tales and many dreams" (S, p. 142). Now that these two examples have served to distinguish between Ratio-bound and Reason-bound ornaments, the area of specific urban experience can be explored.

2. THE MASS ORNAMENT AND THE METROPOLIS
The Ornament between Ratio and Reason

As is typical of Kracauer, he does not undertake any final conceptual clarification of the relationship between Ratio and Reason. As a consequence of his skepticism regarding the abstract solution of problems with concrete effects, he shifts the amplification of the issue to a field of experience where Ratio and Reason meet. If such mediation between Reason and Ratio is at all possible, it must be assumed to take place in a visually established intersection of the two forms of reason. In this way, the theoretical considerations are once more in the domain of the ornament (here, the mass ornament).[13]

With its two-dimensional spatiality, the ornament allows a number of different forms of abstraction. The ornament is subject to a general ambiguity: "The mass ornament is, like abstraction, ambiguous" (O, p. 59). This ambiguity consists of being able to help both Ratio and Reason develop. When looked at more closely, it turns out that Kracauer's definitions of the two aspects of the ornament correspond roughly to a transposition of the opposition between Reason and Ratio. On the one hand, he defines the ornament as a sensitive abstraction or, to use a formulation from "Das Ornament der Masse," as "a reduction of the natural that does not allow the human to languish but—as long as it is completely implemented—on the contrary presents what is essentially human" (O, p. 59). The ornament represents an *"extraction"* (O, p. 59), which implies an exteriorizing anonymization of the nature on which it is based. This basis (in an almost visual sense) is illuminated by Reason, finding expression in an abstraction that, by means of its form, nevertheless remains in accord with the thing itself.

On the other hand, the ornament can be the extreme opposite of a sensitive abstraction. It can express a *"mythological cult"* and thereby—as was the case in an aggravated form in the Nazi mass processions of the 1930s—present itself as "the crass manifestation of lower nature" (O, p. 60). Kracauer advances the hypothesis that what appears to be rational in certain ornaments most often conceals that the natural basis which ought to be made abstract in and by the ornament is not illuminated at all. On the contrary, nature is subordinated by a concept that is exaggerated and only formally abstract. As a reaction to the brutal grouping within an insufficiently sensitive concept, the concrete material turns to a paradoxical means of expression. As its answer, it assumes the forms of the mock-rational ornament in order to complete its "regression into mythology" in the guise of a rational form of appearance:

> Ratio, which gives rise to it [the mass ornament], is large enough to call forth the mass and to squeeze life out of the figures. It is too small to find the human beings in the mass and to make the figures transparent for cognition. Since it flees from Reason into the abstract, uncontrolled nature expands violently, under the guise of a rational mode of expression, making use of the abstract signs to present itself. (O, p. 61)

Kracauer's basic idea places the ornament at the theoretical and analytical center, at the same time as it creates an awareness of a theoretical problem that is of great importance for the conclusions to be drawn from his deliberations.

Kracauer's text states clearly that the ornament as a *general form* and as a *concept* has the potential both to give "the human" expression and—in a radically opposed move—to manifest "the empty form of culture" (O, p. 61). On the other hand, one point of Kracauer's presentation remains unresolved, when dealing with the ornament as a concrete visual form. Is it possible that the same concrete ornamental form can express both Reason and rationally disguised mythology? Or, another basic possibility, is there a systematic link between the visual form of the ornament and its affiliation to Ratio and Reason, respectively?[14]

Since theoretical fixed points are lacking, our judgments must be based on Kracauer's examples of ornaments. Using his list of the ornaments that are unambiguously linked to one of the two types of reason, it is possible to see a clear link between form and type of reason. The Tiller Girls mentioned earlier are still the stock example of the cultic function of the rational ornament. Conversely, nonperspectival Chinese landscape paintings can serve to illustrate a form—admittedly historical—of ornamental abstraction that was capable of transforming the originally organic object into an illuminated ornamental state.[15] This process was completed without the use of illegitimate force.

The formal idiom of the ornament contains an intersection of both the authentic and the "darkened" versions of reason. But the precise form of the ornaments is not a matter of indifference. Given the examples mentioned, it would seem that "light," dancing, and dreamlike ornamentation mainly corresponds to Reason. Ratio, on the other hand, has to make do with ornaments that are brutally linear and geometrically totalizing. So there are reasons to assume that for Kracauer differentiated and complex ornaments, to a greater extent than "curves and circles that are to be found in the manuals of Euclidean geometry" (O, p. 53), are able to articulate "the human." This position would be an extension of Kracauer's stylistic judgments of various examples of Berlin wrought-iron work in his doctoral thesis of 1915.

The Status of Urban Ornaments

This analogy between ornamental forms and types of reason makes it possible to understand the perspective adopted by Kracauer when dealing with ornamental fragments of the urban world. Unlike the real culture industry[16] (Tiller Girls, etc.), the social and cultural forms of urban life take shape at a considerable distance from the capitalistic production process. Civil life can thus be assumed at its horizontal levels to modify capitalist rationality, which attempts to make an impact vertically. In any case, in the life-world both the visual and the interpersonal aspects take, on the whole, more "poetic" and composite forms than they do in the capitalist production process. Because of this richness of forms they must also—despite their place in societal reproduction—be assumed to be more closely connected to Reason. In short, urban ornaments are made up of more distinct parts and thus can offer greater potential than the production process for the development of Reason.

It is therefore my hypothesis that Kracauer's many-faceted and extensive work on urban motifs constitutes a coherent attempt to set in motion or give support to a historical and cultural movement. The medium of this movement is subjective reflection. As a process it stakes out a path whose point of departure is an ornamental cross section of a visual, social, or otherwise experienced reality. Via an essayist's interpretation, conditions are created that enable Reason—at the expense of Ratio, to a greater or lesser extent—to be introduced into both individual and collective reflection.

This hypothesis is in accordance with the perspective that Kracauer himself took on ornament as a category and an object of interpretation. In "Das Ornament der Masse" it is his basic conception and point of departure that the ornament possesses vital but as yet undeveloped forces relevant to developing a honed awareness of contemporaneity. The ornaments are made up of "insignificant surface utterances" (O, p. 50). "Because of their unconsciousness" they grant access—if developed in a sensitive analysis—to understanding, even to a full perception of "the basic content of what exists" (O, p. 50). So the writer has to seek to establish a link between the ornamental surface signs and a possible "basic content." By means of his commentary he processes—as if he were one of those individuals ostracized from society for whom the ornaments are like "the prongs of a rake" that "sink down between the layers of the soul" (O, p. 51)—selected urban fragments of experience. They then assume the nature of what Simmel called "objectivized spirit," since as literary ornaments in essay form, they offer themselves to the larger public's own everyday interpretation. This point will be dealt with in more detail in the introduction to the next chapter.

The Analytical Strategy

Kracauer's formulations, which indicate the framework of his personal strategy as a social analyst and writer, are expressed—particularly toward the end of "Das Ornament der Masse"—in a general program of cultural criticism. Here he links social analytics, historical development, and the two basic forms of the ornament. In just a few sentences the themes of the essay are gathered together, since they are used—once and for all—to mark the theoretical possibility of distinguishing between capitalistic Ratio and humanistic Reason. These two poles are the extremes of a movement both analytical and historical from the mythic and repressive ornament to an ornament capable of abstracting the essence of things. Here is Kracauer's historico-philosophical conclusion:

> The process passes directly through the mass ornament—and not back from it. It can move forward only if thought limits nature and presents man in the way he is on the basis of Reason. Then society will change. Then the mass ornament will also disappear and human life itself will assume characteristics of the ornament, in which it, in fairy tales, expresses itself in relation to truth. (O, p. 63)

The relationship described here between the ornament and history ascribes a major role to intellectual practice. Carrying out a historical development presupposes that a movement of thought is taking or has already taken place. Practical and real History must, so to speak, be prepared. It must have undergone a meditative process *before* it can carry out decisive movements at a social and material level. To put it metaphorically, the social world would in principle have to undergo collective psychoanalysis in preparing for its historical development.[17]

3. CONCLUSION: THE METROPOLIS AS A FIELD OF ANALYSIS

In the cultural context after the First World War, which was dominated by the mass ornament, Kracauer's concentration of his efforts of social and cultural analysis on, among other things, the urban sphere seems to result from his choice of strategy. The most condensed expression of this sphere, the metropolis, is, if anything, *the* place for "das Ornament der Masse." The mass ornament in all its dimensions belongs to the metropolis. Kracauer himself stresses how cities with a million inhabitants differ from both the industrial city and the provincial town by addressing themselves, in their considerable cultural market, less to a group well defined in terms of culture or class than to a general and apparently neutral public:

> Berlin's four million people cannot be ignored. The mere necessity of their circulation transforms the life of the street into the unavoidable street of life, produces decor that penetrates even the four walls of the home. But the more people feel themselves as a mass, the more the mass also develops powers in the intellectual field whose financing is rewarding. The mass is no longer left to its own devices, but makes an impact in all its desolation; it does not tolerate its remnants being thrown away but demands to be served at ready-laid tables. Next to this, there is only little room for so-called cultural layers. They have to eat or snobbishly keep their distance; their provincial isolation comes at any rate to an end. By their inclusion in the mass the homogeneous world-metropolis public comes into being, in which every member, from the bank director to the clerk, from the diva to the typist, has the same importance. Moans and complaints about this turn toward a mass taste are belated. For the cultural baggage that the masses refuse to pick up has, as far as some are concerned, become only an increasingly historical possession, since the economic and social reality to which it was assigned has changed. (O, p. 313)

Thus cultural *mass production* has as its counterpart a *public* that is itself mobilized as a uniform *mass*. This meeting takes place within the framework of the mass, both physical and social, of the metropolis. All in all, the metropolis—represented by Berlin in Kracauer's interwar Germany—constitutes the place where the mass ornament is concentrated as a culture industry, a mass public, and an urban spatial mass.

The challenge to the reflective, writing individual that follows from this is considerable. The following three chapters will show what axes of articulation Kracauer finds possible in the 1925–1933 period. The level of abstraction is a different one, however. Kracauer's thoughts concerning Ratio and Reason contribute—without his mentioning the word "resubjectivization" a single time—to an understanding of the conditions underlying this. In the same way, Ratio and Reason provide discreet but noticeable grounding for his essays on urbanity. No matter whether the themes are taken from the fields of Ratio or of developed Reason, the perspective is the same: to underpin Reason. Kracauer makes this attempt using as a point of departure both Berlin and Paris and the Mediterranean cities, whose urban modernity is made the subject of a number of journalistic essays. His childhood city of F. (Frankfurt) is admittedly where these studies were published (in the *Frankfurter Zeitung*), but from the point of view of urban experience it belongs at a personal level to his provincial past.

Urban Ornaments and Subjective Experience

I. THE CRITICAL REFLECTIVE GAZE

Among Kracauer's writings, his *Straßen in Berlin und anderswo* (*Streets in Berlin and Elsewhere*) provides the best basis for uncovering an inner systematics in his urban analysis. This collection of essays contains a balanced selection of the urban essays he published in the *Frankfurter Zeitung* in the period from 1925 to 1933. Considered as a whole, the book represents a comprehensive, complex attempt to evoke places in the metropolis related to human consciousness. Through a written interpretation of over-looked phenomena, the uniform, considerable spaces of the city are transformed into limited and significance-laden points, a systematization of which will be attempted in the next three chapters.

The Basic Elements of the Interpretive Situation

The basic structures of the interpretive situation do not deviate all that much from those previously investigated. The single individual stands directly opposite a totality of a social and physical nature that surrounds him, but that can still be the subject of interpretation. This is achieved by the *fragmentation of the whole into ornaments.*

The ornaments that serve as models for Kracauer's urban essays are mostly of a different type than the Tiller Girls. That mass ornament had been consciously created as a rational whole, which remains alien to the complex and not quite so thoroughly rationalized metropolis that is Kracauer's point of departure. His essays thus deal with visual sections of the metropolis whose interpretation can create a link between various types of ornaments, since these are sought to be made accessible to Reason.

The staging in essay form is the means whereby Kracauer articulates the abstract and neutral spaces of the metropolis. Its principle facets will be briefly listed. First, his comments on the "superficial forms" allow the visual aspect, which is crucial for de-limiting the original ornament, to survive in the final text. This enables him to main-tain a special contact, rare in texts with a philosophical slant, with the parceled-out spatiality of the city. Second, Kracauer's introduction of a subjective link with this space must be emphasized. The spatial form of appearance that often (because of the density of buildings) is identified with a city does not of itself guarantee that there actually is an *urban* unity.[1] For that, a place is needed that is invested with both linguistic and social practice.

The intellectual critic can contribute to the creation of place by his commentary, which gradually joins together to form an essay. In other words, it is the task of the essay to provide the urban "superficial form" with a discursive interpretation, thereby introducing that element of subjectivity that can transform the abstract urban *space* into a *place,* hedged in by consciousness. The rest of part II in this book seeks to uncover the three forms of subjectivization that are prevalent in Kracauer's texts in *Straßen in Berlin und anderswo.*

These three forms of subjectivization all express a central feature of *Straßen in Berlin und anderswo.* Although the point of departure for his analyses is still, as mentioned, a polarization between the individual and the totality of the metropolis, the essays in that book—more clearly than does the novel *Ginster*—adopt a social perspective. This is already apparent from the titles of the four sections of the book. They show a movement from the streets ("Straßen," part I) via the discrete forms of the social ("Lokale" [Rooms], part II, and "Dinge" [Things], part III) back to the open city, this time seen in a social light with the title "Leute"—people. The point of departure that sounds inorganic (the street) is thus finally resolved in its social definition (people)—a movement, by the way, that at a microlevel takes place within the great majority of the short single essays in the book.[2] The subjectivization of the visually limited element is thus the form in which Kracauer seeks in his essays to provide the fragmented city with a social-reflective perspective, with the intention of transforming its spaces into places.

The Self-Centered City

Kracauer's bringing into perspective of individual phenomena in the metropolis is enhanced by the fact that no attempt is made to view the urban universe from the outside. There is, in fact, only one essay in *Straßen in Berlin und anderswo* in which the metropolis is opposed to the surrounding expanses of countryside. This clearly reveals that Kracauer is well aware of what can be criticized in the self-centered urban form of culture, but also recognizes its powers of fascination and its status as historical reality.

The essay, which is in the form of a narrative, has the title "Lokomotive über der Friedrichstraße" ("Locomotive above the Friedrichstraße") and was the last of those collected in the volume to be published. It takes the form of a metaphor of urban culture, having as its point of departure—in accordance with the above characterization of Kracauer's form of writing—a visual impression: a train that finds itself unnoticed above a street in Berlin's entertainment district that is most animated at night. The text unfolds in a seeming identification with the train driver, who has traversed open landscapes at great speed. Suddenly he (and the train) stand still above a dazzling main street, whose evening life displays a completely different form of visual and cultural acceleration. The city constitutes its own "world axis." Its ocean of light gives the impression of "a huge dissolute party that, like the arc lamps, has neither beginning nor end" (S, p. 43). With its "brilliance and tumult" the cityscape has burned itself into the train driver's gaze as "the place for reddish life" (S, p. 43), and the image stays on his retina while he continues his journey eastward. This is how the city's dazzling—and for an outsider brutal—self-reflection is established as a central theme for Kracauer's analysis, with Kracauer, unlike many German intellectuals, never expressing the wish for a historical unraveling of the metropolis but instead dealing with urban culture from the inside.

Kracauer abandons the traditional opposition between country and town, investigating much more intensely instead the city as a universe that is not above criticism, but that cannot be explained as simply the antithesis of rural life. To promote a subtle understanding of modern urban culture, the analysis has to take on the city's inner oppositions and seek to expose some of its vital patterns of movement.

The essay "Ansichtspostkarte" ("Picture Postcard") illustrates this endeavor. The forceful, even violent, aspect of the modern metropolis is still represented by the neon advertisements of the entertainment and commercial districts, while the critical, potentially dynamizing element is now localized not in a rural consciousness but in a visual impression. This view reconciles opposites, like one of tourism's simultaneously embellishing and stereotyped postcards, although it here shows itself as a possible source of culture critique.

The motif of "Ansichtspostkarte" is the Kaiser Wilhelm Memorial Church in Berlin. This accords with the secular character of life in the metropolis, in that it no longer functions as a church. The building has been closed to the public and now lies like a trace of times past, blocking the traffic. But in Kracauer's presentation, the church building is a sign that the urban culture of the mass ornament produces opposing forces. The essay, for example, expresses surprise at "a gentle radiance that is just as soothing as it is inexplicable, a clarity that has nothing in common with the profane, reddish gleam of the arc lamps, but that detaches itself from its surroundings and seems to spring from the memorial walls of the Kaiser Wilhelm Church itself" (S, p. 47). But "the gentle radiance" comes not from the church but rather from its diametric opposite: "an uninhibited glittering that in no way only serves the advertisement but is furthermore an end in itself" (*Selbstzweck;* S, p. 47). The gentle rays come from the mass ornament's light pendant in the metropolis. Even so, the afterglow of the church walls is interpreted as a reflection and as an unintentional leftover, as the expression of the existence of a nonidentical element on the surface of the metropolis. By their beauty the walls articulate a repressed—in terms of both humanity and Reason—element in the city evening that is otherwise so raw: "That which is rejected by the spectacle of light and is expelled by the economic setup—is conserved by empty walls. . . . Not in the hidden interior—[but] right there in the street, the unnoticed and insignificant are gathered together and transformed, until they begin to gleam—a consolation for each and every one" (S, p. 48).

A deep humanity thus returns as an immaterial surface, as a visual source of an ornament produced via thought. Although they both contrast with the ocean of light found in the metropolis, the gently reflecting walls of the memorial church are of greater theoretical weight for Kracauer than the previously mentioned dazzled gaze of the train driver. For the reflections on the walls of the memorial church indicate the possibility of producing a metropolitan reality other than that generally recognized, thus expanding the framework for an understanding of the city.

The Abstracting Gaze

The observer's abstraction from the city's symbolic and functional hierarchy is a compulsory element in Kracauer's conception of critical urban analysis. The observer's field of vision—and thus the aesthetic part of his sphere of reality—is explicitly determined by being demarcated from consciously produced urban images: buildings, street perspectives, fine squares, and so on. In all their complexity the unintentional, often overlooked urban images correspond to the ornamental form of dream-reason. For they

> come into being . . . without having been planned in advance. They are not compositions . . . but creatures of chance that cannot be accounted for. Where masses of stone and streets converge—since their elements result from completely differing interests—an urban image arises that has never been the subject of any interest. It has been shaped as little as nature has and resembles a landscape in that it asserts itself unconsciously [bewußtlos]. Unconcerned about its own appearance, it slumbers through time. (S, p. 51)

In this analytic strategy Kracauer allows himself to look away from urban spaces that can be ascribed an artistic or political intention as totalities. Instead, he draws attention to spatial unities "which appear unintentionally" (S, p. 51), supported only by the observer's attention to random spatial formations that are nonetheless compositions—both visually and in terms of interest. There is a double shift: he seeks to displace not only that which is observed but also the way in which observation takes place, the point of view, in relation to the traditional urban commentary. This results, when most

successful, in certain urban images whose demonstrably anonymous nature makes one think of scenes in nature, whereby they—in their apparent innocence—offer a potentially freer gaze at the cityscape of everyday life.

Kracauer's description of the view from the high location of his apartment must be understood in this connection. Nothing is further from his mind than an attempt to write a nostalgic reproduction of an all-dominating, divinely tinged gaze familiar from the premodern city maps' bird's-eye view. The vertical angle of the text "Aus dem Fenster gesehen" ("Seen through the Window"; originally called "Berliner Landschaft," or "Berlin Landscape") is if anything connected to the avant-garde within contemporary photography (Rodchenko, László Moholy-Nagy), which investigated the new vertical vistas of the metropolis via the medium of photography. Kracauer observes from a distance the formless confluence of numerous streets and streams of traffic that are the point of departure for an endless gaze out across the considerable "iron fields" of the railway network (S, p. 52).

The description of this view naturally contains certain references to Berlin's reality (the destinations of the trains, the radio tower in the distance). But above all the image of the well-known dissolves into abstract streets, lines, and movements that, in the darkness of the evening and night, seem to condense into "a great field of light." The cityscape becomes the space for an ornamental "tumult that has no depth" (S, p. 53). The essential thing in this disinterested, naturalizing gaze is not that it seems at first glance to ignore the social and historical nature of the metropolis but that it exposes the outer regions of culture—its random, eccentric expressions—as material for urban reflection. Modernity's equivalent to a natural landscape is an urban space.

A number of Kracauer's texts display a type of image analysis that, without necessarily naturalizing space, carries out a visual abstraction with the aim of making the city the subject of interpretation. The inclusion of few, limited elements of action creates a discursive description, which results in an urban dream-space. Using Marseilles as a starting point, Kracauer thus confronts two forms of space—on the one hand, the mazelike pattern of the streets; on the other, the open expanse of a square that is introduced during the city stroll in a form of movement recalling the time sequence of dreams. In the process, the particular discoveries are replaced by a courtroom atmosphere: "by the might of the square the captive is forced into its center. . . . A court is in session on invisible chairs around the square. It is the moment for the announcement of a sentence that is not passed" (S, p. 27). It is evident from a letter to Kracauer from Walter Benjamin that the source of this quotation, from the section "Das Karree" ("The Quadrangle") in the essay "Zwei Flächen" ("Two Planes") from autumn 1926, is a shared nocturnal walk and not a solitary dream.[3] Nevertheless, the coincidence of space and psyche occupies a prominent place in the actual text.

The reference to the mental level is even more pronounced in "Die Bai" ("The Bay"), the first half of "Das Karree," in which the dockland area of the city of Marseilles, le Vieux Port, forms the basis of a characterization of the city as "a dazzling amphitheater" (S, p. 24). The harbor is "the sea-cobbled square, which makes incisions into the city with its depth" (S, p. 24). At the same time, however, the city, led by "the street of streets" (la Canebière), has repressed the harbor's fundamental role for Marseilles's urbanity. The harbor's constitutive importance is pushed into the background with a reference to its loss of any useful function in an age of ocean liners, when the bustle of sailing ships has disappeared. The city streets, however, continue to open out onto this space, whose empty surface still leaves its impression on the city. The city's origin and basis for existence—the motherly harbor—has on the surface perhaps lost its raison d'être, but it is far from having lost its symbolic importance for the city's basic sociospatial structure. This is retained, despite the fact that the city has turned its back on the aquatic stage: "The full rows of seats in the amphitheater overlook a hollow space. The standing audience has turned its back on it" (S, p. 26).

In this interpretation of Marseilles, the figural interpretation of the city scene thus refers both to a conception of the city's origins and to the loss of this original structure. This paradoxical construction is of general significance in Kracauer's urban analytics. An extensive series of modern urban feelings of loss (at both the individual and collective level) are located in this opposition. This interpretive structure will be dealt with in greater detail in the rest of this chapter.

2. SUBJECTIVITY AND URBAN EXPERIENCE

Inspired perhaps by French surrealism, which with André Breton's novel *Nadja* and Aragon's essay *Le paysan de Paris* (*The Parisian Farmer*) had placed the investigation of the metropolis under the sign of the dream—but also in accordance with contemporary writings by his acquaintances Ernst Bloch and Walter Benjamin—Kracauer goes so far in 1931 as to allow, in a programmatic formulation, the cognition of the city to be linked to an interpretation of its complex, dreamlike space: "The cognition of cities is linked to the deciphering of the dreamlike outlines of their images" (S, p. 53). This is how Kracauer concludes his previously mentioned distinction between intentional and unintentional spaces.

The formulation indicates the perspective in which the connection between the individual and the metropolis must be understood. According to Kracauer, Marseilles acquired its urban form from its relationship to the antiquated yet foundational dockland area. There is more evidence in his other writings to support a hypothesis of an intimate connection between subjectivity and urban experience.

Repetition and Melancholic Self-Contemplation—The Urbanized Subject

The finest example of the fact that the individual, during his walk through the city, moves in a spatiality that corresponds to basic structures in his own psyche is found in Kracauer's story "Erinnerung an eine Pariser Straße" ("Memory of a Paris Street") from 1930. As the title implies, the stage of the memory is set in Paris—more specifically, a street in an unassuming precinct that the narrator "by chance" and "when intoxicated" reaches in the course of his endless walks: "Chance led me there, or rather not really chance but intoxication. An intoxication with the streets that always seizes me in Paris. By the time I met that street I had spent four weeks completely on my own in Paris and had walked for several hours each day through the city districts" (S, p. 9). These city walks are of a libidinal nature, replacing both social and sexual contacts. Furthermore, their lack of an immediate destination is presented as an echo of the narrator's feeling of also, more generally, having lost his goal.

The possible recapture of the goal now becomes the overall reason for the walk, animating his restless search through the most mazelike areas of the metropolis: "Filled with the desire to finally reach the place where what was hidden would once more be revealed to me, I could not brush past the smallest of side streets without entering it and then turning around the corner. My utmost wish was to search through every house, room by room" (S, p. 10). So manic walking through the city is ascribed a function similar to the one occupied by the dream in Freudian psychoanalysis. By means of verbal constellations of images, the dream (i.e., the walk) can produce points of support for memory's path back toward the unconscious (and what therefore is not immediately accessible).

In this context, the intoxication of the city walk, which, as described, is not to be separated from a dream sequence, increasingly takes on the nature of a compulsion. In his unpremeditated choices of subsequent movement the narrator seems to be obeying an outer structure that causes him to lose every sort of spatial overview. To an ever-increasing extent he is controlled by a subjective (i.e., achronometric) time that appears during the confrontation of the individual with urban elements, by analogy with structures in his own psyche. This is the basis for the central intrigue of the story.

"Erinnerung an eine Pariser Straße" reconstructs at a considerable distance (and with a precision that sometimes wavers with regard to both space and time) an afternoon walk that takes place from before 3 P.M. (S, p. 11) to a later point in time that can be deduced from the advanced darkness and—a more reliable piece of evidence—the herds of schoolchildren on their way home after the end of school (corresponding to 4:30 P.M.–5:00 P.M.). So it is a walk of some two hours. During this time, the narrator has twice been through the same side street, which has given him certain shocks. The narrator is first convinced that this street comes to a dead end, but this is not the case.

It leads past a deserted suburban theater (which on his return journey presents itself as being a normal dwelling), some unspecified properties, and a hotel just as deserted-looking, finally ending up in a busy shopping street on the outskirts of Paris. Although this street is seen from opposite directions during the two visits, the repetition is presented as fatal, not only because of the involuntary, apparently chance return but also because of the structural content of the visits.

First, the theme of the meeting of the individual with the collective during both sequences is handled in a form already outlined in the analysis of "Das Karree" (Marseilles). The sporadic looks of certain residents from the street windows in Paris is also interpreted as a sign of a silent court case.

Second, as a new element, the narrator meets "a live image" (S, p. 12), which is the unifying shock motif of the sequence. During his first walk through the side street the narrator notices a young man sitting on a chair in a hotel room overlooking the pavement with his face buried in his hands. The windows are open, making the already half-public interior accessible to gazes from the street. A washbasin, an unmade bed, a cupboard, an open suitcase with dirty clothes are the primitive, almost emblematic furnishings of the hotel room. "I am standing in front of the window, which has long since vanished into thin air, but the young man with the unkempt hair is looking as little at me as he is at his suitcase. For him, nothing exists—he sits then completely alone on his chair in the empty space. He is afraid; it is fear that paralyzes him thus" (S, p. 13), is how the narrator describes his first contemplative but involuntary[4] meeting with a person that invites a comparison with Rodin's sculpture *The Thinker* (*Le Penseur*)— Kracauer's analogous figure being a secular, modern (and nonheroic) version.

On the narrator's subsequent return walk back through the side street (which has suddenly opened itself to his gaze),[5] he is accompanied by a herd of schoolchildren. Their laughter has banished all menace and fear until the instant when he once more is opposite the young man on the chair in the hotel room. The narrator's attempts to repress this image by interpreting the person as a criminal on the run (S, p. 13) have been in vain. The image is insistent, as if he were looking at the image of his own self: an isolated individual, his head averted, on show to an unknown public that nonetheless does not hinder his introverted, frozen speculation. The idea cannot be dismissed that Kracauer is giving us here his interpretation of the figure of the modern melancholic:[6]

The young man in the hotel room—the overdistinct image had remained untouched by time. The young man was still sitting on his chair in the middle of the room. As before, his suitcase was half-packed, the water from the basin had not been emptied. And still the sitting figure had his head in his hands. Perhaps it is a different young man? The thought strikes me that I have not seen his face.

Against my will I feel the wall of the hotel building—it is firm and of brick. (S, pp. 14–15)

Kracauer's story offers some basis for confirming that the perplexity of the narrator on meeting the young man might correspond to a self-recognition and thereby represent a "live image" of his own melancholy. This anonymous, in principle replaceable, figure is the only thing (apart from what is felt to be the collective hostile threat from those in the windows) that is capable of slowing down his frantic walking through the streets of an unknown city. The urban compulsive contemplation of the narrator, which is duplicated in the likewise speculative and contemplative figure in the hotel room, is thus a form of *active self-observation*. The unsettling aspects of the city, which are emphasized by the freezing of the narrator in front of this image, seem to be closely related to a decisive but not necessarily well-known or accessible subjective structure in the strolling individual himself.[7]

Between Reality and Mental Representation

The impossibility of clarifying the relationship between the actual city scene and the mental reflections of the narrator is confirmed time after time in the story. Within its framework, the opposition between reality and concept is resolved in a third materiality constituted by the literary text. At the story's linguistic level, a coincidence between the urban and the mental space becomes possible. The literary representation produces a realistic fiction that nonetheless is also able to present itself as a fictionally articulated reality.

This ambiguous nature of the course of events ought not to be understood—whether from a sociological or historiographic point of view—as a weakness or a sign of its lack of relevance for an understanding of urban culture. On the contrary, this status, beyond the sharp lines of division between psyche and materiality, is to be seen as one of the qualities of Kracauer's writings that enable them to call attention to central mental structures in urban culture.

The indivisibility of representation and referent, of "reality" and literary treatment, is emphasized in other texts by Kracauer that likewise investigate the state of tension between reality and dream. The course of events in "Der verbotene Blick" ("The Forbidden Look") from 1925 takes place in a dusty, dingy pub, where a waiter in a dinner jacket at regular intervals starts up two alarming machines, to the distraction of the public. The "phantom," which the narrator has announced early on to be the anchor of the text, is, however, neither directly linked to the "demon," roused from his sleep in a *pianella*, or to a mirror case with a pair of dolls that move to the accompaniment of a "hellish music" (S, pp. 95–97). All at once, though, fairly late in the story, the two machines are reduced to elements in a dream world, while "you"[8] wake up "on the border between dream and reality" (S, p. 97), in the middle of a decisively identity-changing decor. Only then does the long-awaited phantom appear, in the form of the "forbidden look":

> At precisely these moments, when this Nowhere holds you close, the forbidden look strikes the ethereal passengers. This is what it is all about: that a meeting takes place between creatures who do not really exist, that you, who are also only a phantom in a space with no content, are haunted by bewitched figures who obstruct [your] passage and drag you into their forlornness. (S, p. 98)

If "Erinnerung an eine Pariser Straße" left any doubt concerning the relationship between walker and image, the individual here, clearly and explicitly, meets his own subjectivity depicted as an ontological void. Like the dancing figures in the hall of mirrors,[9] the human individual in the evening atmosphere of the pub is like a doll without its own satisfactory substance. Both the machinery of entertainment and the individual mental reality suffer a loss of character, without its being possible to determine the precise relationship between cause and effect, between "reality" and "dream."[10]

The Subjectivized City Space

A collective and societally oriented version of this feeling of fear that arises when an empty space is confirmed is described with reference to Berlin. In the text "Schreie auf der Straße" ("Cries in the Street") from the summer of 1930, Kracauer deals with a feeling of unrest and fear that seems especially prevalent in the fashionable areas of Berlin, dominated by wide streets and individuals who are anonymous to each other. Although the unrest expressed by the narrator is accounted for—for example, in a sudden street disturbance (a group of Nazis attacks people at a café; S, p. 28)—this manifest violence only partially covers the shared widespread feeling of fear. Particularly typical of this fear is that it is abstract and, though not without an object, yet unverifiable and inexhaustible.

The link between ontological emptiness and fear is the main axis for the initial attempt at interpretation on the part of the narrator. By emphasizing the endless perspectives of space and the individualizing and anonymous nature of social ties, he has said something without, however, having convinced himself about the real state of affairs: "Is it this emptiness that in a few seconds makes [the streets in Berliner Westen] so sinister? I repeat, that I do not know" (S, p. 29). The link between the individual and collective space proves difficult to establish, especially when occasioned, as here, by a diffuse feeling. But its explanation is sought under all circumstances at a social level, which perceptibly distinguishes "Schreie auf der Straße" from the other texts just analyzed.

The hypothesis finally advanced is in this connection even more radical. It involves a total reversing of the subject relations. After first having taken as his starting point his own fear, which he linked to phenomena at a group level, the narrator, in an attempt to explain three events that are completely independent of each other—and that seem to share only the characteristic that they find expression in an apparently senderless cry— assumes a third model of subjectivity. He then offers an explanation that stresses a superior, that is, urban, level: "Today, I assume that it is not people in these streets who cry out but the streets themselves. When they cannot stand it any longer, they cry out their emptiness. But I'm not completely sure of this" (S, p. 30), Kracauer concludes. As this last sentence makes clear, we are dealing with a hypothesis that underlines the analogy between an individual and an urban-collective subjectivity. Continuing on from the fact that an individual confirmed his own fear during his feverish walks through the city, the narrator feels able to go so far here as to subjectivize the city. The city as an entity, which is at the same time both less and more than the sum of its parts, is made into a subject that expresses, even screams out "the emptiness" (*die Leere*) of its social and cultural basis.

Neither individual nor city-collectivity is based on an integral mechanism; they build their life utterances on a constitutive loss.[11] Without first overemphasizing a psychoanalytic interpretation of the relationship between individual and metropolis in Kracauer, it is nevertheless important to underline the active interaction between these two levels. As a duplication of mental structures, the streets of the metropolis make it possible for the individual to reflect unconscious—and thus not easily accessible—entities in his own frail identity.

The conception of the metropolis is also affected by this interaction. As mentioned, the city encompasses and dominates the individual. But the individual's selectively interpretive relationship to the totality of the metropolis means that the image of the city cannot be maintained in spatially and functionally continuous terms. Because of its active links with the frail individual, the city itself becomes a fractured framework around a social and subjective practice. In dreams or intoxication the anonymous collective is perceived as bringing coercive measures to bear, while fear's true articulation is concentrated in the individual. On the other hand, the wide-awake, soberly analyzing individual is in a position to locate fear in the metropolis at a social level that is not merely reduced to a simple opposition between the individual and the surrounding masses. Because of its link with the negatively ontological constitution of both the subject and the city (see the Marseilles analysis) as a reaction to lost origins (the mother and the harbor, respectively), fear constitutes a basic structure in Kracauer's conception of the metropolis. Fear is the dystopian counterpart to the utopian signs of (at least sporadic) redemption, which will be dealt with in chapter 8.

The Objects—Aesthetic Reflection and Flight

The intense interaction between psyche and metropolitan space has consequences even within the apparently city-free field of private life. In the same way that the individual—in order to defend against an inner structural crisis—mirrors his psyche in (and thereby forms an image of) the overall spatial structures, he also finds compensation for the "emptiness" Kracauer confirmed in the metropolis through a network of private articles of daily use. The *macrocosm* of the city and the *microcosm* of the private space are thus symmetrically located around the axis of the individual. This world of objects is both the negative image of the public space and its condensation.

As it suggests an original analytical perspective—which also finds expression in a special genre of essay, the "grotesque"—the position of the objects in Kracauer's urban analytics must also be briefly dealt with. His special interest in the links connecting city, individual, and objects can be confirmed by the presence of a group of texts, "Dinge"—the third of the four sections in *Straßen in Berlin und anderswo*. Despite some internal differences, these texts illustrate an affection for everyday objects. To refer to Simmel's concept of the urban blasé state of mind, Kracauer can also here be said to be attempting a resubjectivization—this time in relation to a world of objects that is historically untopical.

Analysis here will be restricted to the most intimate and also the most paradoxical text, which presents a relationship between an individual and an object in his possession. The story "Das Schreibmaschinchen" ("The Dear Little Typewriter") depicts the relationship of identification and love between the narrator and a typewriter. The narrator personifies the object. He honors its functionally divine design—the machine is raised to the level of a myth-laden fetish.

This worshipful devotion means that the typewriter is not used to produce messages to a third party (a recipient). But it does serve as a medium for written images, whose intention is not to give meaning.[12] The dyadic relationship between the narrator and the machine is so intense that it increasingly excludes the narrator from social life. The symbiosis is broken when a bent typewriter key makes the intervention of a professional imperative. The impersonally brutal treatment by the repair man—aside from solving the problem—causes a loss of the typewriter's aura. Only when he has recognized the machine as being a mass product does the narrator gain the ability to treat it as a functional tool, as a means of pursuing secular ends.

In the description there are elements of a fetishization process that is not reserved for children or for the melancholic,[13] but that can also be found as a fascination in an adult consumer life that is not as yet completely blasé about new acquisitions (computers, houses, cars, clothes, etc.).

"Das Schreibmaschinchen" (the diminutive of a typewriter) is only one example of Kracauer's analyses of everyday objects. Both Ernst Bloch and Walter Benjamin express enthusiasm for this new type of essay in their letters from the latter half of the 1920s. As early as 1926, Benjamin broaches the idea of collecting these articles in a book.[14] Among their qualities both he and Bloch emphasize the "grotesque" aspect, which defies any form of classification according to genre.[15] In connection with the essay "Falscher Untergang der Regenschirme" ("The False Demise of the Umbrellas"), Benjamin writes the following:

> In "The Demise of the Umbrellas" I see the same intention at work as [that which] so intensely occupied my mind when you showed me "Das Klavier" in that ill-fated Berlin café. You paint the demise of the petits bourgeois in a truly remarkable, loving description of their leftovers. That is quite magnificent. The grotesque gains a clear, legitimate political position, liberates itself from any affinity with arbitrary mysticism, and rubs shoulders with the theory that it has in all distinguished examples of this sort.[16]

The article "The False Demise of the Umbrellas," which Benjamin uses as a point of departure for a political interpretation of Kracauer's essays, is characterized precisely by a critique of the petits bourgeois: "The material of the bearer is distinctly impaired— the petits bourgeois control the area" (S, p. 121). Their relationship to the umbrella's sound universe that almost imitates nature has become less and less close. This is a great pity: "Because only under the shelter of the umbrellas can the subtle difference between daytime rain and springtime drizzle be experienced and truly enjoyed" (S, p. 120). So the theme is less the demise of the petits bourgeois than their transformation into a wage-earning metropolitan mass. In this connection, Kracauer is mainly against the loss of sensitivity in the petits bourgeois to the aesthetic qualities of objects and nature.

Admittedly, Kracauer does not recommend that the petits bourgeois go off on city walks instead of going on excursions into the countryside. It is nonetheless obvious that the culture of the petits bourgeois is being criticized, insofar as their open-air excursions seek to renounce their nature as bound to the city and mass ornament.[17]

In retrospect, Kracauer's object analyses are of importance, first because they insist on the microlevel of urban culture as an indirect but significant area of investigation. Second, this collection of essays demonstrates the extent of the connection between individual and city—the theme of this chapter. It shows how closely the individual and the group-psychological, the mental and the cultural aspects are linked poles in

Kracauer's perception of the city. Far from excluding each other, these two points of view are necessary for understanding the metropolis as the place where different but mutually analogous forms of subjectivity exist that, each in its own way, are part of the *joining of the cultural layers of the urban.*

Until now, the individually reflective aspect of Kracauer's essays on the metropolis in *Straßen in Berlin und anderswo* has been given a privileged position. This makes it obvious that the collection of articles, despite its orientation toward a social perspective, never annihilates the *individual*—who experiences and analyzes as well as writes. On the contrary, the social perspective is constituted on the basis of an analogy to the individual's particular articulation of experience. The following chapter will deal with the sociosubjective effects of the city in a different light. This means not that subjectivity will be pushed aside, but only that it will be viewed from the standpoint of *social spatiality.* Chapter 7 differs in that it places greater emphasis on the social significance of space than on the mental structures of the individual.

Space Analysis and Social Critique

I. THE SPACE OF SOCIAL REPRODUCTION
Space Analysis and Social Cognition

The analysis of urban space is subject to a social perspective, not only because such a perspective transcends the isolation of individually experienced space but also because it enables a new look to be taken at society as a whole. Through his analysis of space, it is Kracauer's idea to consider societal reproduction in a way that is both more immediately concrete and potentially more in-depth than that typical of, for example, statistical and sociopolitical discourses. In one of his articles he is more precise about the basis for the social and urban development of what he referred to in "Das Ornament der Masse" as an analysis of "surface phenomena":

> Every typical space is brought about by typical societal relations that express themselves in it without the distracting intervention of consciousness. All that is denied by consciousness, all that which is otherwise deliberately overlooked, takes part in its construction. The spatial images are the dreams of society. There, where the hieroglyphics of some spatial image or other have now been decoded, the ground of social reality presents itself. (S, pp. 69–70)

In the same connection, Kracauer expresses the hope that by an analysis of space he will be able to avoid social discourses, which are "ideologically colored," in favor of real cognition of the "position . . . in the social system" of a social group (S, p. 69). Because the socially defined "space is produced by reality itself" (S, p. 69), this reality's "spatial images" will be, at one and the same time, concentrated and unrepressed expressions of societal conditions. The analysis of these potentially makes it possible to uncover the "ground" of reality (S, p. 69).

"The spatial images are the dreams of society," Kracauer writes in the text quoted above. This formulation ought not to be understood as a hypothesis that social spaces possess a special predictive, utopian, or in some other way imaginary nature. But this interpretive possibility is implied by Theodor W. Adorno when, in a letter to Kracauer from 1930, he links Kracauer's intention to Walter Benjamin's contemporaneous works on nineteenth-century Parisian urban architecture: "With amazement and, especially, with approval I have noted that you have accepted the Benjamin formulation of the houses as being dreams of collectivity—only without the word collective, which I do not like either. The matter is really extremely aggressive and striking."[1] In his reply, Kracauer insists on the perspective that is critical of ideology in his undertaking, dissociating himself from conceptions that see society at this level of a totality as being organically cohesive.[2]

This limitation does not, however, prevent Kracauer's programmatic formulation from being crucial for a number of articles about various spatial forms in the metropolis. The spaces to be dealt with in the following share their socioreproductive nature. This means, in the concrete historical situation (Berlin in the early 1930s), that they contribute to the reproduction of a society in which certain *groups,* because of unemployment and their cultural and economic impoverishment, are excluded from social recognition,[3] without this exclusion necessarily being noticed. Kracauer's analyses invite the unifying hypothesis that the function of certain spaces in the metropolis is to isolate, make invisible, and homogenize disfavored groups. The analyses thereby form a subcategory of the general theme of his articles from the period in question: the contribution of the various spatial forms to the production (and differentiation) of the metropolitan mass.

It is possible within this series of articles to distinguish between two main types of space, using the social criterion of whether *money* is the decisive medium giving access to the analyzed spaces or not. The importance of money is decisive in both instances insofar as those in the first group, consisting of the employment office and daytime shelters and other institutions, are characterized precisely as including persons without financial means, while those belonging to the other spatial form, represented by daytime cinemas, pinball arcades, and amusement park rollercoasters, involve paying a sum of money before they can be entered and can contribute to temporary forgetting and to a symbolic conversion of social need.

The Reproduction of the Penniless Individuals as a Mass

Both the employment office and the daytime shelters for the unemployed and the homeless are by nature socially isolated rooms that organize and to a certain extent neutralize the social misery of Berlin in the 1930s. At the same time, their spatial forms are analogous to overall social structures. The employment office maintains a link to the capitalist production process by being its shady side, its negative image, and its continued reservoir of labor. The daytime shelters, on the other hand, are so far removed from paid work that at most they resemble urban society in a wider context.

The role of the employment office as the shadow of the production process is a crucial motif in Kracauer's article "Über Arbeitsnachweise—Konstruktion eines Raumes" ("On Employment Offices: Construction of a Space"; FZ, June 17, 1930), in which precisely these fundamental remarks concerning the analysis of society's spatial dream images occur.

The raising of awareness about the social role of this spatial form takes place at three different levels, which together outline "the aspect . . . under which the production process appears" for the unemployed (S, p. 72). In this way a critique is made of the *spaces,* the *speech,* and the *writing,* respectively, that establish the waiting room at the employment office as a social institution.

To begin with, Kracauer emphasizes that the mere location of the rooms of the employment office in a depressing framework, far from the centers of professional life, expresses the disfavored position of the unemployed. "The relationship between the dole and real wages is like that of the employment office to the proper office" (S, p. 70) is the striking analogy used. As "waste products" from the production process, the unemployed have to make do with a "box room" (S, p. 71), rooms in a distant backyard permanently in shadow—in more senses than one.[4]

Furthermore, Kracauer analyzes the socially reproductive characteristics in the conversation between the unemployed. This takes place in "a whisper" (S, p. 72), dealing with social misery in neutral, resigned confirmation of their futile situation. The existence of unemployment spatially and as social shadow is reinforced on a spiritual and ideological level.[5]

Finally, Kracauer deals with the way a number of signs influence the behavior of the unemployed. The signs hung up, giving warnings and orders, are thought of as expressing the double standards of the place. For example, its alienating purpose is underscored by the following warning sign: "Those out of work are to guard and protect public property," property that is thus confirmed as being far removed from the unemployed.[6] It is one of Kracauer's hypotheses that language in these social spaces is disciplining by nature: "It carries out assignments that have not been given it, *establishing bastions in the unconscious*" (S, p. 74; my italics).

This reading of the institution of the employment office is an example of how, through a staging of the city's concrete spaces in essays, it becomes possible to expose with precision the link between public space and the production process, with its capitalist organization.

The daytime shelters, which are the point of departure for the essay "Wärmehallen" ("Heated Halls"; FZ, January 18, 1931), are, in contrast, not so directly characterized by the polarized relationship between employers and unemployed. Not the hope of being reintegrated into paid work but merely survival stands out as the apparently natural[7] main purpose of this huge hall. The several thousands of daily visitors, "young lads, men, and old men," make material the social space of the hall. They

> stand . . . together in groups, just as those on the waiting room benches in the employment office sit enjoying the warmth, . . . a prerequisite for naked life, like a special benefit. It is dispensed by a stove in the middle of the room, whose pipe carefully picks its way past the pillars and that only by means of its immense spread symbolizes the main purpose of the hall. (S, p. 80)

The stove (and not the production machinery) organizes life around it in the former tram hall: "Originally it had been a depot, in which trams were stored instead of people," Kracauer notes when characterizing this form of space. In its confusion of the public and the private it brings back memories from his military service of barracks, where lavatory doors, the last primitive sign of an individual private life, were also lacking (S, p. 80). The tram depot, however, is to an even greater extent the place for a restricted life. The presence of shoeshine men and hairdressers turns the hall into a despondent microcosm of civil life in the city outside. The difference is underscored, for example, by the lack of mirrors, for which there is at least one good reason: "who would want to display his own poverty in a mirror?" (S, p. 80). There is here a situation of social emergency, where mythic conditions are fostered in the form of constantly repeated conversations and a local small retail business with fetishized objects (soles of shoes, cigarettes) that "cease being merely wares and become irreplaceable goods[;] . . . nothing could be more moving than the gleam that surrounds their wretchedness" (S, p. 81).

Without any particular reliance on theoretical categories, an image of literary journalism and social criticism is produced, capturing an enclosed society that, thanks to its isolation from the writer's and the average reader's world of experience, can be described in a simultaneously objectivizing and historicizing light.[8] Employment office, heated hall, and daytime shelter all appear screened off from the public nature of production, politics, and the city.[9] In inner isolation, they escape the medium of money in a way that, if viewed globally, helps pass on the world of signs and norms found in the production process.

Social Reproduction via Entertainment Procured with Money

While Kracauer, in presenting certain institutions whose social legitimacy might at first glance seem to be unassailable, criticizes their spaces and underlying social mechanisms, a couple of his articles on spatial types procured with money show a tendency

to moralize at the expense of the less-well-off public that lets itself be seduced into wasting money on ideological deception.

This moral condemnation is especially obvious in the article "Kino in der Münzstraße" ("Cinema in Münzstraße"; FZ, April 2, 1932), which deals with the special daytime cinema phenomenon in Berlin. One might have expected a positive judgment of this exceedingly urban and antinaturalistic institution, but the opposite is found. The break with cosmic rhythm, which turns day into night, light into darkness, appears to Kracauer as a *flight*, less from nature than from a socially binding reality.

The initial description of the waiting crowd admittedly has the same sympathetic tone that had earlier been used in describing the unemployed at the employment office and in the heated daytime shelters.[10] But as soon as the scene inside the dark cinema interior itself is described, one can sense a certain contempt for those spectators, almost down-and-out,[11] who identify themselves with a film star's bold display of force:

> Characteristic of the audience there are places where they laugh. Special hilarity is provoked by a scene where Albers [a star from the 1920s] unconcernedly makes use of his muscle power. He jumps down to the scrawny man in the bath tub and ducks his head under water several times. There are unemployed who laugh at the uncouth joke, people adrift for whom any form of entertainment compels gratitude. They are outside the work process and thus increasingly lose the ability to discriminate. One ought not even make a fuss if they also clap their hands at the wonderful course that their favorite Albers normally runs in a film. (S, p. 94)

Kracauer is well aware that the social conditions of Berlin in the 1930s are the immediate backdrop making it possible for such entertainments to become more widespread. But a number of sociophilosophical reasons—apart from traditional intellectual ambivalence concerning the common people's tendency to lapse into "unserious" activity—urge him to insist on the necessity of a more active attitude toward time passing.

The philosophical and speculative tone of the social analysis can already be seen in "Glück und Schicksal" ("Happiness [or 'Good Fortune'] and Fate"; FZ, October 10, 1931), which deals with the entertainment industry that has resulted from the crisis. Kracauer's treatment of the various facets of fortune as a category thus has as its starting point how "small speculators in happiness" (S, p. 85) have taken over empty shops and converted the premises into a kind of amusement hall. With the assistance of machines, graphologists, fortune-tellers, and so on, the entertainment industry addresses itself in particular to "those masses . . . who have no other chances nowadays than good fortune" (S, p. 85). The social basis of the explicatory model is stressed with all possible clarity in connection with, for example, graphology: "That the reading of palms and graphology have become articles of fashion can be explained by the terrible poverty that forces people to make a final, last-ditch appeal to their powers of luck" (S, p. 87). Yet the quality of the article consists in its going beyond making general social deductions. It depicts several layers at which a quite simple technique of entertainment is able to spread a socially unmotivated confidence in man's natural power—thereby strengthening the individual's belief in a chosen link to good fortune.

"Glück und Schicksal" thus investigates the social and historical slant put on the category of good fortune by entertainment procured with money. Kracauer underlines the alien nature of good fortune. The nature of such spaces—"deserted rooms" (S, p. 85)—indicates from the outset that their present function is external, diametrically opposed to that of the original shop interior. The illusory good fortune and fate do not deserve their names, since their form is not only extremely limited but at root distorted. Within the framework of a merchandise economy, good fortune becomes like a *refuge*. The space "serves . . . good fortune as a refuge" (S, p. 85). The public's fascination is linked only to "the traces of happiness" (S, pp. 86, 88), not to happiness itself or to luck in any real sense.

At this point, the moralizing tone is almost completely absent. The nature of the illusory happiness as trace and refuge has not completely destroyed the possibility of true happiness. The idea of it is maintained in a refuge via its traces, even though the conditions are not present to transform these into reality. Kracauer's final reversal of the two concepts of the title "Glück und Schicksal" into their historical opposites, "Unglück" and "nicht nur Schicksal,"[12] does, however, attempt to maintain the link to a historical and practical reality beyond imaginary substitutes and fragile illusions.

Kracauer emphasizes the maintenance of even the most fragile (subjective) link between an illusion-creating scene and the seeds of transformation of a burdensome reality. So he searches for a possible critical force in the existence of these spaces of entertainment and exclusion, whose effectiveness he tries to explain. Using a trip on a rollercoaster as his starting point, he seeks to present the abrupt transitions between belief in and insight into the merely superficial nature of the illusions in his article "Berg- und Talbahn" ("Mountain and Valley Railway"; FZ, July 14, 1928). Kracauer observes how Berlin employees on a Saturday evening seek refuge in an amusement park outside the city in order to forget their everyday lives in the metropolis in something that in certain ways spatially reduplicates them. The rollercoaster has a backdrop that resembles New York, thereby confronting the Berliners with a vertical urban form. The backdrop adds an element of dimensional distortion that—from the passing car—makes possible a constant shifting between identifying with, seeing through, and feeling triumph over the intoxicating cardboard landscape:[13]

So this is New York—a painted surface and nothing more? The small pairs of loving couples [in the cars] are at the same time enchanted [*verzaubert*] and disenchanted [*entzaubert*]. Not in the sense that they should simply take the exaggerated city painting as humbug, but they see through the illusion, and their victory over the facades [via the passing and surveying look] is not so important from now on. They linger at this place where things show themselves to be double [i.e., ambiguous], they hold the shrunken skyscrapers in the palm of their hand, they have broken free of the world whose magnificence they nevertheless are familiar with. (S, p. 45)

The sudden changes between enchantment and disenchantment are characteristic of Kracauer's understanding of the culture of the mass ornament. These changes are violent yet also fascinating, and they express the disappointment of the hopes of those involved. The opposite finds expression in the structures of fragmented and compressed time ("Arrival. All over. The trip has only lasted a couple of minutes"; S, p. 46). Utopia and fantasy are held within a perverted mass presentation. The wordless cries that are forced out en route are almost automatic and, in an anthropological sense, primitive. They are replaced after the trip by a mixture of brief intoxication and a reestablished position of inferiority to the surrounding stage effects.

This Tivoli world can seem far removed from the backyard offices of the employment office because of its public and festive atmosphere, but it is related to pinball arcades, daytime cinemas, and heated daytime shelters as well as the employment office. A social function links these urban spaces.

2. SOCIAL AND CULTURAL WAITING
Part-Time Spaces and Waiting Rooms (Critique of Passive Waiting)

In his written staging of these anonymous forms of spaces, Kracauer has stressed their contribution to the reproduction of a crisis-stricken capitalistic sociality behind the scenes of Berlin, the metropolis. These spaces are all more or less concealed, surrounded by various temporal structures. While establishing a certain basic framework for social cohesion, they nevertheless present a predominantly fragmented image of life in society.

This quality of disintegration, which expresses a basic state of lack, is to a great extent linked to their nature as part-time public places. There is no hint anywhere of a space that is human or in some other sense domestic that could make possible a lasting and mutually mediated relationship to the components of the city. The storage function of the heated halls is taken over during the afternoon by the night shelter, and the pinball arcades in the Berlin shops temporarily rented for such activity are alienated from their spatial surroundings.

The spaces described all simultaneously have a framing and a disintegrating function. But added to these two is a third quality that particularly influences the spaces' subjective component, their "population," and their relationship to time. The space of social reproduction—from employment office to pinball arcades—places the social groups and their single individuals in a *generalized waiting position.*

This waiting position is most clearly stressed in the analysis of the employment office, where the general feeling of the lack of any aim or purpose is found in its purest form: "At the employment office the unemployed employ their time by waiting. Since the number of jobs is at present being neglected compared to the number of unemployed, waiting almost becomes an end in itself [*Selbstzweck*]. . . . I know of no [other] type of place where waiting would be so demoralizing" (S, p. 74). Under such conditions we can talk of an "enforced idleness" that has lost "its social nobility" (S, p. 74). The formal freedom of unemployment is placed in the light of a social sanction that consists of poverty and a lack of recognition.

Another form of waiting becomes apparent in the repetitive conversations that ensue at these places of mass storage: "The idleness . . . produces a whispering that fills the hall just as the stovepipe does. This whispering can time and time again be heard to be repeated conversations that have to do with tobacco, shoes, sweaters, and other items" (S, p. 80). The repetition and the lack of any personal or political meaning in the conversations are further demonstrated in connection with the pinball arcades and the rollercoaster. Here smiles (S, p. 86), laughter (S, p. 94), and screams are almost compulsory—"everyone has to scream. And even if they are clenching their teeth, they have to scream" (S, p. 45). To the outside observer—the journalist engaging in social critique, for example—the oblivion-enhancing (and only in this sense liberating) function seems to assume an ominous tinge: "It almost looks as if everyone is screaming because they imagine that they have finally been redeemed" (S, p. 45). Which Kracauer does not find well-justified.

The waiting position does not involve freedom and reflection; it "is completed in the shadow" of society (S, p. 74) and expresses a basic characteristic of modernity. Yet it is possible, when not waiting for anything specific, to wait in a variety of ways.

The Waiting Intellectual (Active Urban Waiting)

The metropolis's spaces for daytime accommodation and entertainment are part of a general social and cultural situation characterized by waiting without any (explicit) aim. For that reason, it can serve no purpose to pass moral judgment on an attitude of waiting generally. On the other hand, what is important for Kracauer is to promote an active, reflecting attitude toward the waiting position as something basic for modernity's intellectual and—who knows?—social practice.

Although the sociopolitical implications of this apology for active waiting, which can be seen as an answer to Nietzsche's active nihilism, have not been explicitly developed, the question is dealt with in one of Kracauer's relatively early writings. In the essay "Die Wartenden" ("People Waiting"; FZ, March 12, 1922) he conducts a defense of an active, analytically reflective attitude toward time. The basic idea here is that the ethics of the intellectual (but also perhaps of the man who is unemployed or is an amusement addict) must take the theological and social situation as their point of departure. At the beginning of the twentieth century and, in a more acute form, after the First World War, this situation is characterized, according to Kracauer, by a general vacuum of belief.[14] Rather than espousing an explicit, hollow-sounding creed (like that of Rudolf Steiner's anthroposophy) on the one hand, or a potentially neutral relativism (like that of Max Weber) on the other, Kracauer sees no other possibility than to recommend a third way: that of the waiting man.

The few fixed points of this third position have no immediate relevance for social misery, though this fact scarcely makes superfluous principled considerations concerning the possible involvement of the intellectual. As Kracauer's answer to the crisis of values and the ethical systems of reference, the waiting intellectual is polemical in relation to the unreservedly positive intellectual. Thus the negative position acquires meaning. It is basically characterized by a "hesitating openness," which Kracauer attempts to define by listing certain fixed points. An "ability to hold on" ("Ausharren-Können") is supplemented by a "pride" at "pedantry and a certain coolness" (O, p. 117). All these characteristics serve the abstract goal "of achieving a relationship with the absolute." This calls for a fundamental attentiveness that is scarcely possible in the everyday life of the urban masses: "Seen positively, waiting means an openness that naturally must not be confused in any way with a relaxing of the mental powers as regards things farthest away; on the contrary, it is far more an intense activity and an industrious self-preparation" (O, pp. 117–118).

Using terms whose theological coloring is far removed from his analyses undertaken a decade later of Berlin's crisis reality, Kracauer is nevertheless already stressing in "Die Wartenden" a practical dimension of intellectual work. In a socially more binding version, the essay is also valid for Kracauer's sociocritical journalism. In general terms he states

> that for the people being considered here [people waiting in a programmatic fashion], it is a question of shifting the center of gravity from the theoretical ego to the generally human ego and [thereby] turning away from the atomized un-

real world of formless forces toward that of *reality* and the world of language included in it. As a result of the overwrought state of theoretical thought, we have,
to a shocking extent, distanced ourselves from this reality, which is full of true
[*leibhaftige*] phenomena and people and therefore needs to be observed concretely. (O, p. 118)

So the waiting intellectual tries to bring about a shift in his thinking and writing toward
practical reality, since he hopes in so doing to establish a link to something that "cannot be mediated as knowledge, since it has to be lived" (O, p. 118).

This is not an allusion to unemployment and so on but to more or less clarifiable
possibilities for development—originally existentialist and theological, to an increasing extent social and cultural—though Kracauer, in his journalistic essays, does not
make them the subject of strategic consideration. Nonetheless, on the basis of his personal feeling of being referred to a metaphysical waiting position that calls for an intellectual and practical answer, he has drawn attention to a far more comprehensive
field for a specifically urban subjectivity—and to a corresponding intellectual opportunity for action. Although the poor urban masses are not synonymous with the relatively privileged middle-class groupings Kracauer referred to in his original essay,[15] the
difference between them can perhaps be contained within the category of a specifically
urban mentality that can be said to be included in the following characterization:

Today, there are a large number of people who, without knowing about each
other, are nevertheless linked by a common destiny. . . . They spend most of
their days in the loneliness of the big cities. . . . But when they step back from
the surface to the center of their being, they are assailed by a deep melancholy
that springs from a knowledge of their being excommunicated [*ihr Eingebannt-
sein*] in a particular spiritual situation. . . . It is their metaphysical suffering at
the lack of a higher meaning in the world, at their existence in an empty space,
that makes these people the attendants of fate. (O, p. 106)

The existential and social crisis is a widespread phenomenon; it cuts across social distinctions, with the potential to create lines of communication between classes and
strata that, despite all their differences, have one unifying characteristic: they live in *the
metropolis* and are confronted by a *culture* that is probably marked by a social and cultural crisis but that offers in glimpses the possibility of a different reality.

Perhaps the discreet formulations in "Die Wartenden" bear witness to the fact that
Kracauer has limited confidence in the potential of the urban masses to re-create a link
with a secular or theological Absolute entity. This is far from certain, however. People
waiting, either actively or passively, unconsciously or consciously, are precisely those

who are not characterized by a manifest community. Rather, they adopt a socially latent form that shows similarities with the "communauté inavouable" of the French philosopher Maurice Blanchot,[16] an (unavowable) community that cannot be proclaimed to be a social movement. The same applies to the people who are included in Kracauer's concept of conscious, and in that sense actively waiting, reflectiveness.

The negative definition of "Die Wartenden" is rediscovered in Kracauer's attempt to locate utopian characteristics in the culture of the metropolis. His work on evoking these aspects of urban culture finds its paradigm in cities on the Mediterranean. These represent an opposing pole to the society to their north that is so burdensome. His attempts at utopian interpretation—which do, however, also find momentary expression in the north—are the theme of the next chapter.

Improvisation and Memory

1. FRAGMENTARY POPULAR CULTURE (SOUTHERN EUROPE)

In Kracauer's essays in *Straßen in Berlin und anderswo,* city spaces are also places where conceptions of a different (and better) society are generated. The utopian force thereby becomes the third overall articulation of urban culture in a series that began with the city's role as a subjective experiential space (chapter 6), followed by its ability to ensure the reproduction of the basic structures of society (chapter 7).

It ought to be made clear from the outset that the utopian characteristics that Kracauer notes in the metropolis at no time join together to form a global utopia. In his form of reflection, modernity forbids Kracauer to suggest a coherent social and spatial alternative to existing conditions, as we find exemplified elsewhere in the history of ideas (More, Campanella, Piranesi, Ledoux, Fourier, Le Corbusier, etc.). It is a question neither of an abstract negation of the existing historico-spatial reality nor of a simple list of principles of order for a future formation of society. Kracauer's approach remains negatively dialectic in the sense that, by reflecting on what actually exists, he indicates points where elements that promote or hinder a marked change of aesthetic or social character are implied. This means that this chapter has a double purpose, stretching between, on the one hand, really utopian aspects and, on the other hand, conditions that are less stimulating but still indicate tendencies.

The implications—positive or negative—differ in nature. An attempt will be made here to map them. A common feature of all the utopian signs is simply that all of them are based on ornaments of the metropolis that, on analysis, prove able to justify conceptions of a future development. By way of introduction, a predominantly aesthetic utopian model will be uncovered, based on observations from the Mediterranean and from popular districts in Paris. Then, with Berlin a point of departure, it will be shown how the aesthetically identified utopian elements meet with social restrictions in the binding reality of Kracauer's hometown. Only by referring to the unsuccessful escape or the discreet strength of what is repressed is the possibility of change hinted at. Finally, a form of critique is examined derived from the opposition between aesthetics and the social search for utopia. This is most importantly developed as a work of memory in relation to urban history. However, the threatened traces of history radically challenge this form of reflection between aesthetics and sociality. These three relations between urban experience and the production of utopias are not mutually opposed, but they make comprehensible the fact that the active historical work of memory can come to occupy a crucial position in Kracauer's later work.

Fragments and Improvisation: The Utopian Paradigm of the Mediterranean City
Completely in line with the liberating significance that Kracauer ascribed to Marseilles in *Ginster*, his utopian gaze at European urbanity is informed by the aesthetic force of Mediterranean cities. But this sensitivity to southern European qualities—as will be seen in the following pages—also sharpens his awareness of a crisis in the northern European cities' ability to produce utopian conceptions.

It is of less importance that the place which serves as a paradigm in connection with an analysis of the street bars of the south is Nice and not Marseilles, since Kracauer's thorough observations are placed under the generalizing title "Stehbars im Süden" ("Stand-Up Bars in the South"; FZ, November 5, 1926). In this article he is primarily interested in the bars as scenery, as stage sets in a theatrical urban reality. When he concentrates on the "comptoirs" of the bars in the title,[1] they are furthermore underlined as places to rest during walks through cities. They are an extension of the street and are in no way opposed to the public spaces of urban culture.

The description of this place splits up the spatial continuity of the stand-up bar into a number of independent elements. Aspects of style, furniture, liqueur bottles, cigarette packs and tall stacks of matchboxes, and so forth all figure in an exhaustive account. The list of these separately colorful and excitingly formed components causes the total image to shimmer in the inner eye of the reader. This shimmering creates a correspondence to reality, as the text's image of the place reproduces a café that, via its wall mirrors, is in a state of continuous, illusion-filled change:

> The mirrors, which take the trouble of multiplying every single pathetic electric lightbulb, expand the bar into a public cave of treasure. It is overflowing with reflections, in which the things that are present are mixed together and quartered. Their independent reality turns out to be a deception, even though the mirrors do not let anything slip through that is more real. (S, pp. 67–68)

The mirrors emphasize the general tendency of the bar space, which lacks inner stability and duration. The outer, indeed split, relationship between the individual objects, which are linked to each other only because they serve to promote enjoyment (S, p. 68), is ethically regrettable, from Kracauer's point of view. At the same time, it is the basis for both instantaneous beauty and a utopian future justice for things in a composite space.[2] It is through the absence of *Seßhaftigkeit* (permanent residence) that objects, as "restless nomads" (S, p. 68), can be part of the subjects' work of visual improvisation. The ensuing social and cultural effects are no less than the utopian work that Kracauer imagines being developed by both the bar guest and the reader of his text.[3]

That development constitutes the crucial theoretical aspect of this text, which also represents the dominant utopian figure in Kracauer's urban essays: the *decomposition* of spaces contains the possibility of an imaginary interpretation that can bring about their transformation into dream images or wishful images.

The central status of this figure of thought is documented by the fact that Kracauer raises the visual inconstancy of the city to the general normative criterion for assessing its value as a city. He concludes, "The value of cities is determined on the basis of the number of places in them that are conceded to improvisation" (S, p. 68). Or, conversely: a city without ambiguities or tensions has neither social nor aesthetic value. This is the radical theoretical and philosophical consequence of a link between dream, fragmentation, and utopia, a link that took the overall characteristic of cities in southern Europe as its point of departure.

> They [the Mediterranean cities] admittedly are purposefully designed, with tracks, cars, benches, and cathedrals. But invisibly spread fingers plunge into the organism, separating all that belongs together. The whole is dismembered into tiny pieces [*das Ganze ist zerstückelt*], and doubts are raised concerning its totality. Nowhere are the places of rupture so frequent as in the cities of the south. (S, p. 67)

By means of their decomposed and internally mobile "dream image strips" (S, p. 67) the Mediterranean cities challenge an imposing and apparently unchangeable image of the city. With exceptional strength the frozen totality is dissipated. It is transformed here into a labile, unpredictable world of images and thoughts that have social and aesthetic perspectives of great importance.[4]

The dynamic breakup of a burdensome urban totality acquires weight by being linked to the ability to produce socially utopian conceptions. The visual paradigm developed in the atomizing description of the type of bar found in the cities along the Mediterranean coast contains sociohistorical forces that will be put to the test on the way from Nice and Marseilles via Paris to Berlin.

The Awakening of the Common People: Popular Street Culture in Paris

The Paris that Kracauer links in *Straßen in Berlin und anderswo* with utopian potential is popular in nature. Only in the districts of the less privileged—"les quartiers

populaires"—and their everyday situations does he find visual and social characteristics that establish a link with the major cities of southern France. The reference to
Mediterranean culture is explicit in two crucial articles, "Analyse eines Stadtplans" and
"Straßenvolk in Paris" ("Analysis of a City Map" and "Street People in Paris," from
autumn 1926 and FZ, April 12, 1927, respectively).[5] It applies to both the concrete and
the social aspects of urban space.

The extension of the analysis of utopia in the bar essay is most clearly expressed in
the diverse studies of situations having to do with street vending in Paris. In accordance
with his sociocultural conception of architecture,[6] Kracauer places much emphasis in
his depictions of Paris on the effects of social conditions (such as the piling up of commodities) on architecture and city planning. The street space has a full claim to existence only when it is filled up with things and human life. With an eye for the special
commodity fetishism of market culture,[7] Kracauer describes the space of Avenue de
St.-Ouen on a Saturday afternoon. It displays the entire southern repertoire of decomposed and yet organic richness that forms transitions between interior and exterior:

> Even if the Mediterranean were to lap the borders of the avenue, its shops could
> not open up more windowlessly. A stream of commodities that serves the satis-
> faction of the needs of living beings overflows from them; it climbs up the fa-
> cades, is interrupted by the street corner, and then soars up again with double
> strength above the crosscurrents of the passersby. (S, pp. 16–17)

The profusion of commodities makes the street look like a fertile landscape.[8] In all their
fragmentary and mutually contradictory dynamism the commodities also possess the
ability to change climate and space:

> From the open shops, commodities push out into the open air. Catacombs-full
> of tinned food flow out of the queue from a delicatessen shop that is reminiscent
> of the secret depot of foodstuffs of a South Seas expedition, so cunningly and ad-
> venturously does it glide out from its depths. Fruit stalls with lemons and roots
> are by nature loggias;[9] they accept their limitations so much the less as their sell-
> ers are operatic tenors in disguise who want to be heard. (S, pp. 128–129)

The commodities turn winter into summer,[10] enabling the broad Parisian avenue to appear "like the narrow streets of Genoa" (S, p. 128), a constricted space for the sea's
imaginary presence in the market culture of the metropolis:[11] "Neither oysters nor es-
cargots are needed to confirm the nearness of the sea. They are present where markets,
splashes of color, and menials meet" (S, p. 129).

The culture-forming forces of life in the market know no bounds, but are distinct
for each new form of retail trade. Kracauer's "Straßenvolk in Paris" stages the most

diverse variants, ranging from the open food shop and its extension on the street (S, pp. 16–17, 128) via the muddle of the shanties (S, p. 129) to tiny stalls (S, p. 130) that are on the borderline between commerce and amusement. To each category is linked a social form of practice that involves fetishistic but also utopian aspects.

Mediated by commodities, the things' detours are places where memory can intersperse the present with moments of happiness that are radically different from a quantitative concept of richness. The street stalls typical of Paris belong together with the "futile strolling," offering "what no one wants to buy because they are not thinking about it" before the unpredictable moment when the buyer makes his reply to "wishes from forgotten childhood years, dark wishes from various regions of the body, wishes that are transient soap bubbles—all the mishmash that otherwise gets lost between day and night" (S, p. 130).

Price setting finally leaves the traditional economic conditions in order to be "linked to the buyer's *happiness*" (S, p. 130), not to a worldly calculation. The symbolic and utopian function is visually supported in a way that also recalls the inventory of street bars in southern Europe. In the absence of substantial coordination, the objects that for Kracauer are surrounded with aesthetic interest are characterized by being *in opposition to "the whole"* (*das Ganze;* S, p. 129), to the ordering totality of the city. Things do not join together to form a surface—they break the urban smoothness in the form of "specks."[12]

For Kracauer's Parisian world of objects is linked to the popular tradition and lifeworld, not to the mass-produced commodities of industrial production. Commodities are things more than units to be exchanged. They are looked at in the borderline areas of the capitalistic commodity-based economy, where their libidinal and psychosocial nature is confirmed.[13] Their importance is due to their ability to mediate between the experiencing subject and his repressed (or in some other way forgotten) past.

In comparison to the analysis of the stand-up bars of southern Europe, Kracauer's studies of the popular market culture of Paris contain further sociological and politically important definitions. Kracauer expresses certain ideas about the "people" who give the world of objects life according to his doubly foreign—both intellectual and German—way of seeing things.

His use of the term "people" (*Volk*) is (consciously?) extremely broad. It refers to a composite group of social layers and classes. These are characterized as "kleine Leute," common people, and they comprise a number of different groups "right from the lower forms of salaried worker to workers, tradesmen, and lives that are called lost, because other people think they have won" (S, p. 16). The aesthetic and social richness that he links to the ordinary people is radically opposed to economic richness, because (among other things) popular richness is not linked to the exploitation of others.

This excessively loose definition, from a sociological point of view, refers to an aspect of urban reality. The common people, who for Kracauer represent the Mediterranean—and thereby the critical and utopian—aspect of Paris, are just as mixed as the districts of the metropolis where they work and live. The popular strata are not—and in an urban context perhaps cannot be—defined on the basis of narrow analyses of class (not to mention Marxist) criteria. They are united more because of their shared belonging to *les faubourgs*.[14]

This exotic mixture is not, however, completely romanticized. Like Kracauer's conception of Marseilles—the city of liberation—his definition of Parisian "street people" has two aspects. On the one hand, it has a number of romantic-naturalizing features, since it is linked with an organic, immediate, and horizontal urban sociality that is reflected in a choice of biological metaphors: "This people has created for itself the urban landscape where it can endure, an indissoluble cell tissue that has hardly been damaged by the architectural perspectives of kings and the enlightened bourgeoisie. The small size of the cells corresponds to the insignificant size of the human proportions and needs" (S, p. 127). Life in *les faubourgs* is regarded as "surplus stock of natural life" (S, p. 16). On the other hand, the naturalizing metaphors contain a critical, negative, even destructive aspect that has already been mentioned in connection with the closing chapter of *Ginster.*

Naturally, there is a touch of romanticism about a people who "do not enter into statistics" and are as "incalculable as their street network" (S, p. 127). But the romanticization is mitigated by an organic horizontal aspect that contains its own ontological opposite. Indeed, the urban culture of the Mediterranean is recalled precisely in a comparison in which the *negativity* of the people is introduced as a corrective to the tendency to view an urbanity composed of cells as idyllic:

> For these common people, who also thrived thus in the cities of the Mediterranean, do not build upward—they break down. Their development is already limited by their mere pressing need [*Notdurft*], their forms break off without forming a surface, their objects stand next to each other, full of color. The nature that is embodied in them resolves itself. A shooting up, a breaking down. This is not synonymous with death, but it is accomplished long before death. Just as if people on the basis of their own decision refused any form of coming together, as if an unknown urge prevented them from joining to form a legible pattern. . . . The image in which common people imagine themselves is an improvised mosaic. It exposes many cavities. (S, p. 128)

The negativity is both spatial (here, horizontal) and ontological (in the form of decay), both formal (in motion) and semantic (an absence of legibility). The social space is broken, even resolved, into ornaments, since popular urban culture in a range of areas is impervious to positive semantic interpretation. It cuts across traditional constructive values and—close to death—then paradoxically develops traces of a real, almost natural (nonimagined) life. Its mosaic is disparate, though nonetheless beautiful, and it supplies material to the ability to imagine in a utopian way. The fascination of the foreign is probably evident, yet it is also marked by the modern feeling of the transience and decay of culture, which emphasizes not the beautifying but the disintegrating forces.

The same love of the commonplace is also found in the political negativity of the urban mass. Its mosaic-like nature acts against its inclusion in a unifying political strategy: "Our [revolutionary] romantics could not make much of a state out of it" (S, p. 127), writes Kracauer, whose theoretical interest (from the period after ca. 1925) in Marx's ideas and general sympathy for the initiatives of social emancipation were never accompanied by any confidence in the Communist Party's organization and conception of politics.[15]

And yet Kracauer, in his praise of popular urban culture, has no doubt that this popular culture is opposed to the power of the economic and political culture of the metropolis at "the center,"[16] whose dominance has to be broken to resolve, on the one hand, the poor but human *faubourgs* and, on the other hand, the unmediated contradiction between glittering but cold main shopping streets.[17] Once again, social structures in concrete urban spaces are being observed, even though their—also political and utopian—articulation remains metaphorical.[18]

2. THE SOCIAL UNCANNY (NORTHERN EUROPE)
Limits to Socioaesthetic Urban Analysis—The Christmas Market in Berlin

This distinction between the *faubourgs* and the city center in Paris makes clear the fact that *Berlin*—the place of neon lighting, social misery, and the culture industry—is seen globally by Kracauer as analogous to the center dominated by a commodity-based economy. The homogeneity of the center of Paris is increasingly also found in other world cities (including Berlin): "Things are like this not only in Paris. The centers of world cities, which are also places of glitter, resemble each other more and more. Their differences are dying out" (S, p. 19), Kracauer writes. As a resident of Berlin (where he was *Frankfurter Zeitung*'s correspondent in the period 1929–1933), he finds it difficult—as indicated in the previous chapters—to locate an independent urban culture that exceeds narrow economic principles. In Berlin the relationship between glitter/emptiness and poverty/humanity is at once closer and more limited, a point made obvious in "Weinachtlicher Budenzauber" ("The Magic of the Christmas Stalls"; FZ, December 24, 1932). This untraditional Christmas article is a piece of visualizing prose that addresses a type of transformation which in Berlin has difficult conditions of existence.

At Christmastime, when the shopping streets are suddenly invaded by street vending involving Christmas trees and all sorts of knickknacks, the otherwise orderly and distinctly non-Mediterranean city undergoes a radical change: "Where smooth streets and squares normally stretch away, wonderful market towns spring up before Christmas consisting of handcarts, stalls, and trestle tables. They are besieged by forests of fir trees, whose rootless trunks conceal the view of the asphalt surfaces and do not permit everyday life to slip through" (S, p. 38). Berlin is transformed into a "Budenstadt" (S, p. 41), a city of stalls, which for Kracauer means that people who are suppressed, collectively or individually, have for a moment returned to the surface of life. The objects, despite their nature as commodities, are not devoted to utilitarian purposes but have the status of "useless bric-à-brac" (S, p. 38). They become signs of a "primitive world of the past,"[19] which has shrunk so much that what "once stretched from the depths of caves to the stars can now easily find room in a corner of the room" (S, p. 39). In this way, the Christmas stalls become an almost exaggeratedly concrete expression of the role of the unconscious and thus the dream in social and subjective life.[20]

Conversely, the importance of psychic factors is spelled out at a more general sociohistorical level. Kracauer turns his attention to the social implications of the sudden resurfacing of the unconscious. The article's fascination and its theoretical meaning are linked to its developing of the relationship between *visuality* and *sociality* in connection with the home metropolis's contribution to a utopian imagination. The utopian characteristics are closely linked to the social repression that, in an immediate way, affects sections of the city's objects and people. Concerning the stalls' wares that are normally sold indoors, Kracauer makes the following remark: "They have been exiled from the shops and now lead in the city of the stalls the same type of vagabond existence as the other outcasts and sellers at the stands and stalls" (S, p. 41). The sellers too are repressed individuals who have been brought out into the light as extra staff: "people out of work who have wages for a few days" (S, p. 41). A person playing music is a blind beggar.

This is how the limits of the aesthetic utopian reflection are shown. The relationship is a double one. The beautiful, identified as that which deviates from the norm, is on the one hand produced by the return of social outcasts to the surface of society. But their continuing poverty—which is the source of the aesthetic break and which for Kracauer suggests elements of a different urban life—is, on the other hand, in opposition to the honoring of the social perspectives that Kracauer can see. Or conversely: social upheaval in the metropolis is limited by the linking of beauty to social inequality and injustice. The melodies of the beggar "will not sound gay until all these poor life-size figures have become as small as the leaping miniature dolls we play with" (S, p. 41) is Kracauer's admonishing observation—symbolically somewhat heavy but basically no less necessary for all that. The social framework of the home city is part of a binding reality that cannot be disposed of as easily as on a journey through Mediterranean cities without considerable ethical consequences.

Digression: Architecture and Utopia

The two poles of this contrast between *formal* and *social metamorphosis* have the status of principles. In connection with Kracauer's thoughts concerning the conditions for experimental architecture, both positions are elucidated. Two essays in *Straßen in Berlin und anderswo* suggest in different ways the conditions under which architectural practice would once more claim his interest. It is no coincidence that the aesthetically reflective architecture is linked to the Mediterranean, while the social and functional principle of reality turns up in Berlin. The weight of the points of view, however, makes the link to geography relatively unimportant.

Though interesting as one of Kracauer's earliest essays (1925) as well as the longest in the book, the first essay is admittedly not immediately linked to an urban world of experience. "Felsenwahn in Positano" ("Cliff Folly in Positano") deals with one of the places in Italy (along with Capri and Naples) that, in the mid-1920s, held an attraction for some critics in the German intelligentsia who were later to become famous: Ernst Bloch, Alfred Sohn-Rethel, Walter Benjamin, and so on.[21] But while Benjamin and Sohn-Rethel, for example, wrote about the distinctly public life-form of the Mediterranean city, using Naples as a model, Kracauer indulged in focusing on one of the exceptions of architectural history, the result of lone individuals who have spent their lives privately erecting a building that, from a utilitarian point of view, is irrelevant but that continues to fascinate the public. Architecture becomes sculpture, a sort of private cathedral that nevertheless lacks any cult functions. It develops outside any social limitations, but thereby also outside the processes that can enable social change to take place.

In this architectural idiom protected by the private sphere, where space and dream approach each other, the constructively utopian element is of central importance. Watts Towers in Los Angeles[22] and Facteur Cheval's experiments in France are today perhaps the best-known examples of the genre. Kracauer's interest, in contrast, is devoted to the lifework of a certain Gilbert Clavel, between Sorrento and Amalfi. In a work featuring the natural elements of stone and sea based in an ancient tower on the coast, this self-taught architect-engineer for decades continued his expansion of a chaotic network of passages and rooms in the cliff.[23] In extending to its limit the question of the subject's reflection in urban space (investigated in chapter 6), Kracauer emphasizes this architecture's connection with the ornamental expression of a child. In this exceptional case, the ornament has gone so far as to be realized as a piece of architecture:

> Gilbert Clavel's cliff locations have nothing in common with human architecture. That they are inhabited is the only houselike quality of this mesentery, which burrows without direction, without a beginning or an end, into the crust. . . . A child scratches squiggles with a quill pen on a piece of paper: their dimensions flutter, become hard, and penetrate stone and atmospheric layers. That is what the house looks like—an amorphous interlacing. (S, p. 57)

By thus avoiding forms mandated by utilitarian and economic requirements, the architectural work places itself outside the socially binding institution of architecture, whose subsequent development is foreseen and even exceeded at certain points. Clavel's architecture "anticipated constructivism, without decoration and crystalline, but only superficially linked to that from the Bauhaus. For passion [*die Wut*] lurks behind the forms; it strikes deep as a man who has gone berserk" (S, p. 62), Kracauer concludes, using the furnishings of the tower rooms as his point of departure.

The necessary social forms are completely in evidence in the other example of an architecture that, for Kracauer, gives rise to reflections on utopian design. But this time, the formulations express themselves via their *demarcation* from the realized—and as an insistence not on an aesthetic or functional but on an aesthetically and socially defined architectural paradigm.

This shift of paradigm becomes understandable when one looks at the spatial models for his reflections. The leap from the dream architecture of the Mediterranean to a tunnel under the tracks at Charlottenburg Station in Berlin is indeed striking. The tunnel space does not produce in Kracauer a feeling that he is viewing a more or less beautiful piece of architecture; rather—on the borderline between aesthetics and ethics—it provokes a *Grauen*—a feeling of horror and loathing: "A clattering hellish passage, a sinister cohesion of bricks, iron, and concrete, joined together for eternity" (S, p. 49). The spatial uncanny is supplemented by the socially depressing atmosphere of the passage space, whose only permanent public consists of beggars. The "horrible unconnectedness" of these people (S, p. 49) is a sign of social lack, but that on its own cannot explain the sense of sinisterness created by the tunnel. That is ascribed to the meeting between an unlovely substantial form and an unjust and dissipated social life, summed up in "the opposition between the closed, unshakable construction system and the fading human confusion" (S, p. 50). Both a spatial and a social factor are found in Kracauer's programmatically formulated attempt at a solution: "The same horror seizes me again and again when I walk through the tunnel. And as a consolation I from time to time devise better, more beautiful constructions. Some whose building materials consist not only of iron and bricks but, in a certain way, also of human beings" (S, p. 50).

This is apparently far removed from Clavel's mentally expressive formalism in Positano, as Kracauer underlines the essential attribute as being mediation between form and sociality. Yet the distance between the two social and aesthetic principles seems less unbridgeable when one considers that the cliff architecture had already greatly honored its utopian definition. The subjectively reflective grounding releases it from the functional requirements that the tunnel has to obey. In that way, Clavel cannot even be criticized for excessive aestheticizing or worship of space. His spatial design is— within the limits of a private piece of architecture—adequate in relation to its psychosocial function. Despite the fact that the sociofunctional requirements are harder to get around in an urban economy, the passage under the tracks has quite a lot to learn from the relationship of Clavel's architecture to human mental space.

Its design remains inadequate in the actual social context. The social requirements get in the way between a beautiful spatial form and its mental realization. Architecture that is both beautiful and collective presupposes that the social problems of a hopeless situation are eliminated, which was not the case in the Berlin of the 1930s. (*End of digression.*)

Back to the Christmas market atmosphere of Berlin in 1932. The beautiful is not necessarily subject to a requirement that social justice be realized, but here it remains fundamentally marked by social injustice. Thus, beauty shows itself as a utopian reservoir for the social field. But in its development the social can hardly follow the same figures as the improvisation-enhancing, fragmentary metropolis, as those are encumbered with societal repression and thus contain an element of oppression.

The Urban Uncanny—Disharmony as Critique

The lack of communication between the aesthetic awakening and the honoring of the social utopia characterizes Kracauer's way of looking at Berlin. As an extension of his criticism of the space of social reproduction, aesthetically established figures for the observation and interpretation of Berlin also differ from the corresponding observations of Paris and Marseilles. A gliding takes place away from what is still—despite elements of finitude (the possibility of death)—linked to the beautiful, toward a field that, first and foremost, contains characteristics of the uncanny.[24]

In "Berliner Figuren" ("Berlin Figures"; a collection of observations from FZ, February 17, 1931, July 10, 1931, and August 6, 1932), social deviation is hardly presented in an enthusiastic light. A person in disguise is sitting alone and unnoticed in the Berlin "U-Bahn," where, as a representative of the carnival tradition, he is not only exhibiting

himself in a completely everyday environment but also appears to be sham, as if he had donned his "glorious colors" out of a "sense of duty" (S, p. 147). The festive dreams have no place in the open urban environment—they assume pitiful forms.

The individuals are so greatly subject to the finality of commodity exchange that, at best, they become supportive of utopia via their grotesquely imitative practice. In a bar typical of Berlin in the 1920s, equipped with telephones and fixtures for the pneumatic post on the tables (as in the film version of *Cabaret,* though here in a more striking analogy to a modern office), Kracauer notices a young man.[25] This person becomes in *Straßen in Berlin und anderswo* perhaps the most consistent expression of what is revealed in "Das Ornament der Masse" as an analogy between the capitalist organization of production (here, though, in the form of office work) and the reactive patterns of the culture industry. He has taken the consequences of the imperatives of business life so far that he has lost the ability to distinguish between life's various facets. He makes use in the bar of the opportunity to simulate a business activity which in no way lags behind that of his working hours when it comes to one-dimensional rationality.

There is a complementary element in the real commercial life in Kracauer's "Berliner Figuren," where "the permanent customer" (*der Dauerkunde;* S, pp. 150–151) is a person who, clad in a succession of new suits, has various fountain pens demonstrated for him at a street stall. This activity once more has the nature of a simulation, only this time consciously, since it is a question of pretending to have an interest—actually nonexistent—in buying the commodities that are on sale. The grotesque elements may appear inhuman and suggest a critique of impoverished life, but they do not necessarily inspire new forms of social existence.

Kracauer's portraits of figures from interwar Berlin also contain critical characteristics, however. A girl at a theater announces, by presenting a numbered sign and mobilizing a smile for the mass audience, what is next on the evening's program. In Kracauer's article her figure seems to have been taken out of the obscurity shared with the theater's other technical staff. By emphasizing her "coquettish and personal" smile and the importance, in retrospect, of the numbers in the story (for example, in the form of dates), he seeks to create an awareness of the unappreciated value and strength of her role. The same idea is developed in the note "Die Stimme" ("The Voice"), where the voice of a Berlin beggar is ascribed so much vehemence (S, p. 149) that it seems to be detached from the beggar's body and to gain its own independent existence in the total environment. This spreading of the uncanny is—apart from serving the beggar's cause—a form of social resistance.

But the importance of this resistance has less to do with socioeconomic factors than with cultural awareness in connection with a meditatively dancing individual who, singing, takes in monotonously laid-out suburban streets with his ability to make this scene seem "uncanny" (*unheimlich;* S, p. 156). Song and dance are perhaps not uncanny in themselves, but they become so in this spatial and social context. The slow body is, as Kracauer sees it, alien to the world, doomed to an existence in a refuge. Just as the uncanny is opposed to the beautiful, life in a place of refuge—which should be understood in a perspective that is theological and existential, and not immediately political[26]—illustrates the possibility of a nonalienated place: "How beautiful it ['a distant sweetness,' caused by the unbroken singing] could be if it had not been uncanny like the unnaturally slow dancer! His hair is reddish, his gaze fixed on the refuge that is reserved for him in this world" (S, p. 156).

Since beauty moves irrevocably toward a state of sinisterness, it stimulates the observer's awareness of a basic repression in the city. In line with the essay "Schreie auf der Straße" ("Cries in the Street," mentioned earlier), Kracauer operates here—as a clarifying intellectual experiment—with a superindividual subjectivity. Its repression of its own urges probably produces an apparently rational organization of space and sociality, but that which is repressed returns in, for example, the form of cries in the street, the beggar's voice just mentioned, and the uncanny nature of the dancer: "Perhaps the street has hatched the dancer. And that which it has to suppress is condensed into this figure" (S, p. 156). In this dancer—the condensed expression of repression—the hypothetical possibility is broached of a different relationship between space and subjectivity.

An overall problem in clarifying the conditions of a utopia lies in the relationship between the affirmative and the critical, the "rational" and the "reasonable" sides of urban life (as it could be expressed, in accordance with "Das Ornament der Masse"). A surprisingly close relationship between these two aspects is deduced by Kracauer in his analysis of a bar pianist, presented under the title "Der Klavierspieler" ("The Piano Player"; FZ, December 2, 1930). The analysis of this form of entertainment, whose strength consists in avoiding positive notice, surprises one by locating the possibility of radical opposites within a phenomenon of utmost conformity. The automatically playing hands—separate from the pianist's body, which, without any real effort, maintains a superficial but variable relationship to the various social groupings (guests, staff) of the fashionable bar—are only one aspect of this figure. The player's innocent childlike face stares out into the room or even looks absentmindedly at his hands from time to time. Already its emptiness—interpreted by Kracauer as an expression of *the force of mnemonic images*—gives a sign of inner contradictions. These, however, break out radically only in situations when the automatic playing of the hands takes on a new quality because of their participation in the pianist's singing:

Then he begins to sing out loudly, bawling a popular song with the dark voice of a drunk. His hands are with him and he is with his hands. A blissful childlike smile suffuses his face, and his song almost disrupts the low bar. But, as if by some miracle, his song seems to the guests to be as silent as his finger exercises, and they go on talking as if they did not hear anything, as if nobody were singing anything at all. And yet this singing changes everything in the room. (S, p. 146)

The writing observer feels—in this as in other situations—that he is noticing something which has been overlooked by the conformist mass. For him, the singing voice involves an element of dissonance that radically changes the atmosphere in the bar and thereby the social significance of the place. Formerly the sign of an unproblematic culture and of social ease, the room is now suddenly tinged with the misery that is both the existential and social reality of the pianist. The repressed sides of his life return as a difference that changes the environment—not in the pianist's own consciousness ("He seems quite unaware of it; he simply sings with a self-forgotten smile"; S, p. 146), but as a result of the writer's interpretation. It seems that the journalist takes it upon himself to be the psychoanalyst of the collective, and the same is true when it comes to discovering utopian forces.

3. THE EROSION OF HISTORICAL MEMORY
The Threatened Historical Sign—Utopia and History

As mentioned in connection with Kracauer's analysis of clowns (see chapter 5), the theater is an extension of the city's public space. On occasion, it also becomes a place where urban reflection momentarily gains conditions more privileged than those found in the wide expanse of social reality. This is emphasized in *Straßen in Berlin und anderswo* in the article "Drei Pierrots schlendern" ("Three Pierrots Strolling"; FZ, October 14, 1926), which supplements the link mentioned above between clowning and society's central forms of thought with a historical (diachronic) dimension. This motif is central to the investigation of the forms under which urban culture can produce fragmentary utopian images as a counterpart to immediately accessible reality. In this piece of work it is absolutely essential for Kracauer and others of his generation that the present age looks "backward" in order to come into contact with and derive strength from history. Consciously or unconsciously, urban subjectivity orients itself toward surviving but often repressed cultural forms. So the question of under which forms this past is accessible for present urban reflection is therefore crucial.

As suggested by the title, "Drei Pierrots schlendern," three surviving examples of the Pierrot figure are subjected to analysis. Kracauer interprets their performance in the Parisian Cirque d'hiver less to promote a distinct message, let alone a philosophical paradigm, than is the case in his analysis of clowns six years later ("Akrobat—schöön"). Here he focuses on breaking up the Pierrot figures' movements into *visual patterns.* Although they are human bodies, because of their costumes and movements they invite one to indulge in a process of visual abstraction: strokes, diagonals on the ground, "airy gleaming ornaments" (S, pp. 135, 136) are produced to the accompaniment of monotonous music. In this way, they become *ornaments,* raised to the level of "lines, points, surfaces of a form [*eines Gebildes*] that itself has brushed off its human shadow" (S, p. 136).

The Pierrot figures are not immediately readable and seem to be meaningless. They can be observed as visual expressions of a time that is now distant and on the verge of becoming history: "This performance may be called historical, since Pierrots no longer exist. They have been fetched from the previous century, three worn-out red costumes," Kracauer notes in his introduction (S, p. 134).

It would seem that by around 1925, the nineteenth century already feels like a part of history. Its concrete cultural and societal structures (not necessarily its general characteristics, which remain general . . .) have disappeared and can be grasped only through what remains—as, for example, these Pierrot figures who, according to the subtitle, are "The Sons of François Fratellini" and thus children of the nineteenth century. Their performance is so powerful that in their mixture of visibility and lack of meaning, they produce spatial abstractions which become "monograms of an unknown language" (S, p. 136). Like some "hieroglyph in a vacuum" (S, p. 137), these figures of urban culture remind one of a historical context, the understanding of which is neither guaranteed in advance nor always possible.

Furthermore, Kracauer has dealt in greater depth with the problem of historical memory in two articles in *Straßen in Berlin und anderswo:* "Abschied von der Lindenpassage" ("A Farewell to the Linden Arcade"; FZ, December 21, 1930) and "Straße ohne Erinnerung" ("Street without Memory"; FZ, December 16, 1932). Both articles are based on a Berlin world of experience and deal with the destruction of cultural traces in urban culture.

While decay in Mediterranean culture was the very basis for improvisation and memory, the converse is true for Berlin. "Time's" dynamic dissolution of the city's spatial structures results here in a newly constructed, homogeneous space that, on the contrary, weakens the conditions for subjective reflection.

The two articles on the Linden Arcade and Berlin's main street, the Kurfürstendamm, both draw attention to a systematic characteristic in Kracauer's conception of Berlin. The Linden *Arcade* is in this instance the place for all that is repressed from the open shopping and traffic artery. At the same time, though, the smoothness of the major city *street* (exemplified by the Kurfürstendamm) provides the foundation for perceiving the heterogeneous space and activities of the passage in a liberating and consciousness-raising light. A certain nonsimultaneity between the passage and the street is thus the basis for the following pages.

Memory Work and Repressed Urban Culture—The Arcade

Thanks to the details of its historicizing architecture and its numerous shops (postcards, cafés, billiards, stamps, waxworks, souvenirs, etc.), the Linden Arcade, which—with a glass roof—was a 130-meter-long, 8-meter-wide, and 13.5-meter-high space between Behrenstraße and Unter den Linden, had long formed a heterogeneous, untraditional space.[27] After having presented Berlin with international luxury (e.g., a Viennese café) in its early days (shortly after 1870), the passage had gradually decayed into a "dark and uncanny" space.[28] In the late 1920s, however, it underwent a face-lift, via among other things a *neusachlich* eradication of precisely the details that for Kracauer had been the place's characteristic features. That which is thus repressed through modernization is the theme of Kracauer's article.

The removal of the many details in favor of cool but clear surfaces has considerable importance for a place's cultural and social functions. In Kracauer's analysis, the passage is typical in that what is already being belittled in the bourgeois commodity-based culture of the metropolis there finds a habitat that is, quite literally, shady but accessible to the gaze of passersby. For

> their [i.e., the arcades'] peculiarity is that of "through" passages—passages through bourgeois life, which lived in front of their openings and above them. Everything that was separated from this, because it was not worthy of being represented or went in general against the official view of the world, built a shelter for itself in the passages. These housed what was excluded or had been included—the sum of the things that were felt to be not right for decorating a facade. Here in the passages these passing objects gained a sort of permit of residence—like gypsies who are not allowed to be in the towns, only in the countryside. (S, pp. 31–32).

Kracauer's remarks apply less to the arcade's shops in their original state, when they still were new, than to their present state, since after the First World War they appear to be "antiquated":[29] physically run-down and, above all, out of step with the present aesthetics of a commodity-based society.

Even from this point of view, the arcade does not necessarily house the opponents of bourgeois society. To a much greater degree it contains society's dregs—the reverse side of the world of commercial facades on the boulevards and the wide streets. But this is sufficient for Kracauer to conceive the passage world as a *subtle critique* of the commodity-based culture that now reigns: "Thus the passage through the bourgeois world was itself a criticism of it, and every real passerby understood," he notes (S, p. 37). The hidden (and forgotten) shops along with their assortment of commodities return as irony, since they present the irrelevant and suddenly less attractive side of capitalist culture. This gives rise to an alien element of the present:

> so were they exiled and cursed to the arcade's inner Siberia. Here, however, they took revenge on the bourgeois idealism that suppressed them, since they played their tarnished existences [off] against its [idealism's] conformist form. Humiliated as they were, they succeeded in huddling together in flocks and, in the twilight of the passage, they instigated an active protest action against the facade culture outside. They exposed the idealism and revealed its products as being kitsch. (S, p. 36)

The object-world of the arcade was so largely determined by its immediate context of production that it very soon appeared to be anachronistic, kitschlike, struck by immobility. Via this accelerating decline, the passage also becomes at the same time a *memory* of a bygone age and a *warning* of the possible future development of the rest of the culture. The historicizing force of the arcade is a criticism of the present (represented by the stroller) that recognizes its heritage in the passage and yet feels alienated from this foundation:

> That which we have inherited and simply called our own—was put on display in the passage as in a mortuary, where it showed its extinguished grimace. We were confronted with ourselves as corpses in that passage. But we also wrenched free that which belongs to us now and forever; that which—unappreciated and distorted—gleamed there [in the arcade]. (S, p. 37)

A final link is added to the already long chain of considerations regarding historical consciousness. What was initially repressed and then seemed to be anachronistic shows itself in the third phase to be deceased and providing the inheritance on which later subjectivity is based, becoming finally an innovative material of cultural construction. Frozen as kitsch, the ephemeral thus becomes a point of departure for utopian activity,[30] making possible the subject's severance from and elaboration of a disquieting past and present.

Yet the spatial and social conditions of this negative dialectic consciousness are impoverished in the modernized passage. Its temporal heterogeneity and divergence from the surrounding cultural landscape are *dissipated* by this modernization. Half a century before the relative consensus about restoration of the 1980s (which inscribes

"historical" spatial structures in present-day material and relationships of use and thereby, indirectly and against its own intentions, denies them), Kracauer has forcefully drawn attention to a paradox in the ideas of restoration and modernization:

> Now, under a new glass roof and with marble decorations, the former arcade is reminiscent of a department store vestibule. The shops are admittedly still there, but their postcards are staple commodities, the world panorama of the passage has been taken over by the film, and its anatomical museum has not been a sensation for quite some time. All the objects have been struck dumb. (S, p. 37)

Even at this stage of anachronism the objects are still being repressed—anew, one could say. The place where they are collected and put on show—the arcade—is made to conform to the architectural idiom of the open city, whose neutral nature and *lack of traces* have radical influences on human consciousness. This is the theme of "Straße ohne Erinnerung," which deals with the wide Berlin street as the framework for an urban consciousness.

The New Urban Memory—The Street

Radically opposed to the frozen time of the arcade, Berlin's Kurfürstendamm is part of a historical development that takes place so fast and so homogeneously that time is described as empty: "Whereas many street precincts seem to be created for all eternity, today's Kurfürstendamm is the embodiment of time that passes emptily by, where nothing is capable of lasting" (S, p. 19).

The shops on this street become the incarnation of a type of progress that is connected with high profits and high rents. For this reason, the turnover in shops is so great that the street conveys an impression of "colonial regions and gold-digger towns, even though there are practically no gold veins left to discover in this zone any more" (S, p. 23). The treatment of the Kurfürstendamm's lack of permanence contains a whole series of literary references.[31] Surprisingly, an echo can be heard of Kracauer's utopian, bright description of Marseilles. But the Berlin shops with their "harbor population that has risen out of nothing," "obsessed by wanderlust pure and simple," convey in all their "transitoriness" an "impression of improvisation" (S, pp. 21, 22; all signs shared with the urbanity of Marseilles) in a way that in its theoretical perspective does not have much in common with the culture of the Mediterranean city. The difference between the two cities is one of historical memory: "Otherwise the past hangs around places where it used to live when alive; on the Kurfürstendamm it retires without leaving any traces behind. . . . That which once was is gone for all eternity, and that which at present asserts itself makes a 100 percent claim on what is present" (S, p. 23). In this commercial street—according to Kracauer's general hypothesis—"eternally constant changing erases the memory" (S, p. 22) of the individual shop and the place that it might have represented in the individual or collective consciousness.

Nevertheless, Kracauer's article represents a refinement of this hypothesis, the radical consequence of which must naturally be that there will be no possibility left for either individual or collective memory. This means that the possibilities for allowing fragments of it—aided by a memory of the city—to be included in utopian conceptions will be considerably reduced.

"Straße ohne Erinnerung" is, however, more an investigation of the conditions under which everyday memory can function when a quasi-natural process of development, whose main example is the medieval city, is replaced by a permanent, economically conditioned change. This motif is investigated using two poles as a point of departure. On the one hand, Kracauer confirms the recurrent shock of encountering a well-known shop (in these cases a café and a confectioner's) and suddenly realizing that only the empty interior is left. On the other hand, Kracauer analyzes the situation in which a memory of the place that has disappeared finds its way to consciousness despite the absence of any immediate referent in present reality.

Both poles make the general hypothesis more precise. For a shock to be able to be produced because the spatial framework has lost its previous function, there must have at least been a practical relationship to the place that makes it possible to register a change. Kracauer gives examples of habitual links to the spaces in question that have served either as places visited at regular intervals (a tea salon) or as a help in orienting oneself in a metropolis (the light from a café). The fact that the reflective relationship intensifies only when the absence of the place is noticed does not contradict the idea that through use and recognition an emotional link to the place in the city street has already been forged.

On the other hand, the possibility of remembering is not necessarily determined by the continuity of the use of the space, as the analysis of the modernization of the arcade might at first glance seem to suggest. In "Straße ohne Erinnerung" Kracauer provides an example of the fact that memory of habitually visited places remains possible even after they have disappeared, although such memory is of a nature more mediated and linked to fragment, less stable and linked to will.

The recollection of the interior of the original tea salon only takes place in an analogous situation established on discovering that the café that replaced it has closed down. Since the narrator has only visited this place once, a year before, when he found that the tea salon had disappeared, the experience of loss is more important than a positive architectural feeling of space. The repetition of this situation of loss is crucial for an image and a feeling of the former tea salon to well up: "all these details emerge afresh from the memory. I see them in front of me, I am their guest" (S, p. 23). Via implicit references, Kracauer is thus giving an example of the fact that the distinction Marcel Proust made between *mémoire volontaire* and *mémoire involontaire*—between voluntary and involuntary memory—can serve to illustrate the development of an urban consciousness. The citizen of the metropolis is, to the same extent as the aging narrator of *À la recherche du temps perdu*, dependent on events that are *random* and not arranged in advance in consciousness in order to experience something that is described by both Kracauer and Proust as the full return of the past.

Memory is involved in a third instance that is able in a structurally grounded way to articulate and shape subjective recall of that which has disappeared. The "instances" necessary for this evocation do not announce themselves via (for a formal consideration) constancy of space but via "repetition of a particular event" (S, p. 23), which to a far greater extent than the narrator's visit to the renovated tea salon is capable of reawakening thoughts of the former interior. Renovation is here the opposite of memory.

Yet Kracauer's overall hypothesis concerning the erasing of memory as a consequence of the constantly changing use of space in the metropolis is confirmed by an architectural observation: "The ornaments, which formed a sort of bridge to the past, have been removed. Now the robbed facades stand without any anchorage in time and are a symbol of historyless change that is completed behind them" (S, p. 23). *The ornament*—this time the term for architectural decoration in a completely immediate sense—is here the unifying example of the anchorage of the particular memory. It is less memory as such than this detailed, individual, and precise form of recall that is threatened by the culture of the metropolis. Rather than simple destruction, a shift takes place from particular, narratable, and organizable memory toward a general *urban subjectivity*. The link to the individual person, moment, or object is lost to a greater or less extent, replaced by a different type of memory. This new type of memory, according to the examples from "Straße ohne Erinnerung," is characterized by being relatively unconscious, fragmentarily linked, and discontinuous in its temporal and discursive location (compared with the consciousness that is linked to "natural" relationships—the country, the small town, the family, etc.).

The continuous change of the metropolis thus has considerable significance for both space and subjectivity. The new abstract framework, according to "Straße ohne Erinnerung," promotes erosion of the type of memory that is based on continuity and thereby represents a shift toward an articulation of the past linked more closely to chance.

In order to make more precise the organization by space of consciousness, Kracauer, in the earlier "Abschied von der Lindenpassage," advances a second hypothesis, the intuition of which would prove to be extremely accurate in predicting historical development: "All objects are struck dumb. Shyly they huddle behind the empty architecture, which for the time being stays completely neutral and which some time later will hatch out who knows what—perhaps fascism or nothing at all" (S, pp. 37–38). But it is not a question of discussing whether there is a necessary connection between detailless, smooth spatial structures on the one hand and, for example, a fascist political development on the other.[32] Kracauer's awareness of the role played by spatial forms in organizing social and even political consciousness must, however, finally be emphasized, since it contains an important contribution to an understanding of utopia's conditions in a metropolis. Homogeneous, extensive space seems to him to strengthen the tendencies toward a mass consciousness without ethical or human points of anchorage. A memory that is borne by ornaments, even in the early, historicist version of the Linden Arcade, means more stable possibilities for both individual and social work with the past, which is lifted out of time's diachronic sequence by the subjective consciousness so that it may enter into new contexts.

From this point of view, there seems to be a general typological opposition between arcade and street. From arcade to street a movement takes place from more coherent to a chance-based work of recollection. The arcade expresses the possibility of working consciously with memory, whereas the wide street means a weakening of this option. In a historical context, where the urban center of gravity is shifted so far toward the open street space that it invades the shadow world of the arcade, it is crucial that the conditions for memory, even in the Berlin street, are not totally eliminated but are simply altered. The importance of this observation increases when the political situation of the 1930s becomes as acute as Kracauer foresaw in "Abschied von der Lindenpassage." Its decisive consequences for the intellectual practice that Kracauer develops concerning urban space will be dealt with in the third and last section of this book.

Chapter 8 has given an account of the understated but permanent place of utopia in Kracauer's urban essays. The utopian dimension is part of the work of urban reflection in such a hesitant, changeable way because the social conditions for honoring the utopian imagination are absent.

Opportunities for urban change are naturally linked in Paris and Marseilles to visual phenomena, which in their fragmented beauty appear to the tourist as a promise of comprehensive, emancipatory development. But the constellation of decomposition and natural urbanity proves to be insufficient for realizing both an aesthetic and a social conception of a different Berlin. The social framework for the aesthetic break cannot be left out of consideration. It has to be included, in all its limiting nature, as a vital condition for utopian development. In Kracauer's analysis of social phenomena in Berlin, the limitation of utopian imagination by social conditions means that he uses an indirect critical strategy. That change is necessary and furthermore ought to be possible is, however, clear from the *dystopian* aspects that—mixed with suggestions of a possible different development—penetrate the mosaics of his texts on Berlin's social figures. In the last part of the chapter, the idea is aired that a social and aesthetic change perhaps cannot be envisaged directly in relation to what already exists. It will have to detour through the medium of historical memory. The changed conditions for historical reflection thus occupy a vital position in Kracauer's urban social analysis.

Conclusion to Part II

Part II has dealt with the issue of ornament from a social perspective. It thereby differs from part I, which demonstrated a use of the ornament that may have been social in its intention (see the anonymously published *Ginster*) but remained at the aesthetic and existential level of individual experience.

Chapter 5 established the decisive theoretical point of departure for an interpretation of Kracauer's social urban essays, since "the ornament" as a cultural and analytical category was separated from the one-dimensional *Ratio*. The thoroughly organized ornament (such as the Tiller Girls) is far surpassed in reflective force by the complexity of the city's horizontal networks. The layer of urban culture is formed by the meeting of various types of ornaments that—even though they do not perhaps correspond to Man ("der Mensch," Kracauer's way of referring to the nonidentical)—are often accessible to Reason. In this context, the *interpretation* of the individual ornament (here understood as a visual or sociofunctional fragment of metropolitan reality) is absolutely vital for determining whether city culture can promote the *resubjectivization of the "objective spirit,"* which was the quest of Simmel's writings of cultural criticism.

Chapters 6 to 8 systematized Kracauer's highly heterogeneous urban essays from this theoretical perspective around three different but nevertheless interlinked axes.

In chapter 6 the interaction is shown between the individual psyche and the city as a spatial and social structure. The wanderings of the individual in the urban maze create links of consciousness to (rather than an exposure of) basic mental structures. Conversely, the individual's recognition of a lack of aims also brings about a changed view of general urban space. Individual and collective space are linked by a widespread fear that is derived from a common subjective constitution.

The ornaments on this axis thus have the nature of selective observations. They belong to what was called the third level of ornament analysis in the conclusion to part I. This type of ornament is the *occasion* of subjective memory. The ornaments' significance quickly widens, however, to imply deeper-lying immaterial mental structures of both an individual and a collective nature. In all instances, they refer to the city's framework of experience. Kracauer's narrative essays suggest an ornamental unity between sections of immediately visual space and structures of subjectivity. A certain reciprocity is adduced, a correspondence, between visuality and subjectivity, which enables a mental dynamics of a psychoanalytical and socioanalytical nature to take place. This unity underpins the assumption that the ornament can constitute a Reason-bearing form of abstraction.

In chapter 7 an investigation was carried out to show how certain social spaces place the individual in a waiting position. A spatial framework for social and individual misery thus illustrated the concrete reproduction of society's totality. Despite the ornaments' connection with societal structures that take into account the individual psyche to only a limited extent, Kracauer still treats the place of the individual in a social context as an important question. The individual is under the dominance of Ratio. In this situation he reacts by identifying himself with Ratio and remaining as a socially conditioned element, as a type, alien to Reason. Reason would mainly seem to be reserved for external interpretation—that is, Kracauer's essays. Only these adopt an *active* stance toward the general fate: to be placed in a waiting position. While the passively waiting individual is *reactive,* the analytically active and attentive individual is *reflective.*

As in chapter 6, the starting point is the visually distinct ornament, whose interpretation is oriented not toward the mental field but toward the sphere of social consciousness. These ornaments are far less ambiguous than those analyzed in chapter 6, since they are characterized by their one-dimensional link to Ratio and by their almost insuperable distance from Reason. Only the reflectively waiting attitude to the ornaments of the metropolis can open up a utopian perspective.

Chapter 8 deals with the conditions for utopian reflection. It investigates conditions under which the essay-writing, reflective individual can locate potential fissures in urban culture. The individual search takes the form of a fragmentation—or decomposition—of urban space, which is transformed into mobile, ornamental shapes. The break, which is first articulated *aesthetically* (Marseilles, Paris), cannot be immediately translated into *social* terms. For that reason, Kracauer seeks to create a utopian reflection in the reader (who is, in all cases, the destination for the written text) by means of an objectivizing, disturbance-producing technique. The utopia is primarily sought via its dystopian opposite. The final remains of a real utopia (understood as the place-without-a-place, a nowhere, and at the same time the best-of-all-places) are relinquished for the expectations that Kracauer links to the reflective process of memory. Memory is characterized by being able to unite the earlier registers of a social and aesthetic nature, respectively, within the framework of a new medium. In all its unpredictability it places itself above the dividing lines between the individual and the collective, the aesthetic and the social.

The three sections of chapter 8 have been linked to changing ornamental models. While everyday *objects* dominate the aesthetic part, the types and *figures* of social life assert themselves in implying societal potential for change. Finally, *considerable urban spaces* (exemplified by the Linden Arcade and the Kurfürstendamm) become the crucial bearers of expectations to the medium of memory.

A general tendency throughout part II thus culminates in its final chapter. At the point where the considerable street and arcade ornaments are introduced, a link backward is also made to the minimal, immaterial mental structures that were dealt with in chapter 6. This confirms the inner relationship between individual, social, and utopian reflection in the metropolis. The relationship implies no identification between the various instances in the triangle but simply a special, changeable dialectical order that states the structures in Siegfried Kracauer's paradigm of urban analysis.

At the level of contemporary society that the texts in *Straßen in Berlin und anderswo* characteristically engage, no break is suspected in the limitation of the aesthetic utopia by the social. However, new perspectives are opened via Kracauer's interest in the reflective form of memory. The threatened position of "voluntary" memory in the mobility of signs of the metropolis does not prevent Kracauer from attempting an analysis of the cultural history of a collective historical past. The past being addressed is linked to nineteenth-century Paris and thus appears both distant and strange—but not enough to prevent Kracauer from finding phenomena that are closely linked to developments in the Europe of the 1930s. It is to his own time's divided subject that he attempts to communicate his analytically based conclusions concerning the nineteenth century. This analysis, presented in the book *Jacques Offenbach und das Paris seiner Zeit,* will be discussed in the third and last part of this book.

PART III

The City—A Sphere
for Collective Memory

History and Urban Collectivity

I. THE INTENTIONS UNDERLYING KRACAUER'S "SOCIOBIOGRAPHY" OF OFFENBACH AND PARIS

Introduction: Kracauer's Last Piece of Writing Focusing on the City

It would be a grave omission to conclude the investigation of Siegfried Kracauer's writings on cities without mentioning his book about the operetta composer Offenbach and the city of Paris. *Jacques Offenbach und das Paris seiner Zeit*, a comprehensive "sociobiography" in its themes and size that dates from 1937,[1] is Kracauer's last piece of *reflection* on issues of cultural and social philosophy that have the urban world of experience as their point of departure. For after his successful flight to the United States in 1941, he devoted himself predominantly—because of considerations that had to do with his new life-space—to the sociology, history, and aesthetics of film.[2] Not until the last five or so years of his life did he return to the general issues of historiography[3]—this time without including the city as an overall theme.

So it is all the more important to stress that Kracauer's book on Offenbach's Paris is a dialectical extension of the novel *Ginster* and the essays that he published as a journalist and later collected and published as *Straßen in Berlin und anderswo*. While *Ginster* dealt with the individual's discovery of the city as a space for *reflection*, Kracauer's articles from the *Frankfurter Zeitung* transformed, as mentioned, this meeting with the social into a form of urban essay writing highly aware of its own time. The book on Offenbach builds further on these first two types of contributions to what Simmel outlined as "resubjectivization" of objective urban culture, since it resolutely returns to History.

This development in Kracauer's writing expresses an attempt to overcome the problems (outlined at the end of part II) involved in locating sustainable utopian forces in contemporary society. Instead of repeatedly being confronted with the impossibility of citing isolated aesthetic and social phenomena in support of particular liberating tendencies, Kracauer hoped that through working with the cultural and social history of the nineteenth century he would arrive at a world of experience with dynamic effects on his own age.

CHAPTER 9

Life in Exile and Historical Reflection

A look at Kracauer's biography makes it easier to imagine why he gave the relationship between Offenbach and Paris the crucial role of establishing a link between the 1930s and a fundamental but forgotten and repressed past. After having regularly been in opposition to the ever less radical editorial and political line of the *Frankfurter Zeitung* for a number of years,[4] Kracauer found himself in a more critical situation when the Nazis took power in Germany early in 1933. In the course of February 1933, Kracauer himself asked to be stationed in Paris (M, p. 70). This wish became pressing when, the day after the Reichstag fire, February 27, 1933, he was warned about his impending arrest by the managing director of the *Frankfurter Zeitung*, Heinrich Simon. Simon agreed to send him on a "working holiday" (M, p. 70) to Paris. This meant that Kracauer left Berlin that very day, February 28, traveling with his wife to the French capital where they were going to live in exile for the next seven years (M, pp. 74–101).

It is thus not so surprising that Paris—which Kracauer had always been fascinated by—is included as a theme of his writings in exile. After having worked intensively during the first period of his exile on his novel *Georg,* a sort of continuation of *Ginster* (the action begins in 1920) that did not appear until 1973 as a posthumous work,[5] Kracauer began in the autumn of 1934 the work of collecting the considerable amount of material needed for his Offenbach book. "Luckily, practically all the material is to be found in Paris," Kracauer wrote on November 3, 1934, to his friend Leo Löwenthal (M, p. 79), as if he was indicating one of the reasons for his choice of topic.

Neither the organizational and practical conditions nor Kracauer's hopes of a sizable international market for the planned biography can satisfactorily explain his precise choice of theme. It is easier to gain an understanding by directing one's attention to the fact that Walter Benjamin, since the late 1920s, had already been working systematically on transforming the surrealists' interest in the nineteenth-century Parisian arcades into a properly historical and critical cultural awareness. Along the lines of his friend Benjamin, who sensed the presence of "revolutionary forces" in that seemingly dusty and slightly antiquated reality,[6] Kracauer now sought to treat basic and still relevant conditions of modernity by means of an analysis of this period of Parisian urban, cultural, and social history.

His *intellectual and sociocritical* intentions underlying the study of Offenbach's Paris cannot be overemphasized. Admittedly, Kracauer rarely mentions truly utopian elements in this connection. But in so key a position as the foreword to the Offenbach book he characterizes French society in the nineteenth century as "the immediate predecessor of modern [societies]," not only "because the birth of the world economy and the republic is completed here," but also because "in various ways it introduces motifs that are still valid today" (P, p. 9). So the nature of the Offenbach study as a politically motivated intervention into the inflamed situation of Europe in the 1930s is of vital importance to Kracauer.

The Offenbach book is intended to have a political function, which is made possible by a striking resemblance between nineteenth-century France and the state of affairs in the 1930s. Kracauer, who is otherwise extremely careful not to exaggerate systematic traits in a concrete situation, sees in nineteenth-century Paris the model for an understanding of his own time:

> And so it [the society of that age] reacts within the framework of foreseeable conditions with such clarity that its reactions acquire the value of models. So observing it becomes all the more useful. For it will undoubtedly be possible to a not insignificant extent to derive the infinitely more complicated thinking and behavior of the present time from the models created in the course of the nineteenth century in France. Or rather—in Paris. (P, pp. 9–10)

The work of drawing such parallels—aside from when, for example, Napoleon III is described as the first of the modern dictators (P, p. 133)—is left to the reader of the Offenbach biography. But the book's ambition to be something other and more than traditional cultural history (let alone a normal biography) is clear from its very first page.

An investigation and a discussion of the common features Kracauer possibly found between the past and the present exceed the focus (and the limits on size) of this book. But Kracauer's general views on the genre of the biography are presented as a basis for an understanding of the historiographical form that he seeks to establish via the "sociobiography" of Jacques Offenbach and Paris.

From "Neo-bourgeois" Biography to "Sociobiography"

In his preface to the Offenbach book, Kracauer emphasizes: "It is not some kind of private biography of Jacques Offenbach. It is a sociobiography" (P, p. 9).

This precise definition is important and is better understood if one reads Kracauer's 1930 essay "Die Biographie als neubürgerliche Kunstform" ("The Biography as a Neo-bourgeois Art Form"; FZ, June 29, 1930). In this article Kracauer takes a critical look at the genre, which was (also) extremely popular in the interwar years. He shows that biography, in all its chronological objectivization of a life's events, is based on quite simple narrative patterns and their attendant outdated psychological theories. According to Kracauer, this form of history writing is less interested in fostering an understanding of the individual in question within his or her historical context than in concealing a crisis over the concept of the autonomous individual—a crisis that had become ever deeper in the period after the First World War (O, p. 76).

In Kracauer's opinion, there is still only one exception to the general type of biography: the autobiography of Trotsky, which succeeds in conveying the outlines of a new type of individual—the historical individual.[7] Kracauer writes about this (auto-)biography: "The description of the life of the historical individual is not here a means of avoiding a recognition of our situation; it serves to reveal it" (O, p. 80). But the historical and, generally speaking, "different individual" (O, p. 80) that emerges in Trotsky's autobiography is to a great extent the consequence of the theoretical dissolution of the individual. The special nature of the individual here is that "it [the individual] has really been exceeded, so that it becomes real only by virtue of its transparency as regards reality; it does not, however, assert its own reality. A new individual outside the atmosphere of ideologies: it exists to precisely the degree in which it has abolished itself in the interest of recognized, current necessities" (O, p. 80).

Already in his work on the novel *Ginster,* Kracauer dealt with and demonstrated the dependence of the individual on history. In his book on Offenbach and Paris he tries to establish the "sociobiography" as a genre. But he never goes as far in it as in this comment on Trotsky's autobiography, where the individual is reduced to a manifestation of the general historical movement. In the Paris book, on the other hand, the theme remains "Offenbach's societal function" (P, p. 11), which clearly (see below) cannot be understood without including considerations of a psychological—even psychoanalytical—nature. The necessity of including such an individual level of analysis is not denied at any juncture.

As can be seen from the actual name of the genre, Kracauer's "sociobiography" still retains the word "biography." In presenting *Jacques Offenbach und das Paris seiner Zeit* it is helpful to note how Kracauer, in spite of everything, makes use of certain principles from the traditional biography that he had criticized only a few years earlier.

Nevertheless, Kracauer can scarcely be accused (as he himself wrote about certain interwar journalists) of contributing to "serial biography production" solely "for economic reasons" (O, p. 77). To be sure, it cannot be denied that the Offenbach biography was begun during a period of straitened circumstances during his exile in Paris, a time when Kracauer was obliged to let financial considerations have a certain influence on his list of priorities regarding work assignments. In letters to Ernst Bloch and Leo Löwenthal he mentions in connection with the project both the general saleability of the biography genre and the possibilities for selling the translation rights for a book about Offenbach, an international figure.[8] The German original version of the book did not, however, enjoy any immediate success (only seventy-five copies were sold in 1938; M, p. 94), though Kracauer did succeed in selling the manuscript for French, English, American, Swedish, Polish, and Czech publication.[9]

Kracauer's outline of the Offenbach book is in no way an uncritical application of the principles of a normal biography. But it is striking that the sociobiography can develop within a historical version of the traditional biographical conception of a statesman's life story, summarized by Kracauer as follows: "It [the life story] is … the guarantee of the composition. Every historical figure [*Gestalt*] already has a figure of itself. This begins at a particular point in time, develops in a clash with the world, gains in contour and substance, recedes in old age, and is extinguished" (O, p. 77). The elaboration of Kracauer's hypothesis concerning an intense relationship between Offenbach, his music, and the development of French society in the nineteenth century differs only slightly from this formula. As will be shown later, Offenbach's period of success and the musical form of the operetta are analyzed in conjunction with the Second Empire. This period of Offenbach's "contour and substance" is dealt with in book II. Book I covers the years 1830–1848, when there was still a conflict between Offenbach and the musical and social life of Paris. Book III corresponds to the period after the Commune (1871), presenting Offenbach's old age as a loss of contact with historical events.

Aside from the fact that Offenbach is not considered as an isolated, autonomous individual, the periods of his life coincide to a great extent with the template-like principle of a life story, or destiny, that Kracauer called attention to in his critique of the traditional biography. An initial, inquiring phase gives way to a second phase that involves the realization—and success—of his musical creativity. From this peak, there is a decline into the third phase: old age, in which Offenbach is increasingly reduced to a musical and social anachronism.

Kracauer, in his attempt to provide insight into the present by means of a historical analysis of Offenbach's relationship to Paris, maintains some of the traditional forms of the biography, including its tendency to legitimize the individual being described on the basis of what he calls the "motif … of deliverance" (O, p. 79). But both the underlying cognitive intentions and the content of the narrative schemes differ considerably from those of the traditional biography.

Academic Criticism's Lack of Appreciation of Kracauer's Writing of History

Since its publication in 1937, Kracauer's book on Offenbach has been much discussed. In many instances, negative criticism has predominated. As has often been the case in the reception of Kracauer's work, the position of T. W. Adorno has set the tone. Adorno's rejection of this book is rooted mainly in his criticism of its nonacademic concept of knowledge, which results in its relatively easily accessible, apparently popular style.[10]

Though I am not in a position to carry out a detailed discussion here of Adorno's points of criticism—developed in an as yet unpublished nine-page-long personal letter to Kracauer—it is clear that Kracauer's book must appear from a number of points of view to be imperfect, even unsatisfactory. Naturally, one would as a reader be disappointed, for example, if one was looking for proper musical analyses or detailed considerations of the history of music. But such expectations are dashed by Kracauer as early as in the preface to his book (P, p. 9), where the socioanalytical perspective is emphasized. A similar dissatisfaction must be felt if the reader expects innovative formulations concerning the theory of knowledge, which Kracauer possibly toned down in the book, in part from a desire to make it generally accessible.

Nor is the professional historian's requirement to explicitly examine sources satisfied in Kracauer's first attempt in the "sociobiographical" genre. This lack is not necessarily due to his not having carried out such a critique of sources, at least for some of the numerous thematic fields of the presentation.[11] But Kracauer, because of the opposition between scientific metadiscourse and narrative presentation, was obliged to sacrifice these methodological considerations.

This decision, which naturally makes it more difficult for the academic reader to judge the basis for the work's many radical hypotheses, is expressed in the preface through Kracauer's hope that "the spirit of the book is not entirely unrelated to that of the true operetta" (P, p. 11). He is thereby referring first to the unpretentious, informal tone, but also to the possibility that its initially inoffensive and comfortable expression would leave room for criticism.

So there are many reasons why this book in an operetta-like style might irritate the traditional academic type of reader, personified in its highest form by Adorno. The problem is simply that the specialized positions from which the book may be unfavorably judged do not take sufficient account of Kracauer's deepest intentions regarding the study of Offenbach. The book is exposed to such heavy-handed criticism that its vital qualities are overlooked. From a *contemporary* historiographical point of view, one of these virtues is that Kracauer, by venturing a number of untraditional presentations of city and individual, created some theoretical historiographical figures that are still of the highest relevance for the discipline of history and the development of the urban history of modernity.

It was possible to write the Offenbach book in just over two years only because Kracauer was so well-versed in the numerous theoretical figures he had developed in connection with his diverse essays in the *Frankfurter Zeitung* (see part II). On the other hand, there is no direct revision and application of motifs from *Straßen in Berlin und anderswo* to nineteenth-century documents of cultural history. The book seems to be fluently written and thus generally accessible, but it can be broken down further into a diversity of theoretical and narrative layers under the discerning eye of the patient reader.

The absence of explicit source criticism and well-developed methodological considerations is thus compensated for by the exceedingly complex "intrigues"[12] developed by Kracauer in order to create transitions and cohesion between, for example, musical, personal, cultural, and political histories. These modes of presentation in themselves ought to justify giving Kracauer's book on Offenbach and Paris a central position among the pioneering historical discussions of recent years on communication between historical research and a wider lay public. To this point, however, Kracauer's book has not received the systematic mapping of its narrative levels that would demonstrate its form of historical presentation.

Nor will any attempt be made in the present book to lessen this lack of secondary literature. On the other hand, the breadth of Kracauer's investigation will be suggested by means of an analysis of three different thematic and theoretical layers. Through their mutual connections one can gain an impression of a crucial part of the analytical, theoretical, and historico-philosophical intrigue underlying *Jacques Offenbach und das Paris seiner Zeit.* In the course of the book, Kracauer, showing his enduring interest in the boulevard, argues in favor of there being a particular tension between (a) the social and cultural environment of the boulevard, (b) the operetta as a musical and sociocultural form, and (c) the social and historical forms of criticism during the Second Empire.

The hypothesis of an interdependence among these three fields also constitutes the framework for joining a number of subordinate *ornamental* motifs. The next section of this chapter attempts to identify these elements in Kracauer's far more comprehensive work on Offenbach and Paris. Instead of relying on criteria of validity from a single branch of knowledge in reading this sociobiography, the investigation will deal with some of the aspects of Kracauer's work that make the City into a central, mediating factor in the social and cultural history of modernity.

2. CRITICAL ANALYSIS: THE BOULEVARD'S MEDIATION OF CITY AND NARRATIVE
Individual and Heimat

The interaction between the boulevard and Offenbach's musical creativity, which in the longer term results in the operetta, is first investigated on the individual and to a certain extent psychoanalytical and existential level. This involves certain considerations of Offenbach's subjectivity, to which is ascribed the ability to create a link between, on the one hand, the environment of the boulevard and, on the other hand, the memory of a lost childhood, far from the animated bustle of Parisian streets.

The main idea of this first level of analysis is that the intense life and noise of the boulevard are a vital source of musical and dramatic inspiration for Offenbach's compositions. At the same time, the space of the boulevard is conceived as an imaginary substitute for the *Heimat*, the familiar hearth and home that Offenbach had to abandon when, while still young, he left the Cologne of his childhood for the Paris he lived in as a young man and an adult. Constantly revived by the boulevard, this memory of his childhood remains the prime driving force behind Offenbach's musical creativity.

The hypothesis that the boulevard is capable of both replacing and activating the memory of childhood expresses the same theoretical figure as that which underlies Kracauer's essay on Berlin's Kurfürstendamm (discussed in the analysis of "Straße ohne Erinnerung" toward the end of part II). In the midst of its constant transformation, this Berlin answer to the Parisian boulevards can conjure up images in memory of street spaces and venues that at the moment in question have no material traces. Correspondingly, in his depiction of the young Offenbach Kracauer places great emphasis on the power of the Parisian boulevard to fascinate and to influence:

> He [Offenbach], if anyone, had to be driven to the surface and to fill himself with the impressions that streamed toward him there. All the sounds, figures, images, and scenes of Parisian life—depicted in such a masterly fashion in his later works—were acquired by him in their basic form at the time when he had just left childhood [and] played in the orchestra of the Opéra Comique. These were what protected him against the danger of sinking to the depths. (P, p. 31)

In Kracauer's attempt to develop a sophisticated cultural and materialistic explanatory model based on the urban sphere of experience, Offenbach's Cologne childhood has already been alluded to as an important source of his later musical universe (P, p. 23). Between these impressions of his childhood and youth and the musical idiom of the mature composer lies a considerable period during which the immediate impressions of urban life are processed, gradually becoming a genuinely musical language. Meanwhile, the boulevard continues to exert a fascination on him, enabling a lasting repression of the need to return to the childhood home he had left behind. The repressive act also has a sublimating function made possible by the particularly intense link that exists between childhood and boulevard. Together, the city and the memory of childhood can constitute a *Heimat*. In other words, in the imagination the childhood home finds its immediate equivalent in the boulevard: "Separated from his home soil [*Scholle*], it [the boulevard] lay like a neighbor of this distant home, to which Offenbach had already referred in his waltz 'Rebecca.' He only had to turn off the boulevard to be at his goal" (P, p. 85).

This goal should be understood as a musical and subjective metaphor for the irrevocably lost childhood home. Just as the operetta is later interpreted as a reply to the widespread boredom and lack of substantial goals to be found in society ("Langeweile"; see P, book I, chapter 8), the human masses and other forms of social mixing of the boulevard become in Kracauer's analysis a productive factor in Offenbach's life. His creativity is portrayed as being determined by the presence of the mass, or rather by Offenbach's presence in the mass. Unlike the individual of the metropolis, who in all his unproductive, blasé, and reserved mental state was at the center of Simmel's analysis, Offenbach found his creative force to be activated by the mass. Conversely, it becomes passive when he assumes the normal working state of the individual artist—solitude: "He came to life when moving among crowds of people, and for him the theater was the epitome of social life. Solitude caused him to wither," Kracauer observes (P, p. 163). The presence of the mass does not prevent Offenbach from giving his music a precise, balanced form: "Often, Offenbach—that strange hermit—was lost in meditation in the midst of the social maelstrom, committing innumerable spidery forms to music paper. Other people would have needed peace and quiet—but precisely the hubbub of throngs of people incited him to concentration and order" (P, p. 170).

The main motif of this first, individual level of analysis can be summed up as follows: The boulevard is probably a replacement for a real *Heimat,* but it also has the power to prompt Offenbach to a musical mediation between past and present. It is thus a fundamental condition for the creative and existential development of the individual.

The Boulevard and the Second Empire: The Sociohistorical Opportunity of the Operetta

Although Offenbach as a creative and reflective individual is a necessary mediator between the boulevard and the operetta, Kracauer does not limit his analysis to this individual subjectivity. A sociohistorical definition of the boulevard also underlies his understanding of the operetta. Boulevard and operetta are brought together via a number of societal considerations, whose principles will be outlined below.

THE EXTRATERRITORIALITY OF THE BOULEVARD

It has already been mentioned that Offenbach's personal rootlessness and homelessness found their social counterpart in the boulevards—from Place de la Bastille in the east to Place de la Concorde in the west. This connection was based not only in a subtle elective affinity between Offenbach's psyche and the atmosphere of the streets but also in the social nature of this space. For the boulevard is the meeting place for many different individuals and groups whose social and existential situation, according to Kracauer, is reminiscent of Offenbach's. They all share the characteristic that their presence on the boulevard is the result of a *flight* from a previous place to which they once belonged.

This flight assumed both immediate and metaphorical forms. The attempt to shun the ruling bourgeois and aristocratic public (the Juste milieu, Faubourg Saint-Germain, etc.; P, p. 74) is advanced, for example, as the main reason for the presence of a considerable *bohème*. The general fascination exerted by this milieu further helped make the boulevards interesting for diverse journalists, whose reality stretched between the life of the cafés and the boulevard theaters.

Both categories—bohemian and professional journalist—are unproblematically part of the "boulevardier type," which Kracauer characterizes as being "quite free, even from a dependence on money, tending its own spiritual nature and enjoying life" (P, p. 76). Kracauer mainly has this group in mind when he suggests that "one lived, so to speak, in an extraterritorial way on the boulevards" (P, p. 74)—that is, in a "role as outsider" (P, p. 75) rather than in a fixed, well-structured social position. But the labile social position of the boulevard, which is at once a negative quality and yet the real strength of the place, is also illustrated by the presence of a "number of genuine emigrants" (P, p. 84): foreigners who were undesirables in their home countries for political reasons. Since we are talking here of "Polish, Spanish, Italian aristocrats" (P, p. 84), they can at the same time be viewed as belonging to the boulevardier type and as exemplifying the critical function that Kracauer ascribes in his book on Offenbach to the social environment of the boulevard.

In Kracauer's essay from the mid-1920s "Analyse eines Stadtplans," dealt with in chapter 8 of this book, the boulevards of the Paris of that period were considered to be part of the city's "center" (O, p. 15). The boulevards constituted the city's "superior world" (O, p. 15), being opposed to the poverty and human warmth of its outer districts. The definition of the boulevard is modified in the historical cultural analysis of nineteenth-century Paris. Here, the boulevards are, on the contrary, characterized by a *double nature* that allows the traits of the outer districts and the center to blend into a new, fluid quality. This double state, combining social exclusion and spatial inclusion, underlies a crucial hypothesis in Kracauer's understanding of the relationship between city and culture. He suggests that the boulevard at the time of Offenbach, during the July Monarchy and the Second Empire, finds itself in a state of sociocultural emergency. Kracauer attempts to capture this state by emphasizing both the boulevard's introverted and illusory self-sufficiency and its socially external, almost extraterritorial condition. These opposing tendencies are summarized as follows:

> So the boulevard came into being via the economic changes, the emergence
> of the newspaper and sex industries, and the damming up of the process of

societal development—the boulevard, which itself was a landscape, but an artificial landscape, surrounded by invisible dams. The ramparts, which were then
beginning to encircle Paris, are an obvious metaphor for these dams, underlying
further the extraterritorial nature of the boulevards. It was a place that escaped
from the dominance of social reality. A neutral meeting place. An unreal area.
(P, p. 83)

In this analysis, the Parisian boulevards of the nineteenth century represent less the
center of an economy based on commodities than a labile cultural and political environment, whose so-called extraterritorial nature is a sign of both impotence and
strength. This hypothesis also underlies Kracauer's conception of the operetta.

THE OPERETTA: THE RESULT OF A HISTORICAL CONSTELLATION

The operetta is the musical offshoot of what Kracauer conceives as the artificial, unreal,
and historically determined landscape of the boulevard. But this musical form is not
only derived from the boulevard. The possibility of the operetta is probably born in the
social space of the boulevard and the mentality that goes along with it. The first book
(chapters 1–8) of Kracauer's Offenbach analysis concludes its elucidation of the early
history of the operetta during the July Monarchy (1830–1848) with the hypothesis that
this musical genre became possible only with the Second Empire. "An operetta atmosphere" is how Kracauer characterizes the final years of the July Monarchy, going on to
say: "The societal constellation from which it [the operetta atmosphere] derived was in
fact related to that which was going to commence during the Second Empire and which
certainly fostered Offenbach's passion for the theater. But no matter how much the atmosphere galvanized him, the door to the operetta form remained closed for the time
being" (P, p. 101).

The emergence of the operetta, which is anticipated in this passage, requires more
than Offenbach's experiences on the boulevard as a young man, supplemented by the
boulevard's state of cultural emergency. Only certain societal conditions can make possible the musical development and public success of this form. Or, as Kracauer puts it,
the operetta "could come into being only in Paris, or rather: only in the Paris of the Second Empire" (P, p. 84). This specific constellation of place and period, dealt with in
book II of the Offenbach biography, needs to be considered in a little more detail.

The period between the 1848 revolution and the Franco-Prussian War of 1870–1871
is the framework for the development of the operetta, its breakthrough and success—
as well as its crisis. The truly effective and, in this sense, vital period is in actual fact even
more limited. While the years 1848–1851 correspond in Kracauer's analysis to "the
breakthrough for the society that was to come to love [Offenbach's] operettas" (P,
p. 124), the heyday of the operetta is to be found between the first two Parisian world

expositions in 1855 and 1867, respectively. The operetta disappears as an adequate cultural form around the fall of Napoleon III (a process that began in the years after 1867 and was completed in 1870), which brought about the annihilation of the empire from which the operetta "was no less inseparable than from international life" (P, p. 277) during the world expositions. In short, the operetta as a genre is born with the Second Empire and loses its raison d'être when this political system falls.

It does not weaken Kracauer's analyses of the boulevard environment and its importance for the emergence of the operetta that Offenbach and the operetta form really make an impact in connection with the world exposition of 1855 and at a spot that, strictly speaking, lies outside the "great boulevards" (*les grands boulevards*). The world expositions and les Champs-Elysées, where Offenbach's success is obvious for the first time, are far from being opposed to the boulevard environment; they merely constitute its ecstatic extension to a yet more temporary though at the same time culturally open and socially external public.

The analysis of the boulevard is thus exemplary for an understanding of the world expositions at both a concrete and a more general level. At first glance, the life of the boulevard and the world expositions appear interdependent. The world exposition of 1855, for example, leads to growth in the life of the boulevard,[13] which Offenbach is quick to turn into an advantage for the operetta (in the Théâtre des Variétés on the Boulevard Montmartre, among others; P, p. 123). Conversely, the cultural rootlessness that was observed at the culturally "extraterritorial" boulevard is largely predominant among the cosmopolitan crowds taking part in the world exposition. Beyond all cultural and national boundaries they are entranced in their distance from the home country by Offenbach's music, which, like "some form of Esperanto," brought forth echoes "from the *Heimat* to which all the inhabitants of the earth belong, no matter how far away it may lie" (P, p. 151). In its collective appeal as well, Offenbach's music is ascribed a recollective as well as a utopian function.

Offenbach's success in connection with an international public is of minor importance, however, since Kracauer mainly analyzes the operetta in connection with the Second Empire. His argument is based on the notion that the economic and political characteristics of this period of French—and especially Parisian—history were well expressed in Offenbach's operettas. The reality of the operetta recalls the conception of reality that thrives in connection with the rentier and finance capital, Kracauer writes (P, p. 186). It is characterized by its distance from industrial production. The developmental traits stressing happiness that Kracauer in other contexts would have cited in support of a utopian perspective in Offenbach's operettas are here interpreted as parallel to something as material as the special brand of Parisian metropolitan capitalism and its results, such as speculation on the stock exchange (P, p. 189). Neither the metropolis nor the speculation-oriented money are granted a footing in a reality other than the specifically distorted one favored in the period in question.

All in all, there is a high degree of circularity in the relationship between music, economy, and society: "The operetta was able to come into being because the society in which it arose was like an operetta," Kracauer (with a sense for the rhetorical effects of tautologies) begins his chapter "The Music of Gold." He continues with a comment on this first circular form of argumentation: "But the operetta-like nature of this society was determined by the fact that it severed its contacts with reality instead of dealing with it in a sober way. During the first stage of the Second Empire the bourgeoisie was in fact surrounded by so many isolating layers that a breath from the outside world scarcely had any effect on it" (P, p. 186).

Though a proper discussion of the reasonableness of Kracauer's hypotheses concerning the mutual dependence of the empire and the operetta is not offered here, it should be stressed that he cannot at any rate be accused of advancing an explanation based on simple causality. In his interpretation, which at times can seem somewhat sketchy, Kracauer always retains a series of levels of differing generality. Their combined aim is to outline the operetta's conditions of existence as a musical and a public form. None of these levels is given unambiguously determining status in relation to the others. As in Simmel's essay on the metropolis, a high degree of relativism is maintained.

Boulevard and Operetta—Dependence on and Critique of the Second Empire

The interplay between individual, economy, politics, music, city, and stage allows Kracauer to advance the hypothesis that the operetta, precisely by virtue of its unreal nature, also had a critical function during the Second Empire. Both the boulevard environment and the operetta form were based on a flight from a precarious cultural and political reality toward a temporary, imaginary, yet none the less effective "home" in the world of the city or of music. Although these refuges have lost their immediate contact with "reality,"[14] Kracauer ascribes to both of them a critical, perhaps even a utopian force in Offenbach's Paris. To facilitate an overview it is necessary once more to distinguish between the intellectual and the social environment on the boulevard and the music public that was established with the operetta.

THE INDIRECT CRITIQUE OF SOCIETY BY THE BOULEVARD ENVIRONMENT

The boulevard environment is not part of the republican camp; even less is it part of the working-class movement. Nevertheless, in Kracauer's analysis it is granted a protest function during both the July Monarchy and the Second Empire. But because these journalists, men about town, courtesans, and so on "clad their protest in the form of inactivity" (P, p. 71), their originally critical function was not recognized by the politically aware republicans of the Second Empire (P, p. 217).

Kracauer's argument in favor of the boulevardiers having played a critical role as early as the July Monarchy points to the fact that they forged links with the French tradition of irony. "For all these homeless persons," Kracauer metaphorically remarks about the culturally rootless and highly mixed population of the boulevard, "the reservation of the boulevards became a home" in the special sense that has been described in connection with Offenbach's time as a young man. He continues:

And where else would this free, highly agile esprit have flourished other than in the rarefied air blowing here. In the same way as the money on which it was dependent, it had a tendency toward the destruction of myths, the disenchantment [*Entzauberung*] of the forces of the dark. Since the esprit of the boulevard was ironical about many traditional powers, it did not demonstrate its lack of tradition but was in fact continuing a still live tradition in France. For the irony by means of which it pierced the establishment had always been the weapon of the French spirit. (P, p. 84)

Especially in connection with the Second Empire, Kracauer argues that courtesans, men about town, and journalists play an overlooked yet subversive role within the established order of society. The courtesans make inroads into the capitalists' fortunes, the men about town mock the morals of the bourgeoisie, and the journalists—some of them, at any rate—have tentative republican sympathies, insisting on the precedence of social reality over Napoleon III's "theatrical" tendencies and "illusions of the empire" (P, p. 226).

THE OPERETTA: THE CRITIQUE OF DEPENDENCY

The same dual nature—deep dependency and discreet criticism of the establishment—also applies to the operetta. On the one hand, the operetta culture is in accord with Napoleon III's principle of joy and glitter. Kracauer formulates it in this way: "joy was to intoxicate, glitter to dazzle" (P, p. 130). On the other hand, the operetta—both musically and semantically—involves an irony, mockery, and absurdity that does not exactly help to shore up the empire. In this connection, the operetta continues an ironic tradition: "Power" becomes "children's pranks" and "life at court a harlequinade" (P, p. 156). The music and action of the operetta "repeatedly took those in power and great opera ad absurdum. Offenbach removed their enchantment [*entzauberte sie*] even before their natural demise came about, and the wonderful thing was that the disenchantment he brought about via the jollity in which he dipped them seems itself to be like magic [*Zauberei*]" (P, pp. 161–162). The enchantment is lifted by means of a new form of spellbinding, Kracauer argues. He assumes the existence of a state of tension as regards both the established musical and political institutions—both the opera and the empire. The operetta constitutes an "attack on the pompous"—for example, in Meyerbeer's operas (P, p. 159). Within the field of meaning it was "as if the veil was lifted long enough to grant one a look at a better order of things before falling once more" (P, p. 157).

The utopian aspect of the operetta is repeatedly stressed by Kracauer. En route, he admittedly expresses a number of reservations regarding the ability of these dream images to take shape and become part of a historical practice. When Kracauer, in developing the ability of the operetta to allude to a *Heimat* (home), states that *Heimat* is "anything but a vacuum" (P, p. 182), this means not that he was going to consider this *Heimat* as positively present but only that it maintains a mediated contact with the forces of what is repressed. These forces can scarcely be converted into a concrete and present project. Thanks to their (from a temporal point of view) incredibly distant—and in fact, atemporal—position (in something that precedes active childhood), they contribute to just as timeless an image of utopia: "So the operetta floats off between a lost and a promised paradise" is how this is summarized (P, p. 207). The utopian images that momentarily become visible cannot, in other words, be precisely fixed and bound:

> This means that the intended kingdom of joy lay neither entirely in the past nor in the future; that it could just as little be fixed in terms of space as of time. It was not for nothing that Offenbach made use of so many folksong-like melodies. Folksongs are like fairy tales in that unlike any product of civilization, they are not limited to any particular space or time but transcend them. . . . Offenbach's joy was assigned to a Nowhere, which it permeated—as light as Ariel. (P, p. 159)

This absence of precision is not directly condemned. On the contrary, Kracauer seems to legitimize and praise Offenbach's treatment of utopian motifs when he comments on the frequent use of folksongs and fairy tales. He himself has tried to make relevant these time-exceeding yet also romantically toned cultural forms in a utopian perspective—as has previously been shown in comments about "Akrobat—schöön" (see chapter 5).

It should be noted that this formless utopia, characterized by a lack of determination and contours, invites a number of conceptions that risk remaining without effect. This increases the risk that the dreamlike elements will be limited to what, using Marcuse's term, one could call a "repressive desublimation" and, in the final instance, will contribute to a stabilization of the Second Empire. This danger is real, since a real strategy of oblivion can actually be documented in Offenbach's case. While Kracauer, throughout his analysis of Offenbach's life and music, emphasizes the importance of personal and musical memory, there are nevertheless formulations by Offenbach himself that point in the opposite direction. Implicitly referring to Baudelaire's conception of modernity as being bound up with the fleeting and transitory, Kracauer can draw attention to a quotation from Offenbach in which his intention to create music on a par with the visual media (here, the so-called magic lantern) is clearly stated:

> No matter how much he tended to include the fleeting and the transitory, the sentences . . . that he [Offenbach] wrote down betray something else: "The work which comes into being allows one to forget the one which died: one does not compare the two, place them side by side, seek any analogy between them: it is a question of a series of images that—as in a magic lantern—float off, and when they have drifted past, the most unqualified success does not weigh any more than the most abject failure." (P, p. 165)

Offenbach, if one is to believe these considerations, is seeking to create music that allows the painful to be smoothly and unresistingly consigned to oblivion. Conversely, his declared aim is to conjure up a state where real differences do not leave any imprint in the sphere of the emotions. In short, subjective *reflection* is to be eliminated.

A composer's intentions regarding the effects of a particular type of music naturally do not guarantee that they will actually be realized in performance. In the rest of his Offenbach book Kracauer tries precisely to show how the uncritical and unproblematic reputation of the operetta matches only one side of its real function during the Second Empire. The operetta was popular in the circles that supported the cause of Napoleon III. But it also had a critical side that, according to Kracauer, was decisive. So it is his fundamental hypothesis that the operetta on the one hand mirrors the empire but on the other contributes to this political form's crisis and downfall: "They [the big operettas] held up a mirror to the Second Empire and at the same time helped to shatter it" (P, p. 184).

In its apparent identity with the structures and forms of consciousness of the existing society, the operetta possesses in a strange way the ability to withdraw its support from this society. In Kracauer's interpretation the operetta is quite reminiscent of the object that, according to Jean Baudrillard's thoughts in *Les stratégies fatales*,[15] on the one hand is subordinate to the subject's urge to dominate and, on the other hand, evades control, in order to display instead the radical impotence of the subject. What appears to be most innocuous turns out to be a fundamental threat to complete dominance. This subtly negative form of criticism is far removed from the paradigms of traditional political radicalism and has only very rarely been credited with having value for analysis or for cultural politics by readers of Kracauer's Offenbach book. Some of its aspects will be mentioned in order to indicate the diverse social critique pointed out by Kracauer.

In his analysis of the historically conditioned cultural form assumed by the operetta, Kracauer is always aware of the fact that its political perspectives are limited. The operetta makes possible the self-criticism of this system, functioning as a hiding place for its bad conscience. But it is unable to suggest how in practice to transgress the empire's culture. This is quite clear in the following passage, in which Kracauer, in a firm distinction between an evasion of and a way out of this period, criticizes intoxication in the operetta for being too little anchored in reality to be able to seriously challenge the political system of the empire: "generally speaking, the operetta does a complete volte-face in its praise of happiness as such. Dissipated life is confirmed and enjoyed in intoxication. Revolution would have been a way out; intoxication is an evasion for those who resist the breakthrough of reality" (P, p. 181).

But intoxication itself is able to express criticism in various ways. When it takes the form of a "hell-bound gallop," the Dionysian characteristics of the empire's culture are marked in a way that allows its imminent "self-destruction" (P, p. 182) to be sensed on the horizon. The unreality of the operetta seems alternately a threat and a dream. At one moment the prospect is darkened and distorted: "It [the operetta] announced a thunderstorm. . . . A whirring, sanctimonious light that dissolved the contours of things made their manifestations ambiguous and favored the appearance of daytime apparitions" (P, p. 255). At the next moment the operetta spreads out a dreamy sleep that is reminiscent of the social reality of the empire. Merely the slightest distance from the spectacle would promote an awareness of this similarity and disrupt the legitimacy of the operetta-reality: "Everything was present, everything. This did not prevent most people . . . from believing that they had been carried off into a dream kingdom via the operetta. If they had been awake, they would have recognized the improbable reality of their existence in [the operetta] *Parisian Life*" (P, p. 262).

There are strong metaphorical touches in Kracauer's mention of *intoxication, dream,* and *awakening.* Intoxication and dream are parallel concepts in the Offenbach book that serve to denote a temporary distance from a binding and unavoidable reality. Awakening, on the other hand, must be seen as a transitional position between a dream and a state of being awake. In all its momentary limitation, the movement toward wakening contains unpredictable and potentially innovative forces. It enables an active link to be established between two different qualities that, in this single moment, flow into each other and cannot be separated.

It is a crucial characteristic of Kracauer that the dream culture of the empire is not conceived of as simply the opposite of sociomaterial reality, which at some point or other is assumed to break through. Not a dichotomy but a dialectic frames this connection. Boulevard, operetta, and the environment associated with them form a *derived reality* during this limited period. It probably has sociocultural and ideological, that is, immaterial functions, but it cannot avoid becoming material, thereby lending this dream-reality a relatively high degree of inertia. The city's physical existence is, however, the most solid framework around this "dream kingdom," as it gains its social illustration in the boulevard and achieves valid paradigmatic expression in the scenic reality of the operetta.

The specific constellation of space, society, and music is linked to a limited historical culture, toward whose decline the operetta and the boulevard itself indirectly contribute. The operetta-reality of the boulevard environment does not survive as long as physical space does. The operetta itself is extremely sensitive to market fluctuations: first, because it is dependent on a paying public; second, because its ability to articulate societal experience, according to Kracauer, is limited to the extremely short and historically specific period between the two world expositions in Paris, in 1855 and 1867. During the empire's crisis, the socially distorted reality dissolves, dragging the operetta's power to fascinate with it in its loss of legitimacy:

> The more the unreality of the regime was revealed, the more the reality of the Offenbachiade became apparent. But so much the more superfluous did it also become as a political instrument. For with the receding of the dictatorship and the upsurge of the opposition of the left, societal forces once again began to join in the play—the forces that the Offenbachiade had represented until then. (P, p. 280)

The reality that is repressed in the political consciousness of Paris at that time cannot be kept at a distance forever. It returns, for example, in connection with the Italian war (P, p. 195), which, on the home front, obliges Napoleon to yield to a liberalism that in the longer term will undermine the authoritarian structure of the empire. That this liberalism initially results in a greater escape into—in Kracauer's eyes—intoxicating cultural phenomena such as the operetta (P, p. 197) is just another element of the complex dialectic between society and the stage.

The connection of the Offenbachiade to the Parisian culture of the Second Empire takes at least three forms. After first appearing in the same dreamlike light as the empire itself, the operetta passes through a short transitional period as a precise, secular expression of this particular ideological and social order. In the third phase its music and drama lose their original raison d'être, turning into an anachronistic institution. If Kracauer's analysis of the function of the operetta in the Second Empire is

well-founded, subsequent developments have inflicted on the operetta a radical loss of its original ability to articulate experience. In the mobile hierarchy of musical genres of the twentieth century the operetta fit into the slot of more easily accessible, simply entertaining, yet still "classical" music. From having once been also dreamlike and critical it has in recent times mainly been reduced to a relaxing, unproblematic form of musical drama that will not be analyzed more closely here.

City and Biography—Synchrony and Diachrony in Kracauer's Narration

The previous three sections have attempted to illustrate the complexity of *Jacques Offenbach und das Paris seiner Zeit.* This was done by shedding light on three different theoretical levels and figures that are central to this product of Kracauer's Paris exile in the mid-1930s.

Kracauer's "sociobiography" provides no genuine *theoretical* mediation between (1) the individual, (2) the social, and (3) the sociocritical fields, which in the analysis are illustrated by (1) the nature of Offenbach's musical inspiration, (2) the central status of the boulevard environment in Kracauer's analysis, and (3) the hypothesis concerning the operetta's simultaneously affirmative and sociocritical functions. The analytical motifs and theoretical figures are ingeniously presented in a progressive narrative that is—at first reading—smooth, even frictionless.

As suggested on the preceding pages, these levels can be reconstituted with the aid of fragments of text taken from the entire book. It is just as important, however, to map the narrative patterns that enable Kracauer to make his presentation of cultural history operate in as many theoretical and thematic fields as it does without making the book more difficult to read—rather the opposite. Such an investigation has relevance for the main issue of this book, since the illustration of the role of urban space in the work of historical presentation is exactly what deserves to be awarded special significance.

In this connection it is hardly a coincidence that the city of Paris is represented in the very title of the sociobiography *Jacques Offenbach und das Paris seiner Zeit.* That Paris figures on an equal footing with and as a counterweight to Offenbach, whose musical life limits the time frame of the presentation, is precisely an expression of the city's central role in the construction of the entire book. No matter how many empirical and theoretical motifs Kracauer might connect in his Offenbach book, practically all of them refer to the French capital.

Paris acquires the status of a point of reference that is simultaneously presupposed and constantly rearticulated, establishing an element of rest and stability in the otherwise varied and lively picture of nineteenth-century French cultural history. Paris becomes the *spatial counterpart* to the *temporally* progressing biographical development. Temporal motifs are not completely absent, but generally speaking the *city* is linked to a synchronic point of view, in which the historical investigation's diachronicity is represented by Offenbach's career and the changing societal structures.

This distinction between synchrony and diachrony, between city and biography, is analytical. A crucial part of Kracauer's efforts consists in his constantly establishing new links between these two aspects. In its concrete form the city is not limited to synchrony, but gains its life and sociohistorical form from its interaction with the temporal pole.

In the Offenbach biography this interaction has assumed a narrative form. But in accord with the urban reality to which it refers, there are many pictorial elements. The nature of the city as a physical and architectural reality is thus revived in the book.

Furthermore, Kracauer has considered the possibility of letting the poles of the Offenbach analysis, city and biography, meet in a feature film. Thanks to his experience as a film critic and film sociologist in the columns of the *Frankfurter Zeitung,* Kracauer was well aware of the new medium's economic importance as well as its ability to form political opinion.[16] The more precise guidelines for such a transformation of the historical work of research into a film production were written down in an as yet unpublished synopsis, completed by Kracauer in his very first years in the United States (see M, pp. 101 ff.). One of his first actions as an immigrant in New York was to investigate, with the help of Max Horkheimer from the Institut für Sozialforschung, the possibilities of realizing this synopsis, prepared together with the photographer Eugen Schufftan. Although the project was not realized (nor has it received comment in previous Kracauer literature), it bears witness to an early-developed sense of the potential value of allowing cultural and in particular urban historical research to find its way to the visually narrative medium of film.[17]

In the Offenbach biography the close and necessarily mutual relationship between space and history finds expression, for example, in the treatment of the boulevard, which was reconstructed above. It is clear from the triangular relationship between boulevard, operetta, and critique that the boulevard solely as physical space, as spatiality in isolation, is scarcely capable of communicating historical experience. Not until the moment it is thought of as a *place,* invested with social, cultural, and historical forces, can the boulevard become the point of departure for a work of historical memory. It is by drawing attention to the specific relations that characterized the boulevard environment at the time of Offenbach that Kracauer hopes to pave the way for an active link between his own age (here, the 1930s) and the forgotten and repressed past: nineteenth-century Paris. By staging it in writing, Kracauer seeks to prepare for the introduction of Reason into the comprehensive network of smaller ornaments—those sociocultural surface forms whose entrance into interpretive relations may allow Reason to be strengthened in a totality that is dominated by Ratio. But the crucial shift

from writing to social awareness is left to the (in principle) unpredictable meeting between present and past.

3. CRITICISM OR HISTORY? — HISTORY AS CRITICISM
Concluding Reservations Concerning Karsten Witte's View
of the Offenbach Biography

It would appear necessary, in conclusion, to insist on the critical perspective of Kracauer's historical presentation, which, on a superficial reading, might seem to be little
more than a historicizing popularization of motifs from *Straßen in Berlin und anderswo.* In his analysis "Siegfried Kracauer im Exil," even the publisher of Kracauer's
Schriften at Suhrkamp Verlag in Frankfurt am Main, Karsten Witte, runs the risk of
contributing to a perception that is just as widespread as it is trivializing—that Kracauer's Offenbach book is basically a piece of hack writing.[18]

Witte's critique of Kracauer is developed in a study that, by his own admission, is
more biographically than critically oriented.[19] His point of view is based on the implicit—and also dubious—assumption that there is an unbridgeable chasm between
criticism and history. For Witte, *Jacques Offenbach und das Paris seiner Zeit* would
thus appear to mark a defeat for the critical perspective.

> The corresponding step was that, in exile, the critic Kracauer became a histo-
> rian—one who in the unfathomable present sought for a foundation in his-
> tory. . . . The critic, who has given up, latches on . . . as a historian. Instead of
> claiming criticism as the realm of the counter-projects, a passage is cleared to
> the [historical] background, whose nature as model can—in its predetermined
> course—relate neither to history nor to the present time, but at most to the path
> that is taken by the venture from the one field [that of history] to the other [that
> of the present time]. Kracauer's intention focused on [the period's status as] pre-
> cursor rather than on its provisionality. The precarious, the incongruous, which
> is not resolved in the methodological transition from the macrofield of history
> to its microfield, fell to the ground.[20]

This tendentious characterization of Kracauer's intellectual project during his exile in
Paris leads to a host of diverse yet all undocumented and highly questionable judgments. Taken as a whole, they deny the real intentions underlying Kracauer's (and
Benjamin's, for that matter) historiographical activity in relation to the Paris of the
nineteenth century.

Kracauer's basic idea, diametrically opposed to Witte's point of view, is precisely
that it is impossible to make any clear distinction between criticism and history. For the

exiled intellectual, historical consciousness is, on the contrary, the most important—if not the only promising—critical possibility in a situation in which traditional political practice is unable to show any positive results as it struggles against Nazism. In the same way as Freud sought via psychoanalysis to articulate repressed but effective experiences in the life of the individual subject, Kracauer makes the above-outlined attempt (via material from the operetta culture of the Parisian boulevard) to elaborate the basic, forgotten elements of the culture of the modern metropolis and the civil and political history that is linked to it.

Kracauer's study of Offenbach has the nature of an experiment and cannot be satisfactorily judged on the basis of its immediate historical effects. Its importance is greater than that alone. Precisely for that reason, it is regrettable that Karsten Witte sees as a weakness in the Offenbach book that it belongs neither to history nor to the present (as these time-markers are traditionally understood). The double, thrilling affiliation to the past as well as the present is both fully conscious and fully intentional in Kracauer, who here localizes his central point in a critical intellectual practice under the conditions he encountered in the Paris of the 1930s. By raising consciousness about the Second Empire's transitoriness and throwing critical light on an apparently harmless urban culture,[21] Kracauer hopes to be able to make historical knowledge an active factor in the present. Witte seems to reject in advance the relevance of this attempt. He does not discuss at all the extent to which Kracauer's topical cultural history within the form of the sociobiography contains elements of value in the 1930s and the postwar years. Instead, he reduces the crucial idea underlying the Offenbach book to a sign of intellectual and political impotence. The experimental work involved in transforming impotence to historical awareness is thus ascribed no major importance by Witte.

As indicated in the previous chapter sections, Kracauer's book on Offenbach and Paris represents a comprehensive, complex narrative work with a historical *staging of ornaments* from the cultural history of the nineteenth century. Despite this, the relative lightness of its style of writing and the absence of explicitly theoretical mediations may have led Karsten Witte to his tersely formulated claim that "the precarious, the incongruous, which is not resolved in the methodological transition from the macrofield of history to its microfield, fell to the ground." That is how it can seem to someone with a traditionally academic point of view, one scarcely shared by the broader public who made up Kracauer's intended readership.

Even if the principal task of a preface to a book is to lay the foundation for a positive reception of the subsequent text, it should nonetheless be noted that Daniel Halévy, a writer and grandson of the Offenbach libretto writer Ludovic Halévy, repeatedly underlines in his *préface* to the French edition of Kracauer's book how the treatment of the Paris of the operetta and the boulevard calls attention to both unknown and contradictory traits from a decisive but overlooked period in recent French history. In a long commentary on the Baudelaire quotation with which Kracauer, at the beginning of his book, underlines the mixture of frivolity and seriousness that existed during the Second Empire, Daniel Halévy remarks that "it is this which Mr. Kracauer allows us to feel on every page of his book. He shows us this Paris with its double face and [how] these two faces breathe together" in, respectively, a superficiality and a "deep sense of nothingness."[22] Halévy—unlike Karsten Witte—stresses Kracauer's talent for historical analysis: "Some people will doubtless find this commentary on a Parisian [form of] entertainment from 1855 somewhat complicated. What do they know about that? . . . Mr. Kracauer has such intelligent antennae that he has found all of it in old, yellowed sheets of paper."[23] Unlike the prevailing somber interpretations of the Paris of the Second Empire, the picture produced by Kracauer, according to Daniel Halévy, is more complex but also more vibrant and coherent: "It is the illusion that Mr. Kracauer resolves. The Paris of the Second Empire is not double—it is a living city."[24]

Daniel Halévy should not be elevated to the rank of soothsayer; he is mentioned simply as a witness to the fact that Kracauer's presentation in the 1930s—thanks to his interpretation of a contradictory Paris and a contradictory historical period—appeared to mark a historiographic renewal. It is clear from Halévy comments that there is a need for an in-depth analysis and not for a general, weakly documented rejection of Kracauer's sociobiography. Otherwise, its value in relation to both its own age and present-day historiography will not be able to be satisfactorily assessed.

Kracauer's sociobiography is of vital importance for the analytical viewpoint of the city that underlies the present book. It rounds off and complements a comprehensive attempt to "resubjectivize" the objective culture of the metropolis. Although the individual analyses of ornaments are more muted in the book on Offenbach than in the essays from *Straßen in Berlin und anderswo*, the historically reflective study should be seen as a continuation of his previous work of introducing *Vernunft* into the rationally reduced surface forms. Only this time, Kracauer deals with fields whose relevance is indirect. By concentrating on Paris and not, for example, the German cities of Frankfurt and Berlin, Kracauer becomes a spokesman for the idea that Western modernity possesses certain common characteristics that are most evident in connection with unconscious fields of experience. It emerges from Kracauer's choice of nineteenth-century Paris as a field of analysis that the basic structures are not unfamiliar only in a geographical sense. Paris in his term of exile there is, generally speaking, just as unfamiliar to Kracauer as the cultural history of this city is for the rest of Europe. In the choice of both time and place for his investigation, Kracauer is moving in the borderland between the known and the unknown. He expects decisive results to come from this double quality.

Whether Kracauer's experiment can be considered successful or not, in the present investigation it has the function of linking Simmel's concept of "resubjectivization" to an entire cultural form: modernity in the metropolis. The idea is to set resubjectivization in motion by confronting the form of culture with its culturally, socially, and historically fundamental locations, in this case exemplified by Paris in the nineteenth century. In this work of resubjectivization, the city proves to be the overall framework for a collective historical consciousness that contains both cultural and political aspects.

A further consequence of Kracauer's urban history should be mentioned. Long before it became a widespread and acceptable idea, Kracauer emphasized in his book on Offenbach's Paris that a city and its cultural existence cannot be reduced to a chronological present. Not until its various components—the city's ornaments—become part of an interaction with its historical basis does the reality of the city become seriously *urban* and *topical.* Thus the Offenbach book makes it possible to underline a characteristic of Kracauer's urban analysis that already had a certain validity in both *Ginster* and *Straßen in Berlin und anderswo.* Let me therefore leave it to the following pages to sum up Kracauer's practice in analysis, interpretation, and writing developed in the 1925–1937 period regarding the urban culture of modernity—within the frameworks of historiography, the novel, and the journalistic essay.

Conclusions and Perspectives

A Composite Corpus: Kracauer's Urban Writings in Book Form

The aim of this book has been to reconstruct Siegfried Kracauer's writings on Western European urban culture in the nineteenth and twentieth centuries. The reason for this study's having become so comprehensive is mainly that the source material on which it is based is so heterogeneous. The reader may well have asked him- or herself while reading whether it would be at all possible to show if not an actual inner system (which has never been my intention) then a thematic coherence and dynamics between novel, essay, and historiography.

In two major sections and a shorter third one I have argued that there exist certain general characteristics in both the development and content of Kracauer's urban writings, insofar as he has made these accessible in book form. This means that the analysis does not include any relevant writings, sketches, or notes in Kracauer's well-organized *Nachlaß,* which is to be found in the German Literary Archives in Marbach am Neckar. Kracauer's numerous articles, signed or otherwise, from the daily newspaper *Frankfurter Zeitung* have also had to be left out of consideration unless included in the volumes of essays *Straßen in Berlin und anderswo* and *Das Ornament der Masse,* published in 1964 and 1963, respectively.

These two volumes were compiled by Kracauer himself and thus represent the part of his total activity as a writer that he, at the age of seventy-five, definitely wished to present to the public—in most cases for a second time. When (re-)issued in book form, the texts were given a general value that had not been immediately guaranteed them in their original state of newspaper essay or serialized novel (*Ginster*). Among the texts analyzed, neither the investigation of wrought-iron ornaments in Berlin nor the sociobiography *Jacques Offenbach und das Paris seiner Zeit* was republished during Kracauer's lifetime. As far as the Offenbach book is concerned, this does not mean in any way that Kracauer rejected the work, which was conceived from the outset to be published in a single volume. For this reason, both titles are deemed suitable for analysis.

In short, the investigation is based on the books on cities undertaken by Kracauer. Its task is thus to arrive at some of the overall traits of the urban writings, in the form in which Kracauer himself left them to posterity. Later, these interpretive hypotheses can be tested against the articles that were not reprinted and the manuscript and note material that Kracauer put in order and left to the archives. It might just be possible that the themes and theoretical focal points emphasized turn out to be part of a whole.

Even just those urban writings by Kracauer that are immediately accessible constitute a rich source of information about the interwar years, which in other fields as well involved considerable and innovative thematization of urban modernity (via the Bauhaus, Le Corbusier, etc.). The social, historical, and analytical relevance of a detailed reading scarcely needs any special form of justification.

Characteristics of Kracauer's Urban Essays

The writings analyzed are mainly from a time that is five or six decades removed from 1989, the centenary of Siegfried Kracauer's birth. In the period in between, the urban culture of modernity has not decreased in importance—rather the contrary. The problems of an individual as well as of a social and historical nature dealt with in Kracauer's writings are also central today. Furthermore, the writings testify in part to an interwar urban consciousness among German intellectual critics and in part to an interest and depth in urban interpretation that the present age would find hard to match. It is largely the conception that Kracauer's urban commentaries and interpretations are a challenge to modern academics and journalists that has animated the analysis of precisely these writings.

Kracauer represents a special kind of intellectual that has never been all that common. Within today's urban sphere of experience his type would appear to be almost entirely absent. What is distinctive about Kracauer is that his view of the city and of the culture of modernity as a whole has a wide and solid intellectual basis. A number of philosophical figures underlie his published journalistic articles, whose literary form and use of socioanalytical modes of thought also mark them off from traditional journalism dealing with events and trends.

At the same time, his sociophilosophical *reflection* is far more interdisciplinary than is the case in past and present university intellectuals. Most of all, these writings are far removed from what, under the name "urban planning" (urbanism), corresponds to an administrative view of the city and its ways of functioning. At no point does Kracauer express his opinion directly on (i.e., in an attempt to master) the technical and legal reality of the three-dimensional city. So his thoughts can be made use of only indirectly by present-day neighborhood groups and grassroots movements that are often indebted to a traditional representation of the city's political and administrative reality.

Kracauer's writings on the city and its culture thus differ in both his age and ours from those in the university tradition as well as the discourses of journalists and political administrators. This distance can be seen as a weakness, since the writings will often appear irrelevant to those narrowly defined discourses and the conceptions of reality that belong to them. Conversely, Kracauer's interest and reflective strength lie precisely in the fact that he goes beyond the specialized points of view and observes, comments on, and interprets the city from a disinterested standpoint. His urban writings, in their immediate unusableness, thereby become relevant—first as a critique of the institutionalized discourses on what can generally be called "the urban," and second as a source of inspiration for a humanistic urban analytics.

Experiments with Written Resubjectivization

Kracauer's disinterested point of view on the social and cultural life of the city does not move his writings outside the urban sphere of experience. On the contrary, one point of departure for the present investigation is that Kracauer's fifteen-year-long engagement as an analyst in and around modern urban culture constitutes an experimental urban practice. He attempts to allow his written thoughts concerning the city's subjectivity to function as elements in the concrete social and cultural process. Kracauer writes about the very field that he is attempting to put into motion by means of his essays and books. Unlike the secular view of the city that thrives, for example, in administrative and financial matters, he does not have any clearly defined worldly aim for his activity. He, in contrast, contributes with his essays to the process of urban *reflection* in a general perspective that can be understood with reference to Georg Simmel's essays of cultural criticism on the "mental life" of cities and on the tragic structure of culture, respectively.

Judging by the part of Kracauer's Simmel monograph published to date, he does not explicitly orient his project of urban analysis by distinguishing himself from Simmel. Nor does he make use of Simmel's concepts when he on occasion uses programmatic formulations with a more general aim. Nevertheless, based on the first chapter of Kracauer's book on Simmel it is possible to sum up his transformation of urban everyday experience into literary and sociophilosophical texts by using tools from Simmel's critique of culture. Like Simmel, Kracauer attempts to revive the subjective factor to its former dominant position. But whereas Simmel saw the work of "resubjectivizing" the so-called objective spirit as a predominantly individual project, Kracauer gives it—even in its individual aspects—a *social perspective.*

Kracauer's contribution to resubjectivization works consciously at a number of levels. While the act of writing must of necessity assume an individual form, since it is carried out with the individual (S. Kracauer) at the center, Kracauer nevertheless always seems aware of the fact that the written word, because it is published in the form of a newspaper, magazine, or book, is part of a collective process of reception that is vital for deciding whether what has been individually observed can be put into general practice.

Kracauer's preoccupation with urban problems can be understood as variations on resubjectivization in both the writing and the receiving phases. To qualify this statement, one could say that resubjectivization takes shape in a constantly forward-moving critique of the idea of an independent and isolated individual (i.e., autonomous) subjectivity. This movement can be detected in the tripartite structure of this book, where each section corresponds to a particular stage, as a precise echo of the attempt at resubjectivization.

Part I can be summarized as the individual's disintegration and expansion of himself in the direction of the city's collective space. The novel *Ginster* provides insight into how Ginster's/Kracauer's dissatisfaction with salaried work as an architect is first compensated for in an ornamental approach to architecture. Later, the fragmentary and temporary observation is overcome when urban space is made an object, indeed the medium, of intensive exploration. When the narrator takes a city walk through Marseilles—simultaneously alive and yet marked by history—this reflective movement can develop fully, since it is detached from everyday obligations. The idea of moving beyond architectural work stands as an insistent utopia.

Kracauer's newspaper essays from *Frankfurter Zeitung*, which are analyzed in part II, have been written from just such a viewpoint beyond salaried work as an architect. They go a step further in the disintegration of individual subjectivity, since the obligation-free observation of the city has been replaced by the application of a social perspective. The fragmentary city is admittedly still described from the point of view of a single individual, frequently marked by the presence of a commenting "I." But the city now only really comes alive as a sociality.

After first exploring the two poles of urban reality, which correspond to a subjective world and a rational, systemic world, respectively, Kracauer becomes able to determine the conditions of a utopia in modern urbanity. As he recognizes social reality as being decisive, the opportunities for a socioaesthetic conception of change prove at the same time to be scant.

The concluding, relatively short part III provides the first commentary on Kracauer's book on Offenbach and Paris. It emphasizes how social subjectivity, which part I sought to confront with an individual's (Ginster's) narration and part II with elements of urban sociality, addresses history in this final piece of urban writing by Kracauer. Individual subjectivity is still doubly present, partly via the author (Kracauer) and partly via Offenbach, who crystallizes nineteenth-century Parisian culture. But the field where Kracauer cherishes a hope for progress in the resubjectivization of urban culture is increasingly less closely linked to the immediate reality of the individual or collectivity. The sphere of experience consulted in order to strengthen the reappropriation by subjective forces of the city in general and of the historical situation in particular finds itself at an increasing temporal (and therefore in a certain sense also spatial) distance from the individual, who, for Simmel, was at the center of the theoretical construction.

Viewing the development from part I to part III as a whole, it is possible to confirm a steady shift in the thematic figures and practical themes with which Kracauer seeks to strengthen the position of the subjective mind. In the movement from the individual awareness of a salaried worker to Parisian history there is on the one hand an expansion of the city's presence in the text, its role in the presentation and in its possible reception by the readers. Conversely, on the other hand, a constriction takes place as the precision of the suggested resubjectivization shrinks. Proposals for a solution are limited but precisely formulated in *Ginster.* In *Straßen in Berlin und anderswo* they are more general but still linked to issues. In *Jacques Offenbach und das Paris seiner Zeit* they assume rather imprecise concrete forms—despite their greater functional importance in the construction and perspective of the book.

Behind this paradoxical development in themes of resubjectivization, whose precision decreases while their tasks and radicalism grow, there lie several real problems in the actual project. These problems were already potentially present when Kracauer expressed reservations about Simmel's polarization of the individual and society. Kracauer seems in his work to have noted the consequence of the fact that the individual can scarcely maintain any autonomy vis-à-vis the surrounding society, instead becoming to an increasing extent a reflection of developmental tendencies at a social and historical level.

This would suggest certain serious limits for resubjectivization, whether it is defined individually or collectively. The basis of resubjectivization can under no circumstances be located in a whole individual or in a coherent social subject. Moreover, the crisis of the individual subject returns in the increasing fragmentation of the social level (which indicates the reality that the analyst must address in order to be on a par with contemporary society). Even if a collective subjectivity should establish agreement at some point about initiatives to undertake resubjectivization, Simmel has already pointed out that objective culture is materially and socially so inert that it would be able to thwart even the best subjective intentions.

As Kracauer's oeuvre as an urban writer develops, it displays an increasing awareness of the limits of concrete resubjectivization. Without going so far as to claim that resubjectivization is impossible (doing so might lead to a rejection of Kracauer's entire work as an urban essayist), it is possible to say that the attempts at resubjectivization possess the interesting theoretical quality that as they pursue and fulfill certain of their goals, they also draw attention to a number of factors counteracting them.

But the dominance, stamina, and cunning of the "objective mind" do not necessarily deprive the subjective factor of any importance. They simply mean that the relations are subtle and that the dialectical relationship between subject and object is a source of permanent dynamism. It would therefore be erroneous to use certain limits as the reason for flatly rejecting the perspective of resubjectivization and its value for urban analytics. On this view, Kracauer's analyses do not become worthless but, on the contrary, acquire the greatest significance, since they reveal problems in the way in which the humanities and the social sciences conceive the city as well as problems in the surrounding philosophical conceptual network.

The difficulties facing the subjective mind under modern urban conditions are the best possible justification for interpretive work to emphasize this aspect of urban culture as much as possible. Traditionally, the objective mind has attracted the greatest interest and has seen its growing power supported in the name of necessity and progress. A number of the problems of modern urbanity must therefore be viewed as caused by the fact that the subjective factor has been insufficiently able to find expression for its heterogeneous but far from illegitimate needs. Without necessarily taking a particularly radical form, experiments in resubjectivization are indispensable for the future development of urban culture.

Kracauer's Echo in French Urban Interpretation

Siegfried Kracauer's commentaries and interpretations follow two principles. On the one hand, he seeks to maintain a connection with general urban experience by using identifiable sections of urban reality as his point of departure. On the other hand, he counters the commentaries' relative silence or predictability by concentrating on the city's distinctive, heterogeneous elements. From this base stem several essays whose theoretical and empirical complexity have no rivals in the urban discourses of later decades.

Even in the abundantly rich French tradition of urban philosophy the positions are both more specialized and more acute than in Kracauer. Two distinguished, original thinkers from the present-day French debate stick to a relatively stable subject-object constellation. The urban philosopher Anne Cauquelin, who has been mentioned several times in the notes, has made great efforts to draw attention to the fact that the "doxa" (general and amorphous opinion), which can be included only with difficulty in architects' and urban planners' grounds for making decisions, is of decisive importance in determining whether physical space gains existence as a "place" permeated by subjectivity. Since she therefore stresses the *linguistic* staging of urban space, there is

naturally a tendency for the *visual* aspect—which in Kracauer survives in the form of detailed descriptions of fragments—to dissolve in the magnetic field of the doxa.[1]

The same undermining of the primitive existence of physical space occurs in the essays of the architect and cultural theorist Paul Virilio.[2] With Anne Cauquelin he shares an interest in the temporal aspects that modify the solidity of the space that the architect has traditionally considered to be his sphere of work. But in concentrating, on the one hand, on the acceleration of speed of transportation and the resulting relativization of the city's physical space and, on the other hand, on the de-spatializing that takes place as tele-technology advances, Paul Virilio sees space from the technical side, that is, from the angle of the "objective mind." The subjective aspect is silenced, being in reality reduced to a reflection of its opposite.

The theoretical positions of both Cauquelin and Virilio are found in an embryonic form in Kracauer's much earlier writings. His analyses of the boulevard environment point forward, for example, to Anne Cauquelin's insistence on the importance of the doxa for the creation of a place. And in his comments on the *Mittelgebirge* (medium-size mountains) around Frankfurt,[3] which Sunday car excursions make (relatively) smaller, Kracauer has formulated in the space of a few lines the idea that is the central tenet of Paul Virilio's urban theory. On the other hand, such locally formulated perceptions in Kracauer tend to disappear in his essayistic, nonacademic discourse. By virtue of a higher degree of theorizing and their links to a university research environment, both Cauquelin and Virilio have more influence on contemporary architects and urban planners than Kracauer did in the 1920s and 1930s.[4]

The Many Registers of Ornament Experience

Up to now, the secondary literature has shown only a limited interest in Kracauer's experiments with the role of the intellectual and in his written attempts to unfold the Simmel-like resubjectivization of urban culture in a social perspective. His practice of urban essay writing has remained relatively ignored. In this book's three analytical sections, whose comments and interpretations are here being considered in conclusion, an attempt has been made to redress the balance a bit. For this purpose, I have made repeated recourse to a particular theoretic problematics to make the presentation coherent. For without being explicitly present on every single page or even in each section, the problematics of the ornament underlies all three sections. Occasionally, the ornament surfaces in the text as a decisive conceptual tool.

It is both directly and indirectly evident from the presentation that the term "ornament" within Kracauer's urban writings is the opposite of an operational concept. Even less than in the present work is a definition of the ornament provided by Kracauer in the context of his urban analyses. From the outset (in the analysis of *Ginster*) it has been obvious that the ornament could not be reduced to what was most frequently a two-dimensional decoration. Yet the ornament was at the same time not devoid of some connection to this visual and surface-bound register. In the course of the three sections of the book, the ornament as a concept has gradually proved to embrace a unifying optics whose task is to articulate visual and social as well as mental and literary aspects of the universe of the city and of urban essay writing.

If one looks back through the individual parts and chapters of the analysis, the term "ornament" can be seen to have been used in connection with a wide range of experiential fields that do not necessarily have much to do with each other. The schoolboy's scrawls in the margin of his notebook, the occasional joy of the adult architect in intense but marginal visual aspects of his work, and the student's abstracting gaze at the creations of art history are all examples of ornaments or ornamental experiences within the circumference of this concept's traditional meaning. The same applies to the patterns formed by the Tiller Girls for the eyes of a mass audience on the stages of German stadiums in the years after the First World War, or to Kracauer's observation, when he mentions the swift changes occurring to the street of the Berlin metropolis, that the ornaments of the houses are removed, leaving behind street space even more devoid of memory.

The distance from the generally accepted meaning begins to become apparent, however, when the ornament is exemplified by considerable urban social spaces, by structures in individual memory, or by Kracauer's typical mode of writing where the interpretation is linked to fragments of reality and the entire text is constructed as if such smaller units were juxtaposed. Many spheres of experience of changing generality are linked to the category of ornament as part of his theoretical considerations. The feeling of polysemy in connection with Kracauer's concept of the ornament is thus well-founded.

The theoretical basis for the ornament's problematics can be divided into a number of levels. Its first level, which is most obviously used in *Ginster*, lies in relative proximity to the ornament, as understood in art history. For Kracauer this surface decoration, most frequently two-dimensional, involves a transgression of the strict division between art craft and *les beaux arts*. The ornament, which is seldom highly valued in art criticism, is emphasized by Ginster as the unconscious common trait running through art history's genres and periods. This link between the ornament and the unconscious already raises the aspect of the problematics that also recognizes unpredictable figures and networks of lines as worthy members of the extended family of ornaments.[5]

Ernst Bloch and the "Searching Form" of the Ornament

In his aesthetic and philosophical interest in the ornamental, Siegfried Kracauer can have found support in an early work by Ernst Bloch, *Geist der Utopie* (*The Spirit of*

Utopia, 1918).[6] Here Bloch deals among other things with the artistic activity of non-geniuses, whose results are exemplified not by embroideries (as discussed in note 5 above on silk and self-memory) but by wallpapers and carpets. In this styleless yet expressive formation of images Bloch glimpses a position beyond art and art craft. He emphasizes "the carpet, the allegory-like, genuine, noncorrupted but searching form" (U, p. 24). In line with Kracauer, Bloch also stresses the aspect of process in the ornament. The ornament is lighter than a proper "construction," expressing what Bloch calls "transcendental joy" (U, p. 34). The ornament has the ability to dissolve matter and yet to let the "deepest, naturally only the deepest object" rule (U, p. 34).

Although Bloch's deliberations (from before 1918) are much more obviously theological in nature than Kracauer's cultural critique from the interwar years, there is—all things being equal—an affinity between the functions ascribed to the ornament by both writers. In Bloch, too, the analysis of the ornament is a possible way of gaining a deeper insight into "Man": "This searching for expression explains precisely the exuberant, violent [*ergewaltigende*] art of the ornament as the method best suited to arrive at Man, that a priori given object of all art history," he writes in *Geist der Utopie* (U, p. 34), a place that could be the aesthetic and theological basis for Kracauer's socioscientific and historico-philosophical deliberations in "Das Ornament der Masse," his program of cultural criticism from 1927.[7]

However, Kracauer can hardly be accused of plagiarizing Bloch's hypothesis that the ornament assumes a third position beyond art and art craft, since he had already outlined this problematics with intuitive clarity in his notes from a lecture given by Simmel in 1907 (see chapter 1). Furthermore, in the period before the publication of *Geist der Utopie,* he had completed his study of ornamental wrought-iron art in Berlin.

The Ornaments of the City and of the Mass—Reason contra Ratio

Apart from these pre-1918 writings by Kracauer, the relation between ornament and folk art is relatively unimportant. The expansion of the concept of the ornament into a central category of cultural criticism is based instead on the affinity between everyday life and the ornament. The decisive social and historico-theoretical illustration of the ornament's problematics is found in the essay "Das Ornament der Masse," which was dealt with in depth in chapter 5.

Kracauer's basic assumption is that an analysis of the surface phenomena of society—that is, of its ornaments—can give cognition access to what is essential in the past and present. In the course of his article, Kracauer shows how these ornaments in real history can be linked to two qualitatively different forms of reason. While *Ratio,* the dominant form in the era of capitalist societies, involves a simplification of matter, *Rea-*

son (with a capital R) corresponds conversely to a true cognition of and regard for the societal and natural conditions that Kracauer sums up as "Man."

As a consequence of this opposition, the analyst of culture and society must support utopian Reason, though the question is how. In this connection it was my hypothesis that the analysis of urban ornaments (whose link to Reason seemed less weakened than that in other areas of the cultural industry proper) assumes a privileged position in intellectual practice, as outlined and pursued by Kracauer.

Kracauer's theoretical treatment of the ornament's problematics is restricted to his essay "Das Ornament der Masse" and, viewed quantitatively, is not particularly elaborate. But the condensed formulations and complex structures of the essay provide a basis for reading Kracauer's urban writings as so many attempts—using urban culture as his material for analysis—to fulfill his ambitious program. Not only the essays from the *Frankfurter Zeitung* but also *Ginster* and *Jacques Offenbach und das Paris seiner Zeit* can be understood as experiments in the direction indicated.

Within the three different genres that have been examined (the autobiographical novel, the journalistic essay, and historiography) the ornament serves as dynamic material for interpretations that aim at strengthening Reason. With support from the many levels of subjective experience, Kracauer seeks in his interpretive work to go beyond the usual disciplines, whose points of view force them to so rationalizing an organization of the object that the link to "Reason" and "Man" becomes seriously weakened.

The Concept of the Ornament in Walter Benjamin's Early Deliberations on Aura

The hypothesis that the ornament is a boundary-breaking form of experience, which plays a central role in the urban writings of Siegfried Kracauer, coincides with certain conclusions I have arrived at in the analysis of another but not completely independent textual corpus from the same period.

It was briefly mentioned above that Kracauer, unlike Ernst Bloch in his treatment of the ornament in *Geist der Utopie*, let the category of the ornament move beyond the field of art history and theology and enter the spheres of the social sciences and history. Kracauer's extension of the problematics also gives rise to another boundary-breaking treatment of the ornament's form of experience. This takes place in Walter Benjamin's notes on hashish from the years 1928–1934 (i.e., after the publication of "Das Ornament der Masse" in 1927), in which the ornament appears at places of theoretical importance.

Though the link cannot be positively documented, everything suggests that Kracauer's definitions of the ornament in "Das Ornament der Masse," which are never commented on in Benjamin's numerous letters, may nonetheless have exerted a considerable influence. In Benjamin's notes on personal experiences of intoxication—based on observers' and even his own notes and written down immediately after the sessions—it is possible to observe, far removed from Kracauer's cultural critique, how the pictorial world of the ornament creates a connection between two registers of thought that Benjamin otherwise consistently keeps apart. The world of the ornament comprises both organic and crystalline forms.[8] These prove to correspond to a euphoric and a depressive register of thought. Thus the ornament becomes a possible common denominator for the romantic reflective mode of thought and for baroque allegory—two never-mediated extremes in Benjamin's aesthetic deliberations, to which he dedicated his "small" and "grand" doctoral theses.[9] While the ornament in Kracauer becomes a meeting place for Ratio and Reason, Walter Benjamin, in his dreamlike states of intoxication, seems also to make the ornament and the ornamental the point of intersection for romanticism and the baroque, redemption and melancholy, intoxication and sobriety, dream and everyday life.

It is crucial that Benjamin's own earliest notes on the concept of the aura (later so controversial), an offshoot of this attempt to mediate, let the form-world of the ornament be the very form of the aura's expression. In distinguishing it from an anthroposophical concept, Benjamin stresses the connection of the genuine aura with the ornament. The mobile forms of the ornament show precisely that the aura is linked to all things. Furthermore, it is at root particular, since it changes with the altered positions of things. Benjamin leaves no doubt about the interrelationship between aura and ornament: "Perhaps the special thing about the real aura is this: the ornament, an ornamental circumference within which things lie embedded as in a case. Perhaps nothing conveys such a correct picture of the ornament as the late pictures of van Gogh, where the aura—the paintings could be thus described—is painted along with all the things."[10] The dynamic multiplicity of the ornament allows it, according to Benjamin, to express the aura to which he ascribes an almost ontological status in the protocols on intoxication. Thus an ontic perspective, one might say, is added to the two-dimensional surface-world of the ornament, which is once more confirmed as being anything but an accidental decoration.

The Relevance of the Double Concept of the Ornament

An overall characteristic is shared by Benjamin's, Bloch's, and Kracauer's interwar deliberations on the ornament. In their development of its problematics—with inspiration from theology, psychoanalysis, social philosophy, and the philosophy of history—the ornament is elevated to the status of the abstracted expression of reality. As such, the naked form of the ornament is exposed to both commentary and interpretation. The formally abstract is thereby enriched by a semantic dimension. The two-dimensional abstraction becomes linked to a third, interpretive dimension. This constellation means that the concrete and the abstract, form and meaning meet. It is only this new—admittedly frail—unity that confirms the ornament's special raison d'être and cognitive value.

In Kracauer the ornament has a double quality. It is at one and the same time surface and an abstraction that conveys meaning. This double definition must of necessity be emphasized at a time when the ornament as form and as concept is fast gaining ground in widely differing areas—from design to single academic disciplines.

The return of the ornament has been especially noticeable in so-called *postmodern architecture.* After its long absence, the ornament has reemerged, first within the field of architectural drawing and construction, where it then attracted the interest of those engaged in other art forms as well as cultural analysis. It became obvious during the debates of the 1970s and 1980s that there are both different reasons for and effects of the ornament, as a concept and as a form, being once more linked to designed objects, buildings, and cities. Not all postmodern versions take into account the double quality ascribed to the ornament by Kracauer and his contemporaries.

Central to the postmodern interest of many designers in the ornament is that it is considered to be an answer to a fundamental crisis in Western semantic systems. A growing doubt concerning the criteria of and possibilities for historical progress is generally assumed to lie behind the breakdown of a cohesive zeitgeist. In the recent architectural debates this has been the explanation offered for why the purified, anti-ornamental, and technical avant-garde idiom of modern architecture seems to be losing the foundation of its legitimacy.

As a reaction to this crisis in modern architecture a number of more or less eclectic tendencies became more widespread. Instead of taking unadulterated, technically adequate forms as their point of departure, a number of architects who think of themselves or who are thought of as postmodern have made it a programmatic principle to "quote" from the catalogue of forms of the history of art and architecture. This sometimes leads to the final building looking like a montage of the design solutions and technical solutions of different styles and periods of history. The ornament assumes the vital position of a category unifying all the highly diverse forms of thought and design.

It seems to me that just as Kracauer distinguishes between the rational and reasonable aspects of the ornament, so one can talk of two different attitudes toward the ornament within postmodernist architecture and cultural debate. On the one hand, there is the widely held view that the alleged breakdown of the zeitgeist makes the quotations of ornament a simulation of meaning. It is no more possible for there to be a genuine reference from various architectural symbols and forms to reality than for a concept of the beautiful to guide the design work of the architect. As a consequence, architecture is elevated above both moral and aesthetic guidelines. In certain architects the design work assumes a frivolous nature and the ornament is easily reduced to its decorative aspect.

This decorative aspect is, on the other hand, very much toned down when the ornament is viewed in a different way. The second position maintains the possibility of a (mobile) connection between the ornamental forms and a semantic dimension, though without using a traditional theory of symbols that would link one image to a particular message and thereby allow the *forms* to correspond to meanings handed down by tradition. On the contrary, a more subtle possibility is maintained of ornaments being able to be an active part of a subjective reflective process. Even though seeing, for example, an ornament cannot necessarily be converted into discursively formulable thinking, certain trends and theorists (including the French philosopher Jean-François Lyotard) imply that visually reflective work with elements of a fragmented space can promote "memory work" of a more general nature.

It is thus possible to find in the Western architecture of the 1970s and 1980s a number of examples of a disassociation from the engineering subspecies of modern architecture (characterized by its neutral and homogeneous spaces) that do not confine themselves to cultivating "decorative quotations." They go further in an attempt to strengthen the link between *architecture, cultural tradition,* and *city.* Their designers seek to inscribe the building as a by no means inconsequential "ornament" into the urban, cultural, and social space around it. The architectural theorist Charles Jencks, who promoted the concept of the postmodern to the field of architecture, emphasizes in his book *The Language of Post-Modern Architecture* the so-called Piazza d'Italia in New Orleans. In this piece of symbol architecture, the architect Charles Moore has attempted to create a link between the architectural signs used (elements of a map of Italy, etc.) and the Italian origins of the population in this particular district of the city.[11]

Another example that might be mentioned of this work engaged with the relation between the ornament and urban cultural memory is the Institut du Monde Arabe (Institute of the Arabic World) in Paris, designed by the French architect Jean Nouvel and completed in 1987. Within the framework of a clear, functional composition, Nouvel has carried out a valuable reflection on the meeting between the Arabic ornamental tradition and the Western understanding of form. The window modules in the south facade of the building, for example, are divided into a number of fields, each of which functions as the diaphragm of a camera. Depending on the light's intensity, the diaphragms are more or less open, forming a rich ornamental texture. Though these windows, the other sophisticated techniques of the building, and its "hard" materials (aluminum, glass, and steel) allow little room for the history of use to make its mark, the result is nonetheless a building that overwhelms the viewer with its visual and

thought-provoking force. The building blends with its quartier in the same brilliant and straightforward way that it challenges its surroundings. Previously, the district was typified by architecturally neutral areas whose only distinctive feature was their traffic density. Slowly but surely, the precinct has become a place that stimulates consciousness.

No attempt will be made to put labels or schools on these two different ways of considering and using the ornament in architecture and culture. They hardly exist anywhere in a pure, self-aware form, although the view of the first version of the ornament given above seems to me to be symptomatic of the many debates concerning the postmodern. The French social philosopher Jean Baudrillard would scarcely recognize his own ideas in this ideology-laden, "conscienceless" position. Nevertheless, it often has sought theoretical legitimacy by referring to Baudrillard's hypothesis that the present cultural period belongs to "the order of simulation."[12] Just as Baudrillard has practically never used the word "postmodern" and at no point has spoken in favor or against any architectural trend, so Lyotard has only marginally dealt with "postmodern architecture."[13] And yet, the rediscovery of the city by postmodern architecture as a contextual and public space, as well as of the central function of memory work in urban culture, emerges with particular force when it is seen in the light of Lyotard's insistence on the necessity of memory work (or "anamnesis").

Perspectives for Interdisciplinary Analysis of the City

There has been an increasing interest in urban memory in recent years among historians and sociologists.[14] But so far it has not resulted in theoretical deliberations that can supply a real *interdisciplinary* framework for exploring modern urban culture. The concept of the ornament, for example, has moved only to a limited extent from the world of the architectural idiom to the areas of the city, social science, and historiography.

The desire for such a framework is what underlies the present study of Siegfried Kracauer's urban essays. An attempt has been made to show how these heterogeneous texts, taken together, can be seen as a three-pronged attempt to resubjectivize the objective culture of the metropolis. This range of experiments explores the various facets of the ornament as possibly creating a conceptual intersection in the analytical work. The concept of the ornament is developed in different ways in the three genres examined, and it has various levels within each of them. Moreover, it cannot be assigned to any single discipline. Only as an exception, in Kracauer's analysis of wrought-iron work in Berlin, does the ornament seem to belong to an established tradition—that of art history. Even there it seems to occupy a border area of a single discipline. The experiential organization of the ornament goes beyond traditional disciplinary boundaries, but the ornament does not display a unified interdisciplinary structure for framing knowledge. Kracauer's position outside the academia of his time freed him from academic constraints.

Nor in Kracauer can one find a general theoretical, interdisciplinary framework for urban research. Despite the programmatic features of his discussion of the ornament, it was never Kracauer's intention to develop a theory and method of urban analysis in the strict sense of the term. The individual writer following the perspectives of "Das Ornament der Masse" is given a considerable degree of freedom in his work on creating a link between "Reason" and the ornaments of the metropolis. Nonetheless, the ornament is an important tool in the memory work of modern urbanity, which once more provides the overall guidelines for a humanistic urban analysis.

At various points, Kracauer can thus be said to have anticipated the discussion of the postmodern. By placing the ornament at the center of his program of cultural criticism he suggested that the one-sided renunciation of the ornamental by modern architecture was neither theoretically nor practically tenable. Kracauer feared that the ornament would then return in a dislocated, unmediated form. As early as 1927, he recognized the theoretical consequence of the fact that the attempt to abandon the pictorial, aesthetic, mental, and societal presence of the ornament would sooner or later prove to be illusory. In his essay "Das Ornament der Masse" he considers what follows culturally and politically as the superficial form of the ornament proves impossible to repress. The ornament's abstraction, based on objects and subjectivity, sets up links—whether one desires them or not—with both Ratio and Reason. This, still according to Kracauer, obliges the intellectual to value the ornament from the perspective of "Reason," "Man," and critical experience.

If Kracauer's defense of the ornament of "Reason" had been better known to a broader cultural and intellectual public, the most simplistic, frivolous-decorative use of the ornament in architecture, and the cultural debate over such use, could perhaps have been reduced. For Kracauer's critique of modern architecture's repression of the ornament contains a warning against allowing the ornament to return in an antimodernist form, dominated by narrow Ratio. This warning had little effect in the 1930s or in the 1980s. Recent years have shown that the ornament is being exploited by what Adorno and Horkheimer refer to as the "culture industry." Here, the ornament loses its experience-organizing force and degenerates into kitsch.

Kracauer's possible intervention in the confrontation of the 1980s between rationalist modernism and the "easygoing" version of postmodernism takes place in the form of a dialectical attempt at mediation. The recommendation to create a link between Reason and ornament, which is the practical and analytical conclusion of his

attempt at mediation, ascribes to the experiential sphere of the city a central role to play, thereby strengthening reasons for developing humanistic urban studies.

From this point of view, Kracauer's considerable, dynamic understanding of the ornament gives us reason to hope for a more comprehensive investigation of how the interwar years treated the city and the urban within architecture, literature, and social science. Siegfried Kracauer is not the only writer from the interwar years who is of interest, seen from the perspective of urban analysis. Walter Benjamin's urban writings from the same period would also seem to be of the greatest importance for our present understanding of the relationship between city and modernity. Others from the Western European urban culture of the interwar years—including, for example, the surrealists and theorists of modern architecture—would be able to contribute to this work.

In the longer term, it will be necessary to consider the work of Kracauer (and Walter Benjamin) on the city in a wider cultural context. Such an investigation can be carried out with sufficient precision only if it takes into account the thematic, genre-related, and theoretical characteristics of the individual authors. If this book has contributed to creating an overview of and insight into Kracauer's relatively neglected urban essays, a vital goal will have been achieved.

Notes

INTRODUCTION

1. Schaukal, however, still wanted to establish a connection between ornamentation and the decorated surface, not merely the disappearance of the ornament: "The ornamentation, if it is to achieve its purpose—to spread the clarity of the beautiful—must be coherent in itself; it must, since it is an addition, cohere with that which bears it" (Richard Schaukal, "Gegen das Ornament," in A. Opel, ed., *Konfrontationen—Schriften von und über Adolf Loos* [Vienna: G. Prachner Verlag, 1988], pp. 32–35; quotation, p. 32; originally published in *Deutsche Kunst und Dekoration,* April 1908).

2. Schaukal, "Gegen das Ornament," p. 34.

3. Such a compromise is proposed by, among others, Karl Gross in 1912, when, on behalf of the German Werkbund movement (which sought a link between industry and architecture), he regarded "quality work" as one of the decisive contributions to the development of twentieth-century "ornamentation" (see Reyner Banham, *Theory and Design in the First Machine Age,* 2nd ed. [London: Architectural Press, 1980], p. 92). Among other quotations from Karl Gross is the following formulation: "If the ornament is to be again what it once was and must remain, a particular distinction that lifts an object out of the general mass, it must be quality work" (ibid., p. 93).

4. The analysis of Loos's critique of the ornament is based on a French translation of "Ornament und Verbrechen," in Adolf Loos, *Paroles dans le vide,* trans. Cornelius Heim (Paris: Editions du Champ Libre, 1979), pp. 198–207 (this edition is hereafter cited parenthetically in the text). This volume is a translation of Loos, *Sämtliche Schriften,* vol. 1 (Munich: Verlag Herold, 1962). For the summary of the original lecture, see *Fremdenblatt,* January 22, 1910; in Opel, ed., *Konfrontationen,* pp. 37–39.

5. English decorative art has also been of considerable importance for Danish design and architecture via, among other volumes, Steen Eiler Rasmussen's *Britisk Brugskunst* (British decorative art) from 1933 (reprint, Copenhagen: G.E.C. Gads Forlag, 1965).

6. To be fair, it must be emphasized that Loos is turning not against the ornament *as such* but against the modern designers' inclusion of it in their creative work. This distinction, which is already suggested in his "aristocratic" tolerance of the use of ornamental figures by "primitive" (and applied) art and in the acceptance of arbitrary consumption of the ornaments of former times by "modern man" (Loos, *Paroles dans le vide,* pp. 205, 207), is confirmed in the much later article "Ornament and Education" (1924). Here, Loos emphasizes, among other things,

that the art of drawing must be learned using classical ornament as the point of departure (Loos, *Paroles dans le vide,* p. 290). Loos there rejects a purist interpretation of ornament critique. He recognizes, for example, the central position of the ornament in the world of ladies' fashion, where the forms are not functionally but erotically motivated and thereby link up with the archaic ornament. "All art is erotic / The first ornament . . . , the cross, was erotic in origin," Loos wrote as early as "Ornament and Crime" (p. 199).

7. The ornament is an important ingredient in design and architecture in the period from the first Great Exhibition in London in 1851 up to and including art nouveau (ca. 1914). Even in the iron-and-glass architecture of the time, which might at first glance appear to be the diametric opposite of the tendency criticized by Loos, the ornamental element is not insignificant. See, for example, the "ruffles" of the Eiffel Tower; see Leonardo Benevolo, *The History of Modern Architecture,* vol. 1 (1971; reprint, Cambridge, Mass.: MIT Press, 1977).

8. Adolf Loos, "Architecture," in *Paroles dans le vide,* pp. 226–227.

9. Benevolo (*History of Modern Architecture,* 1:168) mentions, for example, Owen Jones's *Grammar of Ornament* (1856), which includes ornaments for decorative art and not for "macro-architecture."

10. Loos, "Architecture," pp. 220–221.

11. Adolf Loos, "Architektur," in *Trotzdem* (1931; reprint, Vienna: Georg Prachner Verlag, 1982), p. 94.

12. Stanislaus von Moos proposes this disagreement as a possible explanation of why Loos's essay "Architecture," which the introduction to *L'esprit nouveau*'s reprint of "Ornement et crime" announced as appearing in the following number, never actually was published there. See von Moos, "Le Corbusier et Loos," in von Moos, ed., *L'esprit nouveau—Le Corbusier et l'industrie 1920–1925* (Berlin: Wilhelm Ernst und Sohn Verlag, 1987), pp. 122–133, esp. 132.

13. Quoted by Stanislaus von Moos from the preface to Le Corbusier's book *L'art décoratif d'aujourd'hui* (Paris, 1925), in "Le Corbusier et Loos," p. 122.

14. Such a comparison is irrelevant, simply on the grounds that Loos's German text had probably not been printed in its entirety before October 24, 1929. As a curiosity it can be mentioned that the first German publication was in the cultural section of the *Frankfurter Zeitung,* where Kracauer held an important position among the editors. See "Notice bibliographique," in Loos, *Paroles dans le vide,* p. 333.

CHAPTER I THE RESUBJECTIVIZATION OF MODERN URBAN CULTURE

1. Simmel's text was first published in *Jahrbuch der Gehestiftung* 9 (1903). In this chapter, the analysis of "Die Großstädte und das Geistesleben" refers to its recent German edition, in Georg Simmel, *Das Individuum und die Freiheit* (Berlin: Verlag Klaus Wagenbach, 1984), pp. 192–204. This book is basically a reprint of Simmel's essays collected in *Brücke und Tür,* ed. Michael Landmann together with Margarete Susman (Stuttgart: Koehler Verlag, 1957). For the convenience of readers who may be using various editions, citations include not just the page number in I but also the paragraph number (§).

2. See Arno Münster, *Utopie, Messianismus und Apokalypse im Frühwerk von Ernst Bloch* (Frankfurt am Main: Suhrkamp Verlag, 1982), chap. 3.

3. Walter Benjamin, "Lebenslauf," in *Gesammelte Schriften,* ed. Rolf Tiedemann and Hermann Schweppenhäuser, vol. 6 (Frankfurt am Main: Suhrkamp Verlag, 1985), p. 215.

4. Repeated mentions of Kracauer's personal acquaintance with Simmel and Max Scheler suggest that the secondary literature takes Adorno's claim at face value. His information, however, is highly imprecise. Adorno's text supplies no dates and is open to a wide range of interpretations. Adorno writes, among other things: "He [Kracauer] is linked to Georg Simmel and Max Scheler. . . . He knew both of them well privately. Simmel, of whom he wrote a study, advised him to go over completely to philosophy. Not only did he train his ability with him [Simmel] to interpret specific substantial [*sachhaltige*] phenomena in relation to that which—according to that conception—appears mainly here in the way of general structures. . . . Simmel's influence on him was really more at the level of a gesture of thought [*Denkgestus*] than of an elective affinity with an irrationalist philosophy of life" (Theodor W. Adorno, "Der wunderliche Realist," in *Noten zur Literatur* [Frankfurt am Main: Suhrkamp Verlag, 1974], pp. 391–392).

Martin Jay repeats Adorno's assumption that Kracauer's acquaintance with Simmel was directly related to his change of profession from architect to cultural journalist in 1920 in the seminal article for the interpretation of Kracauer "The Extraterritorial Life of Siegfried Kracauer," first published in 1975. Except that here, Max Scheler is now also directly involved in Kracauer's development: "Encouraged by the eminent philosophers Georg Simmel and Max Scheler, with whom he was personally acquainted, Kracauer turned to philosophical and sociological analysis as a new career" (reprinted in Martin Jay, *Permanent Exiles: Essays on the Intellectual Migration from Germany to America* [New York: Columbia University Press, 1985], p. 155).

In *Text + Kritik*'s 1980 special issue devoted to Kracauer, the link between his acquaintance with Simmel and his change of profession is elevated as it now figures in Kracauer's "vita" for the year 1889, i.e., it is also valid for his period of study (the next entries are under 1915). Kracauer is listed as "a pupil of Georg Simmel, who advised him to change completely to philosophy" ("Vita Siegfried Kracauers," in Heinz Ludwig Arnold, ed., *Siegfried Kracauer,* Text + Kritik, vol. 68 [Munich: Text + Kritik, 1980], p. 82).

Rolf Wiggershaus's excessively ambitious historical study *Die Frankfurter Schule: Geschichte, theoretische Entwicklung, politische Bedeutung* contents itself with illustrating Kracauer's relationship to Simmel by paraphrasing Adorno's essay on Kracauer. Wiggershaus mentions "Georg Simmel's advice [to Kracauer] to devote himself completely to philosophy," adding that Kracauer "was not able to carry this out" but compromised by becoming a cultural journalist and editor on the *Frankfurter Zeitung* (Wiggershaus, *Die Frankfurter Schule: Geschichte, theoretische Entwicklung, politische Bedeutung* [Munich: Carl Hanser Verlag, 1986], p. 84).

In the finest investigation to date of Kracauer's work, Inka Mülder develops further this conception of a link between Kracauer and Simmel during the former's period of study, stating briefly: "Already while studying to become an architect, Kracauer had studied sociology and philosophy as minor subjects, under Georg Simmel and Max Scheler among others, whom he also got to know well personally" (Mülder, *Siegfried Kracauer—Grenzgänger zwischen Theorie und Literatur. Seine frühen Schriften 1913–1933* [Stuttgart: J. B. Metzler, 1985], p. 8). Mülder's note at this point does not document the relationship to Simmel, let alone to Scheler, whom Kracauer, according to the *Marbacher Magazin* biography (M, p. 27), met for the first time at a lecture during the First World War, on November 20, 1916.

5. Leo Haenlein writes: "Kracauer must have been an industrious student since, as Kracauer mentioned in a letter of February 15, 1962, to Erika Lorenz, Simmel gave him the advice, while he [Kracauer] was studying under him [Simmel], to turn to philosophy" (Haenlein, *Der Denk-Gestus des aktiven Wartens im Sinn-Vakuum der Moderne: Zur Konstitution und Tragweite des Realitätskonzeptes Siegfried Kracauers in spezieller Rücksicht auf Walter Benjamin* [Frankfurt am Main: Peter Lang, 1984], p. 161 n. 71). So Adorno can have based his observation on something other than a conversation with Kracauer himself.

6. *Siegfried Kracauer 1889–1966,* ed. Ingrid Belke and Irina Renz (Marbach am Neckar: Deutsche Schillergesellschaft, 1989), a special issue of *Marbacher Magazin* (no. 47, 1988), abbreviated throughout this volume as M.

7. David P. Frisby, "Georg Simmels Theorie der Moderne," in Heinz-Jürgen Dahme, ed., *Georg Simmel und die Moderne* (Frankfurt am Main: Suhrkamp Verlag, 1984), pp. 9–79.

8. A more profound reading of "The Metropolis and Mental Life" would have to involve, at the inner, theoretical level, a comparison (not yet undertaken) with one of Simmel's main theoretical works, published just before it: *Philosophie des Geldes* (The philosophy of money, 1900). Furthermore, Simmel's links to contemporary single disciplines—first and foremost physiologically oriented psychology—would have to be investigated in an attempt to determine their influence on such crucial concepts as a blasé state of mind, a reserved state of mind, and eccentricity.

9. See Nils Gunder Hansen, "Georg Simmel—sociologi og livsfilosofi" (Ph.D. diss., University of Copenhagen, 1989). Special emphasis is placed in the dissertation on Simmel's concept of the metaphysical individual.

10. Cf. Walter Benjamin, "Über einige Motive bei Baudelaire," in *Gesammelte Schriften,* vol. 1.3 (Frankfurt am Main: Suhrkamp Verlag, 1980), esp. pp. 612–613.

11. It is therefore doubtful to assert—as do Stéphane Jonas and Patrick Schweitzer in "Georg Simmel et la ville"—"the indisputable existence of a tendency in Simmel toward spatial determinism, used in the study of the metropolis: scope, density, heterogeneity" (Jonas and Schweitzer, "Georg Simmel et la ville," in Patrick Watier, ed., *Georg Simmel, la sociologie et l'expérience du monde moderne* [Paris: Méridiens Klincksieck, 1986], p. 171). In an incidentally dubious anthropomorphic analogy between the city as space and man as body, Simmel distances himself precisely from this spatial definition of the metropolis by underlining that the city/metropolis first becomes such via its extreme and internal effects of a sociomental nature: "so, too, a city first consists of the totality of the effects that reach beyond its immediacy. This is first its real scope, within which it expresses its being" (I, p. 201, §21).

12. See Anne Cauquelin, *Essai de philosophie urbaine* (Paris: Presses Universitaires de France, 1982).

13. Georg Simmel, "Der Begriff und die Tragödie der Kultur," in Simmel, *Das individuelle Gesetz,* ed. Michael Landmann (Frankfurt am Main: Suhrkamp Verlag, 1968), p. 118.

14. Ibid., p. 142.

15. Ibid., p. 147.

16. According to Inka Mülder (*Siegfried Kracauer,* p. 152), the Simmel expert David Frisby views Kracauer's book as "the most sensitive assessment of Simmel's work by any of his students."

17. The introductory chapter takes the form of a broad portrayal of Simmel's work. In it, Kracauer insists on the important position of everyday experiences in Simmel's research material (O,

p. 210). In his frequent comparisons of individual phenomena, Simmel makes considerable use of analogy (O, p. 221), and in his experimental attitude toward concepts ("Experimente mit dem Begriff"; O, p. 230) he is diametrically opposed to the traditionally cultivated "systematic deduction of individual conditions in a conceptually strict form from general concepts" (O, p. 247).

The "contemplative reflection" noted by Kracauer in Simmel is an important element in Kracauer's own form of thinking and writing. Adorno makes the following, subtly distancing comment on this state of affairs: "In a sense that is hard to comprehend, his [Kracauer's] thinking always had more contemplation [*Anschauung*] than thought about it, obstinately determined not to limit by explanation anything of that which the hard things in the estimation [*Aufprall*] had imprinted on him" ("Der wunderliche Realist," p. 392). Adorno is not without distance from the not-completely-conceptual way of thinking.

18. Adorno, "Der wunderliche Realist," pp. 391–392.

CHAPTER 2   THE EVERYDAY LIFE AND URBAN PERCEPTION OF THE ARCHITECT

1. Throughout the discussion of *Ginster,* all references (cited as G) are to vol. 7 of Siegfried Kracauer's *Schriften* (Frankfurt am Main: Suhrkamp Verlag, 1973).

2. Inka Mülder, *Siegfried Kracauer—Grenzgänger zwischen Theorie und Literatur. Seine frühen Schriften 1913–1933* (Stuttgart: J. B. Metzler, 1985), p. 201, has only found two independent treatments of this novel in recent literary history. Thomas Mann writes, among other things, that Kracauer describes "the war experienced within the country's boundaries and not at the front, as also on his own body, with dry veracity. . . . I believe this testimony will last" (quoted by Karsten Witte, "Nachwort," in Siegfried Kracauer, *Schriften,* 7:496: Mann's comment was first published on September 1, 1928). Joseph Roth writes, "It is a book for simple individuals, very simple, i.e., humane individuals" (quoted from Witte, "Nachwort," p. 497; originally printed in *Frankfurter Zeitung,* October 25, 1928).

3. This review is reprinted in M, pp. 52ff (quotation, p. 53).

4. Kracauer does not identify himself by his own name—especially his first name—without unease. This can be seen from his reaction to Ernst Bloch, in a letter from January 1928 that alters (as if quite spontaneously) the somewhat formal tone of address. After first having signed himself "Yours, Bloch," Bloch adds immediately afterward "or may I write what I actually feel as regards you: Ernst" (Bloch's first name, which means "serious"; quoted from *Ernst Bloch: Briefe 1903–1975,* ed. Karola Bloch, vol. 1 [Frankfurt am Main: Suhrkamp Verlag, 1985], p. 287). Kracauer replies to this declaration of friendship with a number of reflections having to do with names and self-criticism, ending with the wish to be called "Krac." The personally burdensome memory connected with "Friedel" and the displeasure at his official first name "Siegfried" lead Kracauer to resort to the onomatopoeic abbreviation of his surname: "Please call me Krac. It is the proper noun that a couple of people who are dear to me use; I feel at ease with it and would like to be called it by you. By the way, I have in my pedantic way used the expression Ginster for the novel's hero in reaction against my own first name. Most cordially yours [signature]" (ibid., p. 289).

5. Ernst Bloch recalls in a letter to Lili Kracauer after Siegfried Kracauer's death (on November

26, 1966, in New York) the retiringly modest nature of "Krac." See letter of December 8, 1966, in ibid., p. 406.

6. Ibid., p. 294.

7. "'What's this?' he [K.] asked the painter. 'What are you surprised at?' returned the painter, surprised in his turn. 'These are the Law Court offices. Didn't you know that there were Law Court offices here? There are Law Court offices in almost every attic, why should this be an exception? My studio really belongs to the Law Court offices, but the Court has put it at my disposal'" (Franz Kafka, *The Trial,* trans. Willa and Edwin Muir, rev. E. M. Butler [1925; reprint, New York: Schocken, 1968], p. 164).

8. See Leonardo Benevolo, "Art Nouveau," chap. 9 of *The History of Modern Architecture,* 2 vols. (1971; reprint, Cambridge, Mass.: MIT Press, 1977), vol. 1. Benevolo takes 1914 as the watershed between modern architecture and its tradition (e.g., see p. 318).

9. Anne Cauquelin demonstrates in *Essai de philosophie urbaine* (Paris: Presses Universitaires de France, 1982) that a long tradition within the theory of architecture from antiquity to the Renaissance has included, e.g., climatic, mythological, and temporal factors in the field of architecture.

10. The song was published as "Deutsches Flugblatt," number 43, under the pseudonym Friedel Kracauer; the first page of the song is printed in M, p. 26. The article "Vom Erleben des Kriegs" was published in *Preußische Jahrbücher* 61 (September 1915). Here Kracauer writes, among other things: "The release that war brings this sort of person consists precisely in a binding of unbound freedom in the idea. Loneliness is flushed away. . . . Joy at serving takes over the soul. At last it may live immediately, suffer, and rejoice in continued community [*Gemeinschaft*] with others without having to fear the self-mirroring caused by reflection. For the immeasurable task of defending the fatherland, always with death lurking in the wings, concentrates all inner forces to such an extent that it [life] no longer comes to the stifling consciousness of the solitary, isolated ego" (M, p. 27). According to this quotation, Kracauer harbors the illusion of being able to go beyond his feeling of loneliness in the myth of war solidarity. This emotion and the attempt to resolve it by means of a close relationship to others or just to one other person form a decisive moral and philosophical theme in Kracauer's early adult years, as seen in the text "Über die Freundschaft," printed in the journal *Logos* 7, no. 2 (1917/1918): 182–208 (published in book form with the same title by Suhrkamp Verlag in 1971).

    One year after the publication of "Vom Erleben des Krieges," the philosopher Max Scheler, mentioned earlier, visited Frankfurt on a patriotic lecture tour. In *Ginster,* Scheler (under the name Professor Caspari) is presented as a hypocritical, war-legitimizing lecturer, whereas Ginster himself stands for an antiwar attitude. In reality it was on that occasion that Kracauer "got to know Scheler personally" (M, p. 27), and later also sent him his article on experiencing the war. According to a letter of thanks sent to Kracauer, Scheler had read the article "with great interest, profit, and approval" (quoted in M, p. 27). The confrontation with Scheler in *Ginster* is a cover for Kracauer's self-criticism, which must further apply to Simmel's original praise of the First World War as a possible break with the dominance of the objective mind.

11. For example, in the novel, the uncle's death toward the end of the war is an event that affects Ginster deeply. In reality, Kracauer's uncle, "the historian of the Jews of Frankfurt" (Theodor W. Adorno, "Der wunderliche Realist," in *Noten zur Literatur* [Frankfurt am Main: Suhrkamp Verlag, 1974], p. 388), did not die until 1923. Kracauer's father, on the other hand, who in *Gin-*

ster is said to die early on in the childhood of the main character, died on July 9, 1918. The affection for the uncle (in *Ginster*) is in stark contrast to Kracauer's (more than) soberly sublimated diary entry on the occasion of his father's death. The diary, however, does reveal great concern for his mother, whose domination of her son is much regretted on many occasions in *Ginster:* "Today, July 10 (corrected to 9 July 23:20), my father died. . . . My father has had a joyless life and his final time was regrettable. He has found release. My mother, who did such a frightful lot in the nature of care, good spirits, housekeeping, and in general experienced so little joy in her life, can now breathe a sigh of relief and must allow herself some rest and encouragement in the years ahead. She has deserved to have some joy in her life for once" (M, pp. 29–30).

CHAPTER 3   BEYOND FUNCTIONAL SPACE: THE ORNAMENT

1. The distinction between the image and the figural is made by Jean-François Lyotard in *Discours, Figure* (Paris: Klincksieck, 1971).

2. Because the passage is placed in chapter 2 (the chapter that instructs the reader through memory), the incident appears to date from before the outbreak of the First World War, though these considerations are programmatic for the entire course of the novel.

3. Kracauer's own choice of architecture was prompted by the mark "very good" in the three subjects mathematics, description of nature, and drawing in his 1907 upper-secondary exit exam at Klinger Ober-Realschule in Frankfurt am Main (M, p. 7).

4. See this chapter's section 3 on Kracauer's doctoral thesis, whose theme was wrought-iron ornaments in Berlin from the seventeenth to the early nineteenth century.

5. In the retrospective sketch under discussion—which, despite its position at the beginning of the novel (in chapter 2), is programmatic for the rest of the novel—Ginster expresses his relationship to the practice of architecture somewhat simplistically: "Despite his talent, Ginster was not satisfied with the profession of architect. The more he sought to adapt himself, the more he realized that the magic of the drawn representations disappeared as soon as they were realized in bricks and masonry" (G, p. 22). In the section on Ginster's relationship to architecture, some attempt is made to add shading to this summary view by the mention of small elements of pleasure as well as the points where Ginster feels disappointed.

6. This metaphor creation finds expression in a passage in which Ginster is confronted with the ornament in a manifestation that is seductive and full of illusion. In the city Q., Ginster has begun a sort of relationship with the bookseller Elfriede. The decisive setback in their passionless attachment occurs just when Ginster has actually decided to seduce Elfriede during a hot August Sunday walk in the forest. The forest and the girl dissolve into ornamental figures: the forest turns into "dots" reflected in Elfriede's dotted frock; the rest of her consists of an accumulation of curls (*Häufung von Kringel*). But as soon as they were touched, "the curls shook and fell apart like dust. Such curls were frequently used as wallpaper patterns" (G, p. 207). Dots and frills—half visual, half metaphorical—enable Elfriede to appear beautiful just as they make what follows unexciting.

If this example of the ornament's visual abstraction and literary metaphorization leads the reader to suggest the risks of such artificial heavy-handedness, no counterarguments will be raised. But these formulations correspond to Ginster's experience. Elfriede's beautifully ornamented appearance dissolves like an illusion and is subsequently made objective and hardly enticing—like the model for wallpaper. From one type of ornament to another . . .

7. The theme, then, is the development of wrought-iron art in Berlin, Potsdam, and, e.g., Frankfurt an der Oder, from the seventeenth to the early nineteenth century. This work is cited throughout as E.

8. Inka Mülder, *Siegfried Kracauer—Grenzgänger zwischen Theorie und Literatur: Seine frühen Schriften 1913–1933* (Stuttgart: J. B. Metzler, 1985), p. 8.

9. Ibid.

10. Jean-Claude Gardin, *Une archéologie théorique* (Paris: Hachette, 1979). Gardin's definition of "compilation" is that its "author first and foremost intends to disseminate knowledge of previously unpublished or highly inaccessible finds" (p. 47). "Explication" has, most importantly, a "cognitive intention" and thus seeks to "advance new views concerning the positioning of objects or classes of objects in the order of historical reconstruction" (pp. 39, 47).

11. A more detailed presentation and discussion of Kracauer's divisions of the chosen period as defined by four styles (1, pre-baroque; 2, baroque; 3, rococo; 4, "wig style"/early classicism) is not relevant here, since the precise stylistic distinctions have only indirect importance for the problematics of ornamentation. What is significant for this issue will be presented in this discussion via central examples from Kracauer's study.

12. A proponent of this urban and sociological revision of the traditional concept of architectural type is the French sociologist and architect Christian Devillers, whose 1974 article "Typologie de l'habitat et morphologie urbaine" (published in the journal *Architecture d'aujourd'hui*) is a (minor) classic in this field. See Henri Raymond, *Architecture, les aventures spatiales de la raison*, Collection "alors" (Paris: Centre de Création Industrielle, Centre Georges Pompidou, 1984), p. 47.

13. Despite the emergence of rolling mills in the seventeenth century, Kracauer emphasizes the continuity of the work process of the smithy: "The real processing of the wrought iron in the workshop has, on the other hand, remained practically unchanged since the Middle Ages. This has to do with its very nature as a craft that, just like the art of the sculptor, is more the exercise of art than a mechanical activity and [therefore] can only to a secondary extent and to a minor degree be underpinned by technical improvements" (E, p. 2).

CHAPTER 4   DISCOVERING THE CITY AS A REFLECTIVE SPACE

1. "The streets and house facades which Ginster knew seemed strange, because he went in clusters. And yet they were not all that strange, for he guessed a number of shop signs without looking at them" (G, p. 141).

2. The nightmare (G, p. 181) will not be commented on in detail, since it appears as a vertical version of the introductory text of *Straßen in Berlin und anderswo*, "Erinnerung an eine Pariser Straße," in which the movement stays at street level (S, pp. 9–15). In *Ginster* the dream also has a circular construction, beginning (1) in a room, continuing (2) through an avenue that (3) leads to the city and (4) into a side street (*Nebengasse*), (5) up a ladder to an attic room, from where the path is through (6) a mirror that takes us back to the point of departure (1). Flight is at that point in time theoretically possible since the door is open. But Ginster is paralyzed by fear. In its prelude, Ginster describes (G, p. 180) a slot machine with dancing dolls in a hall of mirrors,

recalling Kracauer's story "Der verbotene Blick," in *Straßen in Berlin und anderswo* (esp. S, p. 96).

3. Criticism of the Marseilles chapter appears as early as in Joachim Maass's otherwise positive assessment in *Kölnische Zeitung,* July 19, 1931. He writes: "Ginster feels it himself: at the end of the book he suggests that for us to feel better, we should imitate the chaotic tumult of the harbor precinct in Marseilles; this attempt at deliverance seems to me to be the only superficial part of the whole book, a final apotheosis without the intellectual weight of the previous portrayal" (translated from M, p. 56).

The omission of the chapter when the book was reissued in 1963 was approved of by Adorno, who regards *Ginster* as Kracauer's "most significant achievement" (Theodor W. Adorno, "Der wunderliche Realist," in *Noten zur Literatur* [Frankfurt am Main: Suhrkamp Verlag, 1974], p. 401). Concerning Kracauer's final chapter he further writes: "Ginster convincingly proves that freedom, positivism, cannot as such be stated at all today [*sich setzen ließe*]; otherwise the idiosyncratic aspect of Kracauer would inevitably become a mania. In the new edition he has wisely renounced the final chapter, which flirted with such positivism" (pp. 401–402). As he did in connection with Kracauer's relationship to Simmel (see chapter 1 above), Adorno has, with this remark, established one of the recurring themes in the literature on Kracauer. Fortunately, the final chapter, whose importance is supported by the dedication "For L., in memory of Marseilles 1926 and 1927" (G, p. 8), has been reintroduced in vol. 7 of Kracauer's *Schriften.*

Everything would seem to indicate that Kracauer allowed himself to be persuaded to make the cut by commercial arguments from the publisher. In a letter to Wolfgang Weyrauch of December 21, 1963, he writes: "The last chapter was omitted because all the heads of acquisitions and certain writers as well at Suhrkamp [Kracauer's publishers in Frankfurt am Main] were of the opinion that it could harm the book's success. Just why I do not know, but I finally, with a heavy heart, gave in to this shared wish, mainly because I did not want to be held responsible for a possible fiasco" (M, p. 121). Thus Kracauer himself did not seem to see any philosophical risk or reason for self-criticism in connection with the Marseilles chapter in *Ginster.*

4. Kracauer to Ernst Bloch, letter dated January 5, 1928, in *Ernst Bloch: Briefe 1903–1975,* ed. Karola Bloch, vol. 1 (Frankfurt am Main: Suhrkamp Verlag, 1985), p. 289.

5. Inka Mülder was the first person to draw attention to a short story "Die Gnade" (Mercy), which Kracauer, according to a note in the manuscript, wrote between Easter and Pentecost in 1913. The story is considered to be a preliminary study of the novel *Ginster* and, like the latter, contains a release (here, *die Gnade*) mediated by a prostitute. See Mülder, *Siegfried Kracauer— Grenzgänger zwischen Theorie und Literatur: Seine frühen Schriften 1913–1933* (Stuttgart: J. B. Metzler, 1985), pp. 126ff.

6. Already in F. Ginster had noticed his love of the harbor, as he referred to "the dismal atmosphere of the factories and the purposeful traffic on the water, which rowing races only decorate further. Nothing, apart from the cranes, had its roots here, while people otherwise spent their time everywhere" (G, p. 47). But in F., Ginster's excursion with his friend Otto is to the greenness of the city woods.

7. The radicalism of Ginster's break with the mother figure is open to discussion, since the figure reemerges in a sublimated form in his identification with certain types of urbanity. But what is crucial in this context is partly Ginster's feeling of freedom and partly its link to the urban sphere of experience, which formerly occupied a relatively minor position in his mental life.

8. Georg Simmel, "Der Fremde," in Simmel, *Das individuelle Gesetz,* ed. Michael Landmann (Frankfurt am Main: Suhrkamp Verlag, 1968), pp. 63–70.

9. Ginster's passion for the harbor in Marseilles is related to the description of the—admittedly rather deserted—harbor in F.: "Opposite the docks stretch the depots, indifferent, yellow warehouses that no one notices. Between them and the quays the dockworkers haul goods back and forth. The storehouses attract me—in broad daylight they are so concealed, and nothing remains in them" (G, p. 233).

10. As early as 1921, Kracauer is a member of the editorial staff of the *Frankfurter Zeitung.* From ca. 1924 his writing on urban themes intensifies, and he visits Marseilles for the first time in 1926, together with, among others, Walter Benjamin.

11. A corresponding position is implied by Walter Benjamin in his essay "Haschisch in Marseille" from ca. 1928.

12. Walter Benjamin, *Der Begriff der Kunstkritik in der deutschen Romantik,* now in *Gesammelte Schriften,* ed. Rolf Tiedemann and Hermann Schweppenhäuser, vol. 1.1 (Frankfurt am Main: Suhrkamp Verlag, 1980), pp. 18–61.

13. In my D.E.A. dissertation "Prostitution et interprétation dans l'œuvre de Walter Benjamin" (UER des Sciences des Textes et Documents, Université de Paris VII, 1986) I have undertaken an analysis of the link between Benjamin's account of German romanticism's conception of the medium of reflection and an important theoretical figure in Benjamin's own urban essays. Benjamin's concept of critique as reflection, though it is not identical with Simmel's idea of resubjectivization, undergirds the present work as an implicit reference.

14. The ring cannot be seen because of its high speed of oscillation. Ginster can use it as an allegory to speculate on the extent to which the bird is in a cage or free.

15. Using Walter Benjamin's memoirs and urban images as my point of departure, I have analyzed the prostitute's role as an allegorical threshold for the bourgeois child's imaginary access to the secrets of the city and of the community. See my D.E.A. dissertation "Prostitution et interprétation dans l'œuvre de Walter Benjamin," pp. 60–74.

CHAPTER 5   ORNAMENT, RATIO, AND REASON

1. "Das Ornament der Masse" (1927) really only became known with the publication of Kracauer's essays from the 1920s and the early 1930s in a book: *Das Ornament der Masse* (Frankfurt am Main: Suhrkamp Verlag, 1963), abbreviated throughout this volume as O.

   The essay, whose programmatic and philosophical importance for Kracauer's work during the period in question can hardly be overestimated, seems (strangely enough) not to have spurred much discussion at the time. In Kracauer's otherwise very intense correspondence with both Walter Benjamin and Ernst Bloch, "Das Ornament der Masse" scarcely figures, not even in a letter to Benjamin dated June 11—i.e., the day after its publication in the *Frankfurter Zeitung* (see Walter Benjamin, *Briefe an Siegfried Kracauer,* ed. Rolf Tiedemann [Marbach am Neckar: Deutsche Schillergesellschaft, 1987], p. 46). On a postcard from Moscow sent January 18, 1927, however, Benjamin expresses the wish to see Kracauer's "latest work (Ornament der Masse), among other things" (ibid., p. 37), but he does not comment on the essay in subsequent letters. In a faint echo of "Das Ornament der Masse," the essay "Die Photographie" is mentioned in a letter from Ernst Bloch, dated September 27, 1927, as an "Ornament der Zerstreuung" (*Ernst Bloch: Briefe 1903–1975*, ed. Karola Bloch, vol. 1 [Frankfurt am Main: Suhrkamp Verlag, 1985], p. 285).

2. This compatibility of novel and essay is not guaranteed by the sole fact that *Ginster* to a very great extent was written after "Das Ornament der Masse." The genre of the novel, despite *Ginster*'s initial publication as a serial in the *Frankfurter Zeitung*, is not the same as that of Kracauer's newspaper essays. Furthermore, both the forms of ornament and the empirical material differ in the two.

3. A selection of these essays was published in 1964 in a book under the title *Straßen in Berlin und anderswo* (Frankfurt am Main: Suhrkamp Verlag). This volume, like *Das Ornament der Masse*, was compiled by Kracauer himself and later will be used as a basis for the detailed analyses in part II.

4. Named after the choreographer John Tiller, who presented this type of show for the first time in Manchester in 1890, the dancers made their entry into Berlin in October 1924, ousting the culture of the operetta for the following five years. These huge troupes of dancing girls, almost boyish in appearance and clad in costumes that neutralized their sex, were trained to parade in columns in military fashion. They were soon imitated throughout Germany. The Tiller Girl had a decisive influence on the German female ideal of the interwar years. See Irmtraut Rippel-Manß, "1920–1929: Die goldenen Zwanziger," in *Chronik des 20. Jahrhunderts* (Braunschweig: Westermann, 1982), p. 328.

5. The numerous forms of fetishization in the relation between mass and ornament are conveyed in the ambiguous genitive of the German title.

6. This theoretical level is a result of Kracauer's increasing interest in Marx's writings, specifically the Marxist critique of political economy (although Kracauer's interest was predominantly in Marx's early writings). This development is dealt with in greater detail in Martin Jay, *Permanent Exiles: Essays on the Intellectual Migration from Germany to America* (New York: Columbia University Press, 1985), and in Inka Mülder, *Siegfried Kracauer—Grenzgänger zwischen Theorie und Literatur: Seine frühen Schriften 1913–1933* (Stuttgart: J. B. Metzler, 1985).

7. "The capitalist production process is, like the mass ornament, an end in itself [*Selbstzweck*]. The commodities that it yields have not really been produced in order to be possessed, but have their basis in profit, which would like to be limitless" (O, p. 53).

8. The civil space of the city, despite its property structures and rationalist elements both in social practice and in technical and administrative organization, does not obey without distinction or resistance the performative logic of capitalist (industrial) production.

9. In distancing himself from snobbish, highbrow values, Kracauer does not spare the apparently progressive (Left-ish) variants of traditional spiritual values. He also criticizes the therapeutic aspects of the "rhythmic gymnastics" that had already become widespread in the 1920s. He alleges that its conception of the human soul as the center of aesthetic expression belongs to a premodern conception of culture.

Kracauer's own attempt to revive wrought-iron work in modern Berlin (in his doctoral thesis published in 1915) must also be assumed to have been criticized as being anachronistic and lacking in historical relevance. Highbrow culture, traditional wrought-iron ornaments, and rhythmic gymnastics are all included in the group of examples "among many other exertions, just as hopeless, to get beyond mass being and reach a higher life. As far as most of them are concerned, they quite romantically recall forms and content that have long since succumbed to the partially justified critique of capitalist Ratio" (O, p. 63).

10. Concerning the medium of film, to whose alienating effect Kracauer attached great expectations in 1926, he writes "that they [the film showings] exactly and clearly communicate the *disorder* of society to thousands of eyes and ears—this is precisely what will enable them to produce and keep alive the tension that must precede the necessary change" (O, p. 315). These formulations are from the essay "Kult der Zerstreuung" (FZ, March 4, 1926), which at several points is a precursor of "Das Ornament der Masse."

11. With these thoughts about the reversal of reason into myth, Kracauer establishes the historico-philosophical figure that twenty years later will be at the center of Theodor W. Adorno and Max Horkheimer's *Dialektik der Aufklärung* (The dialectics of enlightenment) (1944; 2nd ed., Frankfurt am Main: S. Fischer Verlag, 1969).

12. Kracauer carries out a concluding opposition between Ratio and Reason at a level of cognitive theory: "It [the abstract nature of Ratio] is the expression of a rationality that becomes obdurate. The determinations of semantic content made in abstract generality—i.e., determinations of economic, social, political, and moral fields—do not give reason what it is entitled to. Through Ratio, empirical material remains unconsidered; every practical application can be derived from the contentless abstractions. Only behind these isolating abstractions do the individual cognitions lie, corresponding to the distinctive nature of the situation that is each time affected" (O, p. 58).

13. Kracauer does not begin with any basic conceptual difference between that which until now has been called "ornament" and his concept of "mass ornament." The latter, however, stresses the place of the ornament in a modern culture. Nor in connection with his discussion of the relationship between ornament and Reason and Ratio, respectively, does Kracauer systematically distinguish between the mass ornament and another form of ornament. Both forms of reason develop within the framework of the mass ornament. Only the concluding lines of the essay show any divergence from this position, but they cannot be ascribed any independent theoretical meaning in the sense of suggesting the need for some third type of ornament. See the discussion later in this chapter.

14. Both of these possibilities are based on the assumption that there actually is a stable relationship between the content of reason and ornamental form, an assumption that—according to, for example, Saussure's linguistic model—must be viewed as theoretically bold. It will, nevertheless, be maintained within this limited field.

15. Kracauer writes: "That nature is desubstantialized in the mass ornament—this is precisely a reference to the state in which only that part of nature can hold its own that does not resist enlightenment through Reason. Such are trees, ponds, mountains in old Chinese landscape paintings, painted only with Indian ink as rudimentary ornamental signs. The organic center has been extracted and the unconnected rest composed according not to the laws of nature [but] to laws that have brought forth a knowledge of the truth—as always—conditioned by time. Remains of the human complex are also part of the mass ornament. Their selection and composition in the aesthetic medium follow from a principle that represents form-exceeding reason more purely than these other principles that retain man as an organic unity" (O, pp. 59–60).

16. "The culture industry" is Adorno and Horkheimer's designation for this sphere of phenomena in *Dialektik der Aufklärung*.

17. The reason for the term being limited here to the metaphorical level is that the idea of collective psychoanalysis is not in direct accordance with the absolutely vital experimental basis of psychoanalysis—the treatment and cure of the individual.

CHAPTER 6   URBAN ORNAMENTS AND SUBJECTIVE EXPERIENCE

1. Confronted by, e.g., suburban buildings or new cities whose construction is based on general, functionally conceived plans, the French sociologist and philosopher Anne Cauquelin asks whether there is any evidence, within the framework of these agglomerations, of an urban context. She doubts this, because "'the place' is lacking, because [the various subjectivities'] memories have not yet been mixed, and because the link between the residents themselves and with their place has only the nature of coercion" (Cauquelin, *Essai de philosophie urbaine* [Paris: Presses Universitaires de France, 1982], p. 190).

2. This movement is not the expression of any inconsistency, but is rather a sign of the fact that in 1963, when *Straßen in Berlin und anderswo* was compiled from a selection of his countless articles from the late 1920s and early 1930s, Kracauer still maintained this basic idea that is found in numerous individual texts.

3. On November 5, 1926, Benjamin sent a thank-you letter for various texts by Kracauer, the fruit of a joint journey in southern France in the summer of 1926. "I felt a mixture of pleasant memories and welcome surprise. I naturally recognized the square, which we came across at night" (Walter Benjamin, *Briefe an Siegfried Kracauer,* ed. Rolf Tiedemann [Marbach am Neckar: Deutsche Schillergesellschaft, 1987], p. 36).

4. "Involuntary" is used here by analogy to Proust's concept of involuntary memory, "la mémoire involontaire."

5. The narrator has not wished to return through the same side street, but after an hour or so wandering around the streets he nevertheless ends up at a place where the street cannot be avoided: "No matter how much I hesitated, I did not doubt for a moment that I would once more have to enter it [the side street], that I had only wandered around other streets in order to find my way back to it" (S, p. 14).

6. Gerwin Zohlen refers without much documentation but with a certain amount of hypothetical evidence and intuition to Dürer's engraving *Melencolia I* (Zohlen, "Text-Straßen," in Heinz Ludwig Arnold, ed., *Siegfried Kracauer,* Text + Kritik, vol. 68 [Munich: Text + Kritik, 1980], p. 70). This association is not as improbable as it might seem, when one considers that Dürer's engraving had been subjected to historico-philosophical analysis in the 1920s—first by Panofsky and Saxl, later by Walter Benjamin.

7. This structure can be explained in its paradoxical form by referring to Freud's thoughts about the relationship between *das Heimliche* and *das Unheimliche*. See Sigmund Freud, "The Uncanny," in *The Standard Edition of the Complete Psychological Works of Sigmund Freud,* ed. and trans. James Strachey, vol. 17 (London: Hogarth, 1953), pp. 219–252.

   This subjectivity-constitutive structure is stretched out during the city walk between two poles in the way memory functions: on the one hand, repetition, on the other, elaboration

(German *Durcharbeitung,* French *élaboration, perlaboration*). The first pole dominates, which is confirmed when the narrator mentions in the final lines that he has never dared to enter this district of the city.

8. The pronoun *du* (you) denotes both the general subject of the course of experiences and the reader addressed by Kracauer's text.

9. As mentioned above, exactly the same type of machine appears, consisting of a "Glaskasten" and an "Orchestrion," in the novel *Ginster* (G, p. 180), where the main character, during a walk in K. (and within the framework of this image), recalls his hometown (F.). This pictorially conveyed memory leads into a dream, a nightmare, that contains many analogous traits of "Erinnerung an eine Pariser Straße" (despite the fact that the narrator in the latter does not immediately pass on a dream . . .).

10. This feeling, absent for most of the guests, is retained by the narrator under the name "the phantom." Their lack of sensitivity is interpreted as an even more valuable indication of the central position of "the phantom" both in the space of the urban pub and in individual subjectivity.

11. Kracauer does not make explicit the extent to which he recognizes a psychoanalytic interpretation of his texts as valid. It would seem, though, to be a fruitful path to take in the longer term—to interpret certain of Kracauer's literary texts on the basis of Freud's ideas about the relationship between narcissism and the Oedipus complex, a relationship whose analysis is further developed by Melanie Klein and, more recently, by Julia Kristeva (in *Soleil noir: Dépression et mélancolie* [Paris: Gallimard, 1987]).

12. The ornamental nature of the activity of writing ought not to be overlooked. "Whereas I had formerly wished to express something with what I wrote, I now began to understand that the mere activity of writing is worth striving for. On large sheets of paper of impeccable whiteness I placed columns of figures and pictures of letters that did not have the slightest suggestion of meaning" (S, p. 111).

The activity of writing and the tools used are thus deprived of a communicative function, gaining recognition instead as a medium of *pure writing.* At the same time, this serves a process of nervous expression and, more or less intentionally, produces a sign-borne visuality. In terms of literary history, Kracauer places himself (unconsciously?) beyond a semantic paradigm and thereby actively anticipates the function of the fragmentary linguistic sign as poetry and image. (In a Danish context, this technique was made use of by the painter Ib Geertsen, within the framework of the art group "Linien II" in the late 1940s.)

13. A vital part of Walter Benjamin's thesis on the origin of the German mourning play (*Ursprung des deutschen Trauerspiels,* written 1923–1925; reprinted in *Gesammelte Schriften,* ed. Rolf Tiedemann and Hermann Schweppenhäuser, vol. 1.1 [Frankfurt am Main: Suhrkamp Verlag, 1980]) consists precisely of a theory of melancholy among the rulers of the baroque. In this connection, Benjamin underlines the *allegorization* of objects by the melancholy prince. The result—allegory—is achieved by removing things from their original functional context to place them in another. In this new constellation things are subject to the contemplation of the melancholic, whose decisive achievement consists of projecting new meaning into the object. This projection of meaning is found to a great extent among the conditions for Kracauer's so-called grotesques, whose basis is not crown and scepter (two baroque elements) but the objects of everyday modern life.

14. See letter 5, in Benjamin, *Briefe an Siegfried Kracauer:* "I can almost guarantee you that these domestic utensils of a dying class will, in an orbis pictus, find a happy fate as a book, once there are such and such a number of tables from your hand. Every requisite that you further incorporate into your cabinet will be a source of great pleasure. What about grandfather clocks? Of course, you will find even better objects" (p. 17).

15. In a letter dated June 6, 1926, Ernst Bloch writes, among other things, "Thank you for the enclosed grotesques. . . . If only one had a name for this new form which is no longer a [form], and which above all derives its power to succeed from not continuing to be one" (in *Ernst Bloch: Briefe 1903–1975,* ed. Karola Bloch, vol. 1 [Frankfurt am Main: Suhrkamp Verlag, 1985], p. 278).

16. Benjamin, *Briefe an Siegfried Kracauer,* p. 17.

17. For Kracauer, outdoor life—as he continues the argument used in "Das Ornament der Masse"—seems to involve a romantic illusion about being able to avoid capitalist culture.

CHAPTER 7   SPACE ANALYSIS AND SOCIAL CRITIQUE

1. Theodor W. Adorno, letter of July 27, 1930; quoted in Inka Mülder, *Siegfried Kracauer— Grenzgänger zwischen Theorie und Literatur: Seine frühen Schriften 1913–1933* (Stuttgart: J. B. Metzler, 1985), p. 181. Attention was first called to this remark by Adorno to Kracauer by Martin Jay, an American historian of the Frankfurt school. In his 1978 article "Adorno and Kracauer: Notes on a Troubled Friendship" (reprinted in Jay, *Permanent Exiles: Essays on the Intellectual Migration from Germany to America* [New York: Columbia University Press, 1985], pp. 217–236) dealing with the development of the friendship between Adorno and Kracauer, Jay interprets the passage as an accusation against Kracauer of intellectual plagiarism: "On occasion, friction would appear in the correspondence, as when Kracauer complained that Adorno had wrongly accused him of borrowing his ideas from someone else, which had evoked the reply that Kracauer was unnecessarily defensive when confronted with the slightest criticism" (p. 222). An endnote here refers to an Adorno letter, dated by Jay to August 6, 1930, though it is probably the same one that Mülder quotes: "the accusation that caused Kracauer to bristle was that he had allegedly borrowed Benjamin's idea of houses as dreams of the collective will in his piece on 'Die Arbeitsnachweise'" (pp. 310–311). The way Adorno's comment and Kracauer's reply are quoted by Mülder, however, seems to make the focus less on accusations of imitation than on the societal status of the dream concept in Kracauer.

2. Kracauer writes on August 1, 1930: "You feel that I have . . . accepted the Benjamin formulation. That is, however, not the case. Certain spatial images I called dreams of society because they represent the being of this society [*das Sein dieser Gesellschaft*] that is concealed in its consciousness. I therefore only coincide with Benjamin . . . in the word dream. . . . The conception of the city as a collective dream still seems romantic to me" (quoted in Mülder, *Siegfried Kracauer,* p. 181).

3. The moral perspective in this expression is not alien to the essence of Kracauer's critique of society, which among other things formulates as its purpose to draw attention—i.e., a social awareness—to unconscious and unjust relationships. But Kracauer does not explicitly use the concept "struggle for recognition," which Axel Honneth, in works such as *The Struggle for Recognition: The Moral Grammar of Social Conflicts* (Cambridge: Polity Press, 1995), has

recently brought back from oblivion in social philosophy. (Taking his point of departure in the early political writings of Hegel, especially the so-called *Jenaer Realphilosophie*, Honneth attempts to establish a theoretical understanding of morality and power in society that assumes a less pedagogical orientation than that of his colleague Jürgen Habermas's *Theorie des kommunikativen Handelns* [Frankfurt am Main: Suhrkamp Verlag, 1981].)

4. "From the windows of the metalworker employment office one looks at the business life that takes place in the front buildings. These, full of the process of production and distribution, cover the entire horizon of the man out of work. He has no sun of his own, he always only has the employer in front of him, who at best does not stand in his light when giving work" (S, p. 71).

5. "Here, where one tempts one's existence in the shadow of the almighty production process, the categories—which have stamped this an unavoidable natural event—still shine in their old glory. Here it [the production process] is still an idol, and there is nothing higher than it" (S, p. 72).

6. The moralizing communicated by signs continues on a number of posters that, by giving advice on hygiene and business, make those present part of a general production process, whose remoteness from their readers is reflected in the scarcely relevant instructions on the prevention of accidents at work. "'Think of your mother' is written under one of them [the pictures], which, like the other ones, warns against the dangers that workers are exposed to when working on the machines. Strangely enough, these few illustrations of potential disaster gleam in a friendly way above people's heads. For nothing characterizes the nature of the room more than that here pictures of accidents become postcard greetings from the happy upper world of wages at trade union rates" (S, p. 78).

7. "In its goodness, nature treats all men equally—despite their unequal incomes—and thus the poor too have to freeze when the temperature falls. Since we are not familiar with the blessed contrivance of hibernation, the people disconnected from the work process are primarily those who now find themselves in a difficult situation" (S, p. 79).

8. The same tendency toward relative autonomy in the form of closed and musty rooms is emphasized in connection with a "day shelter" for various social clients. This room, which in itself is a reaction to trends in outside society, has been set up in a private apartment. For Kracauer it is like a "cul de sac" (S, p. 83). This place tamps down forever the power of individuals to revolt, since those visiting it generally hang on to their petit-bourgeois badges of rank of former times. "Impoverished lower middle class—it has no desire to rise up again" (S, p. 83), Kracauer writes about the population in this modest yet nonetheless human-looking framework. "Like a bulwark against the emptiness outside, the home actually has a certain cosiness that seems to be infinitely more cheerless to the onlooker from outside than . . . [the tram] hall's unpleasant nature" (S, pp. 83–84).

9. The enclosed nature of the storage spaces largely corresponds to the superficiality of the sphere of the media and politics. In the urban spaces these—according to the final section of "Wärmehallen"—appear as contrasting signs without any substantial depth. There is no real connection to urban life: "A cold wind sweeps through the streets, which are without gentleness. At Bülowsplatz, streamers gleam with the names of Lenin and Stalin. And yesterday, yet another German beauty queen was crowned" (S, p. 84).

10. Kracauer stresses the burdensome nature of unemployment (S, p. 92), characterizing the fasci-

nated but also critical loafing of the masses in front of the still photos in the street as something that "is less a pleasure than a means of driving away the apparition of an unpleasant time" (S, p. 93).

11. The description of the break rituals confirms that Kracauer actually censures the rootless cinema audience: "Apparently, the dessert is sometimes used as a substitute for the main course," he concludes. He leaves the dark interior before the end of the film. "The sun is shining, but how does the sun concern these people?" (S, pp. 94–95).

12. The article concludes: "Young men and young women, men and women expelled from the work process—those whom life has once discarded, follow at play the traces of good fortune. And its faint smile compensates them for a while for the miserable existence that is probably a misfortune but certainly not merely a destiny" (S, p. 88).

13. "Workers, common people, employees [*Angestellten*], who during the week are held down by the city, now overcome by air a hyper-Berlin-like New York" (S, p. 44).

14. "Faith, yes, almost the ability to believe has slipped through their [modern individuals'] hands, and for them religious truths have become colorless thoughts that at best they are still able to *think*" (O, p. 107).

15. Kracauer mentions "these educated people, merchants, doctors, lawyers, students, and intellectuals of all types" (O, p. 106).

16. See Maurice Blanchot, *La communauté inavouable* (Paris: Editions de Minuit, 1983).

CHAPTER 8   IMPROVISATION AND MEMORY

1. The term *Stehbar* can be seen as a counterpart to the German phenomenon of *Stehbierhalle*, which Walter Benjamin made the point of departure for an aphorism in the 1928 book *Einbahnstraße* (now in Benjamin, *Gesammelte Schriften*, vol. 4.1 [Frankfurt am Main: Suhrkamp Verlag, 1980], pp. 83–148). This institution still exists in the present-day Federal Republic, although it now goes by the name *Trinkhalle*, which is used of kiosks that sell beer, chocolate, canned food, etc., in the street long after closing time. These venues often become rendezvous for a solid beer-drinking male culture.

2. It might appear surprising to link the concept of justice with everyday objects (furniture, drinks, cigarettes) in a bar. We are dealing with a theologically inspired basic view that Kracauer to a great extent shares with Walter Benjamin (and that can also be found in Georg Simmel). Theoretical research on the problematics of baroque allegory in Benjamin's already-mentioned work *Ursprung des deutschen Trauerspiels* (in *Gesammelte Schriften,* ed. Rolf Tiedemann and Hermann Schweppenhäuser, vol. 1.1 [Frankfurt am Main: Suhrkamp Verlag, 1980], pp. 203–430) constitutes—when transposed to modernity—an excellent comment on the following passage from Kracauer's article on the stand-up bars of southern Europe: "Only the enjoyment they concede in moments links the tobacco goods to the gleaming aperitifs. The other things, too, exist at short notice [*sind für kurze Frist*]. Tables and chairs lack the permanent residence forced on them in rooms of dwellings. Their meaning is denied them by the guests, who keep moving them around. They have scarcely entered before they discard all signs of social dignity and transform themselves into restless nomads. Like the words in a crossword, they stand straight and without links next to each other" (S, p. 68).

3. Kracauer has sought to promote the reader's ability to improvise by almost leaving out the

guests in his description of the bar universe. The objects dominate, inviting the reader to combine their aesthetic and cultural qualities.

4. In his comments on Kracauer's bar essay, Benjamin, who had shared part of his journey along the French Mediterranean coast in the summer of 1926, is very sensitive to Kracauer's depiction of the dynamic aspect of the bar spaces, which retains its textual mobility in the "final" interpretation. On November 5, 1926, Benjamin writes in a letter to Kracauer, after some remarks praising other articles from the *Frankfurter Zeitung:* "But my surprise was complete when reading 'Stehbars im Süden': quite simply a definitive decoding of this never-ending melodic text. . . . I will put it [the article] aside for future journeys rather than as a memento of a past journey. The magic of these spaces cannot be reflected more beautifully" (Walter Benjamin, *Briefe an Siegfried Kracauer,* ed. Rolf Tiedemann [Marbach am Neckar: Deutsche Schillergesellschaft, 1987], p. 33).

5. In both *Straßen in Berlin und anderswo* and *Das Ornament der Masse* the year of publication given for "Analyse eines Stadtplans" is 1928 ("aus dem Jahr 1928; genaues Datum nicht feststellbar"; O, p. 349). But Benjamin comments on Kracauer's analysis of Avenue de St.-Ouen as early as in a letter of November 5, 1926 (Benjamin, *Briefe an Siegfried Kracauer,* p. 33), which means that its dating to 1928 must be assumed to be incorrect.

6. Kracauer's conception is articulated in connection with the tunnel under Charlottenburg Station in Berlin (see the discussion later in this chapter).

7. This is not identical with the genuinely consumer-capitalist and even less with the Marxist concept of commodity fetishism, which refers to the general form of consciousness in the capitalist economy.

8. Kracauer stresses the function of commodities as "underbrush," "treetops," and "captivating flora."

9. The loggia—a large balcony with side walls to keep out the wind—is an important spatial and social element of upper-middle-class German apartment building of the latter half of the nineteenth century. Via its special status, with one foot in the exterior and one in the interior of the apartment, it marks the first—as yet "confined"—meeting of a number of writers with a nonbourgeois urban reality. Walter Benjamin, for example (in *Berliner Kindheit um neunzehnhundert*), has written his literary self-portrait under the title "Loggien" (reprinted in *Gesammelte Schriften,* vol. 4 [Frankfurt am Main: Suhrkamp Verlag, 1980], pp. 294–296).

10. The section "Die Basarstraße" in "Straßenvolk in Paris" seems to have been directly inspired by Walter Benjamin's essay on Moscow in winter. Kracauer remarks: "They [the bazaars and/or their goods] grow out of the houses; for them winter turns into summer" (S, p. 128). Using Moscow as his starting point, Benjamin has observed how market trading on the main shopping street in Moscow mentally and socially neutralizes the temperature of minus 25 degrees, replaced by "a wonderful Neapolitan summer" (Benjamin, *Gesammelte Schriften,* 4: 320). The published correspondence between Benjamin and Kracauer makes it clear that Kracauer was familiar with Benjamin's essay. Benjamin complains in a letter of April 13, 1927, for example, that he has not yet received Kracauer's comments on his essay "Moscow" (*Briefe an Siegfried Kracauer,* p. 41).

11. The inspiration provided by Walter Benjamin's essay "Häfen und Jahrmärkte," published in FZ, July 9, 1926, is obvious and could be demonstrated on a number of points. A sufficient indication of this connection is evident in the following passage from a letter from Benjamin to

Kracauer sent from Paris (April 27, 1926), which in the space of a few lines lists themes that, in the following seasons, were also to become Kracauer's: "Under the title 'Ships and stalls'— unless you can help me at all with a better title—I am preparing certain notes on markets [*Jahrmärkte*] and sailors' voyages [*Matrosenfährten*], in which the secret connection between an amusement park and a harbor are to appear, with certain indications of the causes of [such] stalls' *attrativa* [powers of attraction]. The subject is not far removed from the children's toy [the theme of an article mentioned earlier]" (Benjamin, *Briefe an Siegfried Kracauer,* p. 19).

12. In connection with the heterogeneous assortment of goods found at Parisian stalls Kracauer writes: "The odds and ends spout out unrestrainedly onto the street, right into the society that has not taken them along with it. The visible surfaces are spattered with them like the bars of nougat a Negro is offering for sale. The common people do not understand the decoration of surfaces. They trundle forward with their carts and set up shop wherever they feel like it" (S, p. 131).

13. It is not by chance that "Straßenvolk in Paris" ends with an analysis of an urban roundabout (in Paris the roundabout is part of the street inventory), where children, perhaps for the first time, abandon themselves to an imaginary journey that is both linear and circular—forward and around, away from and back toward their parents. In this way, the urban experience is linked to the subject-promoting mental separation from one's parents.

14. These can be described as the Parisian equivalent of Copenhagen's *brokvarterer.* The Parisian *faubourgs* are not suburbs in the traditional sense (those are referred to as *la banlieue* in French). *Les faubourgs* lie within the present city limits of Paris and, to a great extent, within the Paris that was done away with in 1860 in connection with Haussmann's inclusion of a number of villages (Montmartre, Belleville, Ménilmontant, Ternes, etc.) in the municipal administrative zone.

15. See, for example, his letter to Bloch from early January 1928, in which Kracauer characterizes Ginster's personality with the words "he is clearly a silent anarchist" (*Ernst Bloch: Briefe 1903– 1975,* vol. 1 [Frankfurt am Main: Suhrkamp Verlag, 1985], p. 289). On this and other occasions, then, Kracauer indirectly portrays himself as anarchistically oriented, i.e., unable to identify himself with any entire political program.

16. The subtitle of "Analyse eines Stadtplans" is "Faubourgs und Zentrum," which does not imply that Paris should have one center (the city has many). The reference is to a relatively cohesive central area, outside of which the streets, for example, have such names as "rue du *faubourg* Saint-Martin," "rue du *faubourg* Saint-Honoré"—the extensions of "rue Saint-Martin" and "rue Saint-Honoré," respectively, outside the late-medieval city limits. This coincided on the right bank of the Seine with the present-day *grands boulevards,* which for Kracauer in "Analyse eines Stadtplans" are the incarnation of the center (S, pp. 18–19)—in his later book on Offenbach (see part III) interpreted as a transitional area without any unambiguous social basis.

17. The inner city, "the upper world of the boulevards," differs from the "both poor and human" outer districts by possessing a "sensory splendor [*der sinnliche Glanz*]" (S, pp. 16, 17). The absence of this outside is a limitation (and at the same time a condition) of heterogeneous urbanity. Within the framework of the city of luxury trading, the splendor further aggravates the separation between people and things, between wish and possession (S, p. 18).

18. The politically important conclusion to "Analyse eines Stadtplans" implies in its metaphorical spatial language a resolving (in a dialectic sense) connection between the *faubourgs* and the

"center." "Wide streets lead from the outer districts [*faubourgs*] to the splendor of the center. This is not the intended [*gemeinte*] center. Happiness, which is intended for the misery outside, is struck by other radii than the existing ones. Even so, the streets to the center ought to be walked in, for their emptiness today is real" (S, p. 19).

19. Mechanical toys are modernity's secularized miniatures of the divine or cosmological objects of former times, whose power is reduced, finding expression in sizes that can be grasped.

20. "A testimony about which we only indirectly know anything forces its way to the surface. It has no name, sweeps through the rooms, and likes to attack us from the rear. At night it comes alive without ever showing itself, and in broad daylight it disturbs things, causing them to play tricks. By assuming visible forms in the stalls these nuisances immediately lose the hold they have over us" (S, p. 40).

21. See, e.g., Momme Brodersen, "Von Berlin nach Capri: Walter Benjamin in Italien," in Brodersen, ed., *Benjamin auf italienisch* (Frankfurt am Main: Verlag Neue Kritik, 1982), p. 122.

22. See Jean Dethier and David Elalouf, "Marginal arkitektur i USA," *Louisiana Revy* 17, no. 3 (1977): 22–23.

23. Kracauer notes in passing: "There is no Minotaur sitting in Clavel's labyrinth, nor is there any labyrinth but chaos" (S, p. 65).

24. This tendency is modified on only one occasion, in the "small moral tale" with the title "Friedliche Lösung" ("Peaceful Solution"; FZ, June 24, 1930; S, pp. 157–159). This story from a Berlin restaurant gives Kracauer the opportunity of suggesting how a concrete, interhuman sociality, because of its immediacy, is able to break through the perverted aspect of the complex institutional structures of social life. An open window in a restaurant apparently cannot be closed, despite the efforts of employees of increasing rank to do so. It is closed immediately, however, when the woman who first complained turns directly to the people who until then had been the excuse of the waiters, etc., for not taking action. Kracauer concludes: "A single person dissolved the state of war that separates everyone from everyone else, broke down the fear of the word that has the power to reconcile. Like a comet, peace was seen on the horizon" (S, p. 158). Apart from this, there are few positive signs to be found in Berlin's urban world.

25. This analysis is to be found in "Spuk im Vergnügungslokal" ("Haunting in the Entertainment Hall"; FZ, October 30, 1930).

26. Since 1975, when Martin Jay's essay was first published, this problematics, advanced in Jay's above-mentioned analysis "The Extraterritorial Life of Siegfried Kracauer" (in *Permanent Exiles: Essays on the Intellectual Migration from Germany to America* [New York: Columbia University Press, 1985], pp. 152–197), has gained prominence, without sufficient distinction always being made between the different theoretical and empirical levels of the concepts of exile and asylum.

27. The information on the Linden Arcade comes from Johann Friedrich Geist, *Passagen—Ein Bautyp des 19. Jahrhunderts,* 3rd ed. (Munich: Prestel Verlag, 1979), pp. 132–137.

28. Ibid., p. 137.

29. Cf. the importance the concept of *le suranné* assumed in the theoretical superstructure of French surrealism.

30. The suggestion of a utopian perspective is made in a parenthetical comment on the passage's "real passersby": "(The person who is vagabonding will at some point find himself together with the man of the changed society)" (S, p. 37).

31. This essayistic narrative can in several respects be viewed as an accumulation of motifs from Kracauer's essays on the city. "Straße ohne Erinnerung" is from the very last phase of Kracauer's time at the *Frankfurter Zeitung* (the article was published just before Christmas 1932—Kracauer fled to Paris at the end of February 1933), which means that it built on the experience of many years of essay writing. It returns to motifs both from Kracauer's book of revolutionary reportage *Die Angestellten* (1930) (he mentions "Asylen für Obdachlose" [S, p. 21] after a chapter heading in *Die Angestellten*) and from the philosophical tract *Der Detektiv-Roman*, from ca. 1925 (the mention of shops as "Hotelhalle" [S, p. 21], the title of a central chapter in that book). Furthermore, a dancing club on the Kurfürstendamm is described based on the model already used in *Ginster* (G, p. 188) and "Der verbotene Blick" (S, p. 97): those dancing appear to be "wound up like marionettes" (S, p. 22).

32. That totalitarian political regimes have used such spaces to organize the masses and to shape an architectural self-conception is, however, a fact. Elias Canetti's analysis of the Nazi architectural projects in Germany in *Das Gewissen der Worte* (Munich: Hanser Verlag, 1976) is just one demonstration of the ideological intentions that are linked to certain forms of space. Various projects were actually realized: some, for example, in connection with the German pavilion at the world exposition in Paris in 1937, as well as with Mussolini's setting for a world exposition in Rome—the EUR district—planned for 1942 but never held.

CHAPTER 9 HISTORY AND URBAN COLLECTIVITY

1. The book was originally published in Amsterdam (Allert de Lange); the edition cited in this volume as P is Siegfried Kracauer, *Jacques Offenbach und das Paris seiner Zeit*, vol. 8 of *Schriften* (Frankfurt am Main: Suhrkamp Verlag, 1976). The original was printed on 490 pages, according to an epilogue (P, p. 363) written by Karsten Witte to the Suhrkamp edition, which itself fills just over 350 tightly packed pages.

2. For film history, see Siegfried Kracauer, *From Caligari to Hitler: A Psychological History of German Film* (Princeton: Princeton University Press, 1947); for aesthetics, see Siegfried Kracauer, *Theory of Film: The Redemption of Physical Reality* (New York: Oxford University Press, 1960).

3. Siegfried Kracauer, *History: The Last Things before the Last* (New York: Oxford University Press, 1969).

4. See Wolfgang Schivelbusch, *Intellektuellendämmerung—Zur Lage der Frankfurter Intelligenz in den zwanziger Jahren* (1982; reprint, Frankfurt am Main: Suhrkamp Verlag, 1985), chap. 3.

5. Siegfried Kracauer, *Georg*, in *Schriften*, vol. 7 (Frankfurt am Main: Suhrkamp Verlag, 1973), pp. 243–490.

6. For an analysis of Benjamin's so-called Arcades Project, including especially its relationship to historical empiricism and its crucial theoretical and philosophical motifs, see my article "Passagernes fragmentariske værk" (The arcades' fragmentary work), *Slagmark—tidsskrift for idéhistorie*, no. 11 (1988): 97–135.

7. Leon Trotsky, *My Life: An Attempt at an Autobiography* (1930; reprint, New York: Pathfinder Press, 1970). This exceptional status is all the more surprising since Trotsky's book, according to the title, is not a biography about a third person but his reflections on the course of his own

life. This means, however, that Kracauer's comparison loses some of its theoretical relevance regarding the genre. A *biography* from such a point of view must be considered as radically different from an *autobiography,* which in turn differs from the perhaps less fact-bound *memoir.*

8. See letter to Löwenthal, excerpts of which are printed in M, p. 79.

9. See Karsten Witte, "Nachwort" (P, p. 363). See also M, pp. 74–101.

10. Adorno's official criticism, published in *Zeitschrift für Sozialforschung* 6, no. 3 (1937): 697–698, is summarized by Karsten Witte in his epilogue to the book on Offenbach (P, p. 365). The present remarks are based on that summary.

11. An investigation of Kracauer's relationship to his comprehensive source material is facilitated by the bibliography categorized by theme and genre at the end of the book. Here a distinction is made between, among other things, "A: Biographies," "B: Literary and Political Testimonies," "C: Memoirs, Diaries and Letters, Speeches," "D: General Period History," "E: The History of Music and Drama," "F: Boulevard, Parisian Life," and "G: Magazines and Journals" (P, pp. 353–359). The general absence of notes and source references would necessitate a great deal of hard work, however, if Kracauer's precise relationship to the sources and secondary literature were to be mapped.

12. In his classic book *Comment on écrit l'histoire,* the French historian Paul Veyne defines the most important characteristic of historiography as "la mise en intrigue" of historical facts. This emphasis on the importance of the intrigue for historical presentation and thus for a conception of time has been returned to by the French philosopher Paul Ricœur. It occupies a vital theoretical position in his four-volume work *Temps et récit* (Time and story), begun in the mid-1980s. See Paul Veyne, *Comment on écrit l'histoire: [extraits]* (1971) (Paris: Editions du Seuil, 1979), pp. 13–14, and Paul Ricœur, *Temps et récit,* vol. 1 (Paris: Editions du Seuil, 1983), esp. pp. 239–246.

13. In connection with his description of the first world exposition in Paris in 1855 Kracauer notes: "For the boulevard, which had already become a refuge for strangers and for those without citizenship during the reign of Louis Philippe, good times now lay ahead" (P, p. 151).

14. This concept runs like a red thread through all of Kracauer's writing, from their earliest instances in the early 1920s until his philosophy of history and film in the late 1950s and early 1960s. It is never fully developed at the philosophical level, but it is concretized at an empirical level in connection with the individual forms of materiality that happen to have his interest at the times concerned. The tendentiously fetishized status of "reality" expresses the fact that for Kracauer it is the basis, point of departure, and goal of theoretical work.

15. Jean Baudrillard, *Les stratégies fatales* (Paris: Grasset, 1983), pp. 161–255.

16. Examples of *Frankfurter Zeitung* columns that unite critique of film with sociological considerations of media are found, among other places, in *Das Ornament der Masse* (O, pp. 269–317). Kracauer's first research projects in the United States had to do with the use of the medium of film by the Nazis for purposes of political propaganda. Already by June 9, 1942—he had arrived in New York at the end of April the previous year—Kracauer completed a study titled *Propaganda and the Nazi War Film* ([New York]: Museum of Modern Art, Film Library, [1942]). Substantial parts of his next book, *From Caligari to Hitler: A Psychological History of the German Film,* were complete in manuscript form in late summer of 1945. It was published in April 1947 by Princeton University Press (see M, pp. 103, 105, 107).

17. An analysis of how the film synopsis connects with, and diverges from, the Offenbach book

would make it possible to assess the position of the City in the communication of historical research. This project is difficult to carry out because the synopsis has not yet been made available to the public.

18. Karsten Witte's lecture "Siegfried Kracauer im Exil," delivered in spring 1987, exists in two published versions: one in the feuilleton (cultural supplement) of the *Frankfurter Rundschau* from Christmas 1987 (p. 2), the other—which is more complete (though not identical with the lecture, which included a number of critical comments on Adorno's behavior toward Kracauer during his first period in exile)—in *Exilforschung—ein internationales Jahrbuch,* vol. 5 (Munich: Text + Kritik, 1987), pp. 135–149. This latter edition is the one cited in the following notes.

19. Witte, "Siegfried Kracauer im Exil," p. 135.

20. Ibid., p. 138.

21. To correct Karsten Witte's reading it should be stressed that Kracauer on innumerable occasions draws attention to the historically limited validity of the operetta culture. Kracauer implies that a link between dream (as well as intoxication) and waking up has already been established during the Second Empire, whereas Walter Benjamin, whose so-called Arcades Project defines itself at crucial points via corresponding concepts, seeks mainly such a connection in the cultural history of his own age—the 1930s.

22. Daniel Halévy, preface to Siegfried Kracauer, *Jacques Offenbach ou le secret du Second Empire,* trans. Lucienne Astruc (Paris: Editions Bernard Grasset, 1937), p. 10.

23. Ibid., p. 11.

24. Ibid., p. 9.

CONCLUSIONS AND PERSPECTIVES

1. Not until her later book *Court traité du fragment* (Paris: Aubier, 1986)—which does not directly deal with urban culture—does Anne Cauquelin take up the theme of the semantically and visually irreducible aspects of the fragment.

2. See Henrik Reeh, "En hommage à la ville du futur antérieur—ville et vitesse dans l'œuvre de Paul Virilio," in Groupe de Travail Interdisciplinaire de l'Ecole Normale Supérieure de St.-Cloud, *Ville et voyage—trajectoires urbaines* (Paris: Editions Didier Erudition, 1986), pp. 65–88. My article concludes by showing that Virilio would be able to base an investigation of the spatial aspects of architecture on his concept of inertia. See, for example, Paul Virilio, *Speed and Politics: An Essay on Dromology,* trans. Mark Polizzotti (New York: Semiotext(e), 1986).

3. See Siegfried Kracauer's essay "Das Mittelgebirge," in *Straßen in Berlin und anderswo* (Frankfurt am Main: Suhrkamp Verlag, 1964), pp. 122–123.

4. Historical research has also systematically investigated a number of the themes that Kracauer and Benjamin raised in their studies of Paris. A broad but still academically sound presentation can be found in Georges Duby, ed., *Histoire de la France urbaine,* vol. 4, *La ville de l'âge industriel* (Paris: Editions du Seuil, 1983).

5. Such a link between the types of ornament that are capable of being categorized and a dynamic, potentially evasive ornamental beauty is a challenge to traditional art history. Therefore, a single example will be given here to show that Kracauer's derived ornament concept is nevertheless able to take into account an important aspect of the ornament in popular art craft.

If one looks at a classic ornamental field such as *embroidery,* Kracauer's observations prove to be extremely apt in aiding description and interpretation. A suitable example can be taken from a fine collection of Palestinian embroidered costumes shown to the public by l'Institut du Monde Arabe in Paris in the spring of 1989 under the title *Mémoires de soi(e)* (*Memories of Silk* or *Memories of Self,* depending on whether *soie* or *soi* is translated). These special costumes from the late nineteenth century and first decades of the twentieth century are a good illustration of the popular "will to art" that, as the highly simple and traditional meets the improvisatory and innovative, creates an anonymous art in constant motion.

One of the effects of the geometrically divided costumes is that they reduce the body to a neutral wearer. The costume then presents itself to the viewer as a surface of geometrical embroideries that unite many qualities. The vast majority of these embroideries are nonfigurative. They range from an organically toned formal idiom to almost pure crystalline forms. As complete works, the embroideries can be observed at all levels of scale; each time one moves from an overarching to, for example, an intermediate level on the way to the individual figure (or even the single stitch), one's perception of the totality of the costume changes. And yet there is a clear link between the global and the detailed levels.

This folk art seems to me, by virtue of its aesthetic power, to go beyond the boundary between applied art and *les beaux arts,* and it shows that such a division has come about historically. So it would be nearly presumptuous to try to typologize this rich formal idiom. The variations of motif evade every such attempt to find typologizing masks. At the same time, tradition is still obvious in the individual costumes. The mimetic aspect of their production is thus central and it really means that serious reception of the works ought to go beyond the visual medium of contemplation. The ornamental embroideries recover their dignity only via an active processing—in, e.g., drawing or sewing.

But since reception of these costumes is nonetheless limited to mere observation, to a distant contemplation, there is sure to be that sort of experience which caused Kracauer to allow both the *limited* figure and the *limitless* to be included in the term "ornament." The gaze at the costumes is split between two poles that are difficult to connect with each other. On the one hand, as general form and in the embroidered main motifs, they are characterized by regularity that, with a certain amount of coercion, could be systematized in a typology and thus be viewed as belonging to the areas of folk art and applied art. On the other hand, one cannot as an observer look at the embroideries of these costumes for very long before the total picture dissolves into moving forms, which eventually become a general shimmering before the eyes.

So regularity and shimmering are found once more in the reception of folk art. For this reason among others, Kracauer allowed the world of the ornament to expand and include forms that cannot immediately be represented in fixed structures. Only in the magnetic field between these two poles does the relationship between the apparently banal and the simultaneously conscious and unconscious memory become clear. The silk embroideries of these costumes can recall a distant culture, just as the vertiginous serial embroidery can give rise in the observer to a more immediate and individual process of remembering. The double title of the exhibition is thus just as well-founded as Kracauer's expansion of the formal idiom of the ornament.

6. Ernst Bloch, *Geist der Utopie: Erste Fassung* (1918), vol. 16 of *Gesamtausgabe* (Frankfurt am Main: Suhrkamp Verlag, 1971), cited throughout as U. A second, radically revised edition of this work appeared in 1964.

7. This hypothesis of a connection between Bloch's and Kracauer's conception of the ornament will not be pursued in detail. Doing so would take too much space, among other reasons because there is no discussion of the ornament concept in the very intense exchange of letters between Kracauer and Bloch. Only on one occasion does Kracauer indicate that he has read Bloch's *Geist der Utopie* (in a letter to Bloch of June 29, 1927; Ernst Bloch, *Briefe 1903–1975*, vol. 1, ed. Karola Bloch [Frankfurt am Main: Suhrkamp Verlag, 1985], p. 281).

8. See Henrik Reeh, "Billede, sprog, begreb—Walter Benjamins hash-overvejelser" (Image, language, concept—Walter Benjamin's thoughts on hashish), *Alkoholpolitik—Tidskrift för nordisk alkoholforskning* 5 (1988): 3–11.

9. These two positions and the relationship between them have been dealt with in greater detail in my D.E.A. dissertation "Prostitution et interprétation dans l'œuvre de Walter Benjamin" (UER des Sciences des Textes et Documents, Université de Paris VII, 1986). See Walter Benjamin, *Der Begriff der Kunstkritik in der deutschen Romantik* and *Ursprung des deutschen Trauerspiels*, both in *Gesammelte Schriften*, vol. 1.1 (Frankfurt am Main: Suhrkamp Verlag, 1980), pp. 7–122, 203–430.

10. Walter Benjamin, "Haschisch Anfang März 1930," in *Über Haschisch* (Frankfurt am Main: Suhrkamp Verlag, 1972), p. 107.

11. See Charles Jencks, *The Language of Post-Modern Architecture* (New York: Rizzoli Press, 1978).

12. See Jean Baudrillard, *L'échange symbolique et la mort* (Paris: Gallimard, 1976).

13. See Jean-François Lyotard, "Réponse à la question: Qu'est-ce que le post-moderne?" in *Le post-moderne expliqué aux enfants* (Paris: Editions Galilée, 1986), pp. 11–34.

14. See, for example, the journal *Traverses*, no. 40, *Théâtres de la mémoire* (April 1987), especially the article by Michel de Certeau, "Les revenants de la ville" (pp. 74–85).

Bibliography

Adorno, Theodor W. *Noten zur Literatur.* Frankfurt am Main: Suhrkamp Verlag, 1974.

Adorno, Theodor W., and Max Horkheimer. *Dialektik der Aufklärung.* 2nd ed. Frankfurt am Main: S. Fischer Verlag, 1969.

Arnold, Heinz Ludwig, ed. *Siegfried Kracauer.* Text + Kritik, vol. 68. Munich: Text + Kritik, 1980.

Banham, Reyner. *Theory and Design in the First Machine Age.* 2nd ed. London: Architectural Press, 1980.

Baudrillard, Jean. *L'échange symbolique et la mort.* Paris: Gallimard, 1976.

Baudrillard, Jean. *Les stratégies fatales.* Paris: Grasset, 1983.

Belke, Ingrid, and Irina Renz, eds. *Siegfried Kracauer 1889–1966.* Marbach am Neckar: Deutsche Schillergesellschaft, 1989. Special issue of *Marbacher Magazin,* no. 47 (1988).

Benevolo, Leonardo. *The History of Modern Architecture.* 2 vols. 1971. Reprint, Cambridge, Mass.: MIT Press, 1977.

Benjamin, Walter. *Der Begriff der Kunstkritik in der deutschen Romantik.* In *Gesammelte Schriften,* vol. 1.1. Ed. Rolf Tiedemann and Hermann Schweppenhäuser. Frankfurt am Main: Suhrkamp Verlag, 1980.

Benjamin, Walter. *Berliner Kindheit um neunzehnhundert.* In *Gesammelte Schriften,* vol. 4. Ed. Rolf Tiedemann and Hermann Schweppenhäuser. Frankfurt am Main: Suhrkamp Verlag, 1980.

Benjamin, Walter. *Briefe an Siegfried Kracauer.* Ed. Rolf Tiedemann. Marbach am Neckar: Deutsche Schillergesellschaft, 1987.

Benjamin, Walter. *Einbahnstraße.* In *Gesammelte Schriften,* vol. 4.1. Ed. Rolf Tiedemann and Hermann Schweppenhäuser. Frankfurt am Main: Suhrkamp Verlag, 1980.

Benjamin, Walter. *Gesammelte Schriften.* Vol. 6. Ed. Rolf Tiedemann and Hermann Schweppenhäuser. Frankfurt am Main: Suhrkamp Verlag, 1985.

Benjamin, Walter. *Ursprung des deutschen Trauerspiels.* In *Gesammelte Schriften,* vol. 1.1. Ed. Rolf Tiedemann and Hermann Schweppenhäuser. Frankfurt am Main: Suhrkamp Verlag, 1980.

Blanchot, Maurice. *La communauté inavouable.* Paris: Editions du Minuit, 1983.

Bloch, Ernst. *Briefe 1903–1975.* Vol. 1. Ed. Karola Bloch. Frankfurt am Main: Suhrkamp Verlag, 1985.

Bloch, Ernst. *Geist der Utopie: Erste Fassung.* Vol. 16 of *Gesamtausgabe.* Frankfurt am Main: Suhrkamp Verlag, 1971.

Brodersen, Momme, ed. *Benjamin auf italienisch.* Frankfurt am Main: Verlag Neue Kritik, 1982.

Canetti, Elias. *Das Gewissen der Worte.* Munich: Hanser Verlag, 1976.

Cauquelin, Anne. *Court traité du fragment.* Paris: Aubier, 1986.

Cauquelin, Anne. *Essai de philosophie urbaine.* Paris: Presses Universitaires de France, 1982.

Dahme, Heinz-Jürgen, ed. *Georg Simmel und die Moderne.* Frankfurt am Main: Suhrkamp Verlag, 1984.

Dethier, Jean, and David Elalouf. "Marginal arkitektur i USA." *Louisiana Revy* 17, no. 3 (1977): 21–23.

Duby, Georges, ed. *Histoire de la France urbaine.* Vol. 4, *La ville de l'âge industriel.* Paris: Editions du Seuil, 1983.

Freud, Sigmund. "The Uncanny." In *The Standard Edition of the Complete Psychological Works of Sigmund Freud,* vol. 17. Ed. James Strachey. London: Hogarth, 1953.

Gardin, Jean-Claude. *Une archéologie théorique.* Paris: Hachette, 1979.

Geist, Johann Friedrich. *Passagen—Ein Bautyp des 19. Jahrhunderts.* 3rd ed. Munich: Prestel Verlag, 1979.

Habermas, Jürgen. *Theorie des kommunikativen Handelns.* Frankfurt am Main: Suhrkamp Verlag, 1981.

Haenlein, Leo. *Der Denk-Gestus des aktiven Wartens im Sinn-Vakuum der Moderne: Zur Konstitution und Tragweite des Realitätskonzeptes Siegfried Kracauers in spezieller Rücksicht auf Walter Benjamin.* Frankfurt am Main: Peter Lang, 1984.

Halévy, Daniel. Preface to Siegfried Kracauer, *Jacques Offenbach ou le secret du Second Empire.* Trans. Lucienne Astruc. Paris: Bernard Grasset, 1937.

Hansen, Nils Gunder. "Georg Simmel—sociologi og livsfilosofi." Ph.D. diss., Department of Comparative Literature, University of Copenhagen, 1989. Later published as *Sansernes sociologi—Georg Simmel og det moderne.* Copenhagen: Tiderne Skifter, 1991.

Honneth, Axel. *The Struggle for Recognition: The Moral Grammar of Social Conflicts.* Cambridge: Polity Press, 1995.

Jay, Martin. *Permanent Exiles: Essays on the Intellectual Migration from Germany to America.* New York: Columbia University Press, 1985.

Jencks, Charles. *The Language of Post-Modern Architecture.* New York: Rizzoli, 1978.

Kafka, Franz. *The Trial.* Trans. Willa and Edwin Muir. Rev. E. M. Butler. 1925. Reprint, New York: Schocken, 1968.

Kracauer, Siegfried. *Die Angestellten: Aus dem neuesten Deutschland.* In *Schriften,* vol. 1. Frankfurt am Main: Suhrkamp Verlag, 1971.

Kracauer, Siegfried. *Die Entwicklung der Schmiedekunst in Berlin, Potsdam und einigen Städten der Mark vom 17. Jahrhundert bis zum Beginn des 19. Jahrhunderts.* Worms am Rhein: Wormser Verlags- und Druckereigesellschaft m.b.H., 1915.

Kracauer, Siegfried. *From Caligari to Hitler: A Psychological History of German Film.* Princeton: Princeton University Press, 1947.

Kracauer, Siegfried. *Georg.* In *Schriften,* vol. 7. Frankfurt am Main: Suhrkamp Verlag, 1973.

Kracauer, Siegfried. *Ginster: Von ihm selbst geschrieben.* In *Schriften,* vol. 7. Frankfurt am Main: Suhrkamp Verlag, 1973.

Kracauer, Siegfried. *History: The Last Things before the Last.* New York: Oxford University Press, 1969.

Kracauer, Siegfried. *Jacques Offenbach und das Paris seiner Zeit.* Vol. 8 of *Schriften.* Frankfurt am Main: Suhrkamp Verlag, 1976.

Kracauer, Siegfried. *Das Ornament der Masse.* Frankfurt am Main: Suhrkamp Verlag, 1963.

Kracauer, Siegfried. *Propaganda and the Nazi War Film.* [New York]: Museum of Modern Art, Film Library, [1942].

Kracauer, Siegfried. *Straßen in Berlin und anderswo.* Frankfurt am Main: Suhrkamp Verlag, 1964.

Kracauer, Siegfried. *Theory of Film: The Redemption of Physical Reality.* New York: Oxford University Press, 1960.

Kracauer, Siegfried. *Über die Freundschaft.* Frankfurt am Main: Suhrkamp Verlag, 1971.

Kristeva, Julia. *Soleil noir: Dépression et mélancolie.* Paris: Gallimard, 1987.

Loos, Adolf. *Paroles dans le vide, suivi de Malgré tout.* Trans. Cornelius Heim. Paris: Editions du Champ Libre, 1979.

Loos, Adolf. *Trotzdem.* 1931. Reprint, Vienna: Georg Prachner Verlag, 1982.

Lyotard, Jean-François. *Discours, figure.* Paris: Klincksieck, 1971.

Lyotard, Jean-François. "Réponse à la question: Qu'est-ce que le postmoderne?" In *Le postmoderne expliqué aux enfants.* Paris: Editions Galilée, 1986.

Moos, Stanislaus von, ed. *L'esprit nouveau—Le Corbusier et l'industrie 1920–1925.* Berlin: Wilhelm Ernst und Sohn Verlag, 1987.

Mülder, Inka. *Siegfried Kracauer—Grenzgänger zwischen Theorie und Literatur: Seine frühen Schriften 1913–1933.* Stuttgart: J. B. Metzler, 1985.

Münster, Arno. *Utopie, Messianismus und Apokalypse im Frühwerk von Ernst Bloch.* Frankfurt am Main: Suhrkamp Verlag, 1982.

Opel, A., ed. *Konfrontation—Schriften von und über Adolf Loos.* Vienna: G. Prachner Verlag, 1988.

Rasmussen, Steen Eiler. *Britisk Brugskunst.* 1933. Reprint, Copenhagen: G. E. C. Gads Forlag, 1965.

Raymond, Henri. *L'architecture, les aventures spatiales de la raison.* Collection "alors." Paris: Centre de Création Industrielle, Centre Georges Pompidou, 1984.

Reeh, Henrik. "Billede, sprog, begreb—Walter Benjamins hash-overvejelser." *Alkoholpolitik—Tidskrift för nordisk alkoholforskning* 5 (1988): 3–11.

Reeh, Henrik. "En hommage à la ville du futur antérieur—ville et vitesse dans l'œuvre de Paul Virilio." In Groupe de Travail Interdisciplinarie de l'Ecole Normale Supérieure de St.-Cloud, *Ville et voyage—trajectoires urbaines.* Paris: Editions Didier Erudition, 1986.

Reeh, Henrik. "Passagernes fragmentariske værk." *Slagmark—tidsskrift for idéhistorie,* no. 11 (1988): 97–135.

Reeh, Henrik. "Prostitution et interprétation dans l'œuvre de Walter Benjamin." D.E.A. diss., UER des Sciences des Textes et Documents, Université de Paris VII, 1986.

Ricoeur, Paul. *Temps et récit.* Vol. 1. Paris: Editions du Seuil, 1983.

Rippel-Manß, Irmtraut. "1920–1929: Die goldenen Zwanziger." In *Chronik des 20. Jahrhunderts.* Braunschweig: Westermann, 1982.

Schivelbusch, Wolfgang. *Intellektuellendämmerung—Zur Lage der Frankfurter Intelligenz in den zwanziger Jahren.* 1982. Reprint, Frankfurt am Main: Suhrkamp Verlag, 1985.

Simmel, Georg. *Das individuelle Gesetz.* Ed. Michael Landmann. Frankfurt am Main: Suhrkamp Verlag, 1968.

Simmel, Georg. *Das Individuum und die Freiheit.* Berlin: Verlag Klaus Wagenbach, 1984.

Traverses, no. 40, *Théâtres de la mémoire* (April 1987).

Trotsky, Leon. *My Life: An Attempt at an Autobiography.* 1930. Reprint, New York: Pathfinder Press, 1970.

Veyne, Paul. *Comment on écrit l'histoire: [extraits]* (1971). Paris: Editions du Seuil, 1979.

Virilio, Paul. *Speed and Politics: An Essay on Dromology.* Trans. Mark Polizzotti. New York: Semiotext(e), 1986.

Watier, Patrick, ed. *Georg Simmel, la sociologie et l'expérience du monde moderne.* Paris: Méridiens-Klincksieck, 1986.

Wiggershaus, Rolf. *Die Frankfurter Schule. Geschichte, theoretische Entwicklung, politische Bedeutung.* Munich: Carl Hanser Verlag, 1986.

Witte, Karsten. "Siegfried Kracauer im Exil." In *Exilforschung—ein internationales Jahrbuch.* Vol. 5. Munich: Text + Kritik, 1987.

Index